Fundamental Concepts and Critical Developments in Sex Education

This comprehensive resource equips emerging and experienced sexuality educators with contemporary frameworks for trauma-informed, equitable, and anti-oppressive education.

It provides foundational principles for development and delivery, emphasizing inclusivity, accessibility, and intersectionality. Editors Malone, Gilbert, Dukes, and Fonte curate chapters by leading voices on topics such as historical perspectives, values, emotional intelligence, professional humility, reproductive justice, neurodivergence, sex work, kink, childhood and adolescent sexualities, faith-based education, social media, and entrepreneurship. Authors demonstrate decolonization, trauma-informed care, and equity in practice.

With practical applications and reflective questions, this book is a vital guide for creating and teaching impactful, inclusive sex education for diverse audiences.

Reece Malone, DHS, MPH is an award-winning sexuality educator, equity trainer, researcher, and therapist based in Winnipeg, Canada. Founder of Sexuality Consultants and Support Services Manitoba and Diversity Essentials, he teaches and informs policy on human rights, gender equity, and human sexuality. He co-edited *An Intersectional Approach to Sex Therapy*.

Tracie Q. Gilbert, PhD, is a sex ed consultant dedicated to socioemotional wellness for Black communities and racial justice in sex education. Formerly an assistant professor, she now focuses on curriculum writing and training. She authored *Black & Sexy: A Framework of Racialized Sexuality.*

Catherine Dukes, PhD, LCSW is an award-winning sex educator and sex therapist. Prior to founding her sex therapy and education group practice www. TheCenterCD.com, she led Planned Parenthood of Delaware's education department, winning national awards. Her work also includes speaking at national conferences, publications, and Bedroom Brainiacs online sex ed.

Justine Ang Fonte, M.Ed, MPH is a Filipina-American sex educator, consultant, and professor. She's taught PreK-12 children and their caregivers for 15+ years. Her Audible Original is *How to Talk to Your Kids About Sex*, and she holds master's degrees from the University of Hawai'i and Columbia University.

"This book is the ultimate guide for sex educators! It dismantles the old, siloed approaches to education, offering instead a liberatory framework rooted in authenticity, collective care, and inclusivity. What sets this book apart is its focus on both the educator and learner, promoting an educational environment where both parties engage collaboratively in a process of healing, mutual understanding and valued shared learning."

Dr. Lexx Brown-James, PhD, LMFT, CSE, CSES, Pioneer Sex Educator, The Couples Clinician, President, The American Association of Sexuality Educators, Counselors & Therapists (AASECT) (2024–2026)

"As our young people increasingly call upon all of us to recognize their beautiful, brave, and diverse lived realities, it is incredibly important for sex educators to have the language, tools, and approaches that allow us to teach to the breadth of human sexual and reproductive experience from a place of love, affirmation, and understanding. This new resource will be invaluable for sex educators committed to doing so."

Christine Soyong Harley, President & CEO, The Sexuality Information and Education Council of the United States (SIECUS): Sex Ed for Social Change

"*Fundamental Concepts and Critical Developments in Sex Education* is an embodiment of what I've always known the field of sex education has the potential to become. Authors address the complexity, breadth, and depth of our field without limit or apology. The tone of this book is direct, respectful, self-aware, and clear in the ways that it prioritizes dignity and joy, and articulates boundaries and expectations – it's no coincidence that those are also the hallmarks of influential, dynamic, effective sex educators."

Sara C. Flowers, DrPH, Vice President of Education & Training, Planned Parenthood Federation of America

"Provocative and insightful, this significant work offers valuable, intersectional strategies that challenge health educators – both within organizations and self-employed – to reflect on their role in creating brave spaces for sexual education. With its depth and practical insights, this book is an essential resource for anyone committed to being their best self in this complex field."

David L. Bell, MD, MPH, Professor of Pediatrics and Population & Family Health at CUMC

"Truly groundbreaking. Comprehensive, accessible and deeply needed! This book isn't just about sexuality education, it's about creating a more just and compassionate world. A must-read for educators who share this vision."

Francisco Ramirez, MPH, co-founder, OkaySo

Fundamental Concepts and Critical Developments in Sex Education

Intersectional and Trauma-Informed Approaches

Edited by Reece M. Malone, Tracie Q. Gilbert, Catherine Dukes and Justine Ang Fonte

Routledge
Taylor & Francis Group

NEW YORK AND LONDON

Designed cover image: Getty Images

First published 2026
by Routledge
605 Third Avenue, New York, NY 10158

and by Routledge
4 Park Square, Milton Park, Abingdon, Oxon, OX14 4RN

Routledge is an imprint of the Taylor & Francis Group, an informa business

ISBN: 978-1-032-60151-9 (hbk)
ISBN: 978-1-032-61543-1 (pbk)
ISBN: 978-1-032-61547-9 (ebk)

DOI: 10.4324/9781032615479

Typeset in Times New Roman
by Apex CoVantage, LLC

Access the Support Material: www.routledge.com/9781032615431

Dedication

This book is dedicated to the people, movements and legacies that laid the foundation for what you now hold in your hands. Before us, countless others showed courage, intellect, and talent, often going unrecognized. We stand humbly on your shoulders, with gratitude and reverence.

To our colleagues and friends in this profession – those included in this volume and those who, for various reasons, could not be – we recognize that this book could have been envisioned just as, if not more, powerfully by any number of you. This makes us special only to the degree that we have been entrusted to carry out the vision. Thank you for being the inspiration by which we continue to strive for excellence.

To new and emerging sex and sexuality educators: welcome, and thank you for joining us. We know firsthand how you navigate paths that are far from easy, while continuing to show up with compassion, resilience, and a commitment to truth, transformation and reconciliation. We applaud your hope, tenacity, and the courage it takes to keep moving forward.

To those – even past versions of ourselves – who will be impacted, and whose lives will be changed by each contributing chapter – the ones who have felt invisible, marginalized, and disconnected from their authentic selves. Our collective commitment to self-actualization has brought us to this moment. May the impact of this book be a source of healing, understanding, agency, and empowerment, offering pathways of knowledge and affirmation they deserve to make informed and fulfilling choices.

To our families, friends, lovers and colleagues who have inspired and supported our critical and renegade work: we thank you for your deep wells of love, understanding, cheerleading and encouragement.

Finally, to our communities at large: we who have celebrated moments of joy and connection, while also feeling the weight of resistance in cultures and systems steeped in colonialism and multilayered oppressions. Let us carry on, doing our best to balance our own well-being with the realities of the system, while holding tightly to a shared vision of liberation for all.

In solidarity,
Reece M. Malone, Tracie Q. Gilbert, Catherine Dukes, and Justine Ang Fonte

Contents

x *Contents*

About the Editors

Reece Malone, DHS, MPH, CSE-S, CST (he/siya) is a first-generation Filipino/x and an award-winning sexuality educator, equity trainer and consultant, community-based researcher, and sexual health program developer based in Winnipeg, Canada. He is the founder and CEO of Sexuality Consultants and Support Services Manitoba Inc. and its subsidiary company Diversity Essentials, which delivers awareness and equity training while maintaining a private practice in intimacy and sex therapy. With over 25 years of experience in the field of human sexuality, Dr. Malone's work spans regionally and nationally, informing policy and laws related to human rights, gender equity, and issues concerning sexual orientation. He is also the co-editor of an *Intersectional Approach to Sex Therapy: Centering the Lives of Indigenous, Racialized, and People of Color* published by Routledge.

Tracie Q. Gilbert, PhD (she/her) is a sexuality educator, writer, and researcher who uses her talents to pursue socioemotional wellness for Black people and racial justice in sex ed spaces. Having recently closed out a 25+-year career in direct youth development and sex ed, Dr. Gilbert can be found working most often now as a curriculum writer and trainer for other emergent educators. Dr. Gilbert earned her Master of Science in Education at the University of Pennsylvania and her doctorate from the Center for Human Sexuality Studies at Widener University, where she went on to serve as Assistant Professor for two years. She is the author of *Black & Sexy: A Framework of Racialized Sexuality*, published by Routledge in 2021.

Catherine Dukes, PhD, LCSW (she/her) is a national award-winning sex educator, an expert consultant, and a sex and couples therapist located in Delaware. She served as the VP of Education and Training for Planned Parenthood of Delaware's Sexuality Education Training Institute from 2006–2009 during which she led her department in winning three national Planned Parenthood education awards. She has had lesson plans published in several curricula including "Teaching Safer Sex," "Sex Ed in the Digital Age," and "Sexual

Orientation." Dr. Dukes is a regular speaker at national sexuality conferences and has over 25 years of contributing to the sex education field. She is currently the founder and CEO of The Center for Connection & Desire (Center CD), a growing group practice of sex therapists and sex educators. The Center CD recently launched its online and in-person sex education series, Bedroom Brainiacs.

Justine Ang Fonte, M.Ed, MPH (she/siya) is the child of Philippine immigrants and an award-winning sex educator, consultant, and professor based in New York City. She received her Master's in Education in Teaching from the University of Hawai'i and her Master's in Public Health in Sexuality from Columbia University. Justine is an instructor at Antioch University for the Sex Education Certificate Program and the author and voice of the Audible Original, *How to Talk to Your Kids About Sex*. On Instagram, she's known as "Your Friendly Ghostwriter" composing the texts you avoid sending about setting your boundaries. Justine also sits on the Advisory Board of EducateUS, a sex ed advocacy organization, advancing progressive sex education policy and implementation across the United States.

Contributors

Kim Andreassen (they/them) is a highly passionate and enthusiastic sexologist with a focus on diversity and inclusion in research and education. Kim holds a BA (Psychology), Grad Cert Education, Grad Dip Business Analytics, and Master of Sexology. Kim is a current PhD candidate at Curtin University. Their thesis focuses on best practice pedagogy and creation of consent resources for people with disability aged 12–16 years of age. They desire to advance the field of sexology, particularly within the intersection of gender diversity, sexual diversity, and intersex variations, disability, and other marginalized populations. Kim is currently working on several queering curriculum projects with the hope to enact positive social change through education, support, policy, and best practice implementation. *PayPal: kandreassenoc*

Tanya M. Bass, PhD, MEd, CHES, CSE (she/her/goddess) Dr. Tanya M. Bass is an award-winning sexuality educator, Founder of the North Carolina Sexual Health Conference, and President/CEO of Optics to Action. She serves as Clinical Instructor and the lead instructor for Human Sexuality at North Carolina Central University in the Department of Public Health Education. Dr. Bass completed her doctoral studies at Widener University and holds certifications as a Certified Sexuality Educator (CSE) with the American Association of Sexuality Educators, Counselors, and Therapists (AASECT), as well as a Certified Health Education Specialist (CHES®) through the National Commission for Health Education Credentialing. Dr. Bass is an active member of professional organizations such as AASECT, the NC Society for Public Health Educators, the Women of Color Sexual Health Network, and the Association of Black Sexologists and Clinicians. She is Vice President of Membership of AASECT and a member of the editorial board for the American Journal of Sexuality Education. tanyabass. com/*PayPal: TanyaBass/Venmo: Tanya-Bass-95*

Courtney Brame is the founder and executive director of Something Positive for Positive People (SPFPP), a nonprofit organization dedicated to supporting individuals diagnosed with herpes by providing stigma-free spaces for education, advocacy, and community. Since 2017, Courtney has been hosting the SPFPP podcast, where he leads candid conversations about the intersection of sexual health, mental wellness, and the societal stigma attached to sexually transmitted infections (STIs). Through his work, Courtney has become a leading voice in the stigma minimization movement, particularly within the herpes-positive community. He is passionate about creating platforms where people living with herpes can share their stories without fear or judgment, promoting emotional wellness and mental health in the process. His mission is to humanize the experience of living with an STI, dismantle harmful stereotypes, and provide tools for navigating stigma in personal relationships, medical settings, and broader societal contexts. Courtney's work has been featured in various media outlets, and his advocacy efforts have helped countless individuals embrace their sexuality and live stigma-free lives. Whether through podcasting, public speaking, or peer support programs, Courtney's approach emphasizes the importance of empathy, education, and community in reshaping the narrative around sexual health. *Venmo: CourtneyBrame/ Cash App: CourtneyBrame*

Sam Carwyn (she/her) has focused on youth, families, reproductive justice, and supporting survivors of violence. She is passionate about providing sex health education to those typically excluded. Body liberation principles are her framework as she works to help build self-determination. She is dedicated to speaking truth to power, artivism, and channeling sacred rage. As an educator, she guides others by naming our roles in coercive systems, challenging default thinking and norms with intentional grace. As an advocate, she reforms systems from within, highlights overlapping injustice, and centers the disproportionately impacted. As an activist, she uses storytelling to promote authenticity, dispel myths, and reject shame. She has a bachelor's in child, youth, and family studies and an MA in teaching. In May 2023, earned an MDiv with a concentration in social transformation. Grounded in her faith, she works towards equity, creating a legacy that honors her ancestors, is rooted in community, and makes her kids proud. basics.gumroad.com/ *Venmo: Sam-Carwyn/Cash App: amCarwyn/PayPal: SCarwyn*

Sam Casanova (she/they) is the founder of The P Word, LLC, a sex educator, and researcher who designs curricula centering the experiences of queer and trans people of color (QTPOCs). Casanova facilitates workshops around Love, Intimacy, Pleasure, and Sex (LIPS) through a reproductive justice lens, informed by their Community Ed Interview Series. They serve on the Denver LGBTQ+ Commission and on the Board of Directors for Soul 2 Soul Sisters. Additionally, Casanova is the events director for Sex Down South and Sexual Liberation and Arts Education (SLAE) and Business Manager for Velvet Lips Sex Ed. Previously a Humanities teacher, Casanova holds BAs in English and theater and an MA in teaching. Their works include "Body Items* for

Body Liberation" (2024), "Centering Black Bodies, Black History and Black Wellness within Sex Ed" (2023), "Cafe con Leche" (2017), and "I Asked Out Molly" (2014). www.samcasanova.com/*Venmo: sam-casanova/Cash App: SamYorkCasanova*

Mariah Caudillo (she/her) is a Latine sex educator and digital learning designer with a profound commitment to promoting inclusivity and equity in sex education. She has worked with a variety of organizations to provide comprehensive sex education to individuals of all ages and backgrounds. Beyond traditional education settings, Mariah's goal is to make sex education more accessible through social media. Her social media presence as the Sex Ed Files allows her to share inclusive, medically accurate, and pleasure-centered sexual health information and make complex topics relatable and informed by youth. *IG: sexedfiles/PayPal: womany/Venmo: mariahcaudillo*

Kai Cheng Thom, MSc, Certified Somatic Sex Educator, Certified Jungian Life Coach, and Certified Professional Coach is an author, somatic practitioner, mediator, and expert facilitator based in tkaronto/Toronto. A noted speaker, practitioner, and trainer in the areas of sexuality, embodiment, leadership coaching, and transformative justice, Kai Cheng is Faculty at the Institute for the Study of Somatic Sex Education as well as The Embody Lab, where she has co-directed several programs. Kai Cheng is also the author of six award-winning books in various genres, including the Publishing Triangle Award-winning essay collection *I HOPE WE CHOOSE LOVE.* kaichengthom.com

Aydrelle Collins, MS, LPC, is a sex therapist, ketamine-assisted psychotherapist, and owner of Melanin Sex Therapy based in Dallas, TX. She helps individuals and couples tap into their sexual power, focusing on strengthening intimate connections, particularly within the BIPOC community. As a counselor at Truth Pregnancy Resource Center, Aydrelle is deeply passionate about reproductive justice, guiding clients through pregnancy-related challenges with compassion and care. Currently pursuing her PhD in Human Sexuality at The California Institute of Integral Studies, she integrates psychedelics and somatic practices into her work, fostering profound healing and transformation. www.melaninsextherapy/*PayPal: melaninsextherapy/Cash App: Aygurl87/IG: melaninsextherapy*

Sarah Dahlston (she/her) is Senior Director of Education at Planned Parenthood Southwest Ohio. She provides relationship and sexual health education and training services to people of diverse backgrounds, with a focus on adult learners and people with disabilities. Sarah enjoys kayaking, going to concerts, and desserts of all kinds. She currently serves as a board member for PFLAG Dayton and is a Certified Health Education Specialist and a Certified Sexuality Educator. She lives in Dayton, Ohio with her partner and their family of animals. *Should you wish to make a donation consider: Planned Parenthood of Delaware:* www.plannedparenthood.org/planned-parenthood-delaware, *Planned Parenthood Southwest Ohio Region:* www.plannedparenthood.org/planned-parenthood-southwest-ohio *or SIECUS Sex Ed for Social Change:* www.siecus.org/donate

Kirsten M. deFur (she/her), a seasoned sexuality educator and trainer for over 20 years, specializes in curricula writing and training on various topics including healthy and unhealthy relationships, pleasure, trauma-informed approaches, client-centered practice, engagement skills and leadership development. Kirsten is currently working on a coaching certification. In addition to her professional endeavors, Kirsten is a momma to two daughters, wife to a loving husband, enjoys riding her bike and making homemade biscuits and muffins. *LinkedIn: kirstendefur/Venmo: Kirsten-deFur*

Jennifer Driver has nearly 15 years in the field of reproductive health, rights, and justice and is currently Senior Director of Reproductive Rights at the State Innovation Exchange. Her work centers on addressing systems that add burdens or barriers to accessing full reproductive health information and services – paying particular attention to communities of color, immigrants, system involved youth, and LGBTQ communities. Previously she served as Vice President of Policy and Strategic Partnerships at SIECUS, focusing on federal and state policy. Her career includes work with Welcoming America, Power to Decide, and the Georgia Campaign for Adolescent Power and Potential. Jennifer serves as an advisory board member for Resound Research for Reproductive Health (formerly Texas Policy Evaluation Project) and The Center on Reproductive Rights and Justice at UC Berkeley School of Law (CRRJ).

Mariotta Gary-Smith (she/her/Queen) is a third generation Oregonian and social justice agitator, with a deep family history of activism. In the fall of 2008, Mariotta was one of five nationally selected scholars for the 2008–2009 Inaugural Class for the Center of Excellence for Sexual Health (CESH) Scholars Fellowship Program at Morehouse School of Medicine. In 2009, she co-founded the Women of Color Sexual Health Network (WoCSHN; pronounced 'wok-shyn') – an online-based, collective organization for women/femme-identifying and gender expansive sexuality professionals of color. With over 20+ years of experience as a respected collaborator, trainer, and educator, Mariotta continues to curate informative, thoughtful, and honest learning spaces that center racial justice in sexuality, sexual health/education, and social critique. Her "passion work" has been and always will be teaching folks about the intersections of social justice, sexual health, health equity and "actionable agitation" and moving the focus of those most impacted from the margins to the center. *IG: BrownSugaSexDoc/Venmo: Mariotta Gary-Smith/PayPal: Mariotta Gary-Smith/Cash App: BrownSugaSexDoc*

Rachael E. Gibson, PhD, MPH, MS, MEd (she/her/ella): Dr. Gibson, also goes by "Dr. G", is an AASECT-certified sex educator based in Miami, FL, and spends much of her time in Brooklyn, NY, and Cape Town, South Africa. She has taught comprehensive health and sex education worldwide, including 17 years as a high school health teacher. She has over 20 years of experience in the field and founded AB Global in 2023. AB Global is a transnational organization that supports educators, youth-serving professionals, and families in their work and relationships with young people. In addition, Dr. G is an adjunct professor at Widener University's Center for Human Sexuality Studies and Wright State University. She also maintains a research partnership with the University of Western Cape in South Africa. Dr. G earned a BS in health science from the University of Arizona, an MPH from California State University, Long Beach, a Master of Science in Educational Leadership from the City College of New York, and a MEd and PhD from Widener University's Center for Human Sexuality Studies. In her free time, you can find her on the dance floor, sunning on the beach, hiking in the mountains, or traveling with her dog Lola. *IG: dr.rachaelgibson/or a donation to AB Global at IG: abglobal_dr.g or* www.abg-global.org

Jennifer A. Hart, MPH is a public health leader, trainer, consultant, and coach with 25 years' experience related to stigmatized health and social justice issues. She specializes in inclusive and trauma-informed programming covering sex education, abortion, HIV/AIDS, and sexual and gender identity. Jennifer excels in implementing strategic vision, developing equity initiatives, and navigating organizational change. With empathy and integrity, she fosters authentic engagement with organizations and individuals to achieve sustainable outcomes and full potential. She is a practitioner of anti-racism and proficient in Spanish and American Sign Language. Jennifer served as Vice President of Education, Learning & Engagement at Planned Parenthood League of Massachusetts; Executive Director of ALFA, an HIV/AIDS service organization in North Carolina; and Director of Training and Education at the National Abortion Federation. She earned her Master's of Public Health from Columbia University's Mailman School of Public Health. www.jennhartmph.com. Please consider making donations to the following organizations, *led by and/or serving communities experiencing marginalization by institutional -isms, specifically racism, homophobia, transphobia, ableism, and sexism. SisterSong:* www.SisterSong.net, *National LGBTQ Task Force:* www.thetaskforce.org *or American Association of People with Disabilities:* www.aapd.com

Dr. LaShay Harvey, is an educator, sexologist, and artist. She has always been attracted to creation stories: those stories that tell how something became. Her work and career interrogates not only how something comes to be (that is to say, born or birthed) but also examines the narratives that surround birth and becoming. Put another way, Dr. Harvey studies the reproductive lives of

Black girls and women. To this end, Dr. Havey holds a PhD in human sexuality studies and a master's degree in education. She has taught and trained on sexuality education for over 20 years with some of her favorite times spent at Morgan State University, the University of Baltimore, Towson University, and MICA. She is the principal and founder of Black Girl Saturday School®, an immersive experience where Black women journey back to their Girlhood seeking sensual brilliance. Dr. Harvey was born in Southeast Georgia and raised in Northeast Florida and likes her grits with butter, salt, and pepper and her tea sweet! www.blackgirlsaturdayschool.com

Kara Haug is an ASSECT Certified Sexuality Educator with a BA in psychology from Hope College in Holland MI, a masters in theological studies from Pacific Lutheran Theological Seminary in Berkeley, CA, and a postgraduate certificate in sexual health education and counseling from the University of Michigan in Ann Arbor, MI. As founder and partner of Reframing our Stories, a sexuality health education business, her goal and passion is for people to have brave and caring conversations about their bodies, health and safety, and sexuality to enable self-awareness, growth, empathy, openness, and positive relationships. Kara is also Adjunct Professor in Human Sexuality at Antioch University in Seattle. She lives in California with her husband and two kids. www.reframingourstories.com/*Venmo: Kara-Haug-1 or reframingourstories*

Anne Hodder-Shipp, CSE (she/they) is an AASECT Award-winning certified sex educator and relationship coach dedicated to providing accurate, expansive, and compassionate care. They are the lead educator at professional development org Everyone Deserves Sex Ed, and in her private practice, she helps teenagers and adults build knowledge and confidence around identity, pleasure, relationships, and communication. Most recently, Anne wrote the highly anticipated love language revamp, Speaking from the Heart: 18 Languages for Modern Love, and its accompanying guide, The Speaking from the Heart Workbook: A Practical Guide to the Modern Love Languages. www.annehoddershipp.com/*Cash App: EDSEsexed/Venmo: annehodder/ Zelle:* anne@annehodder.com

N. Jasmine Johnson (she/her), a psychotherapist and co-owner of Royal Fetish Films, is a prominent figure in sex education, mental health, and adult entertainment. With master's degrees in clinical social work from Florida State University and gerontology from the University of South Florida, she brings over 15 years of experience to her therapeutic approach. Founder of Blue Pearl Therapy, Jasmine is known for her innovative Path and Pathways method, blending medical mental health tech, CBT, and narrative therapy. An advocate for marginalized communities, she focuses on decolonizing sex and pleasure as a human right. As a mother of four, Jasmine balances her professional life with family, often incorporating her family's voices into her work.

Her commitment to fostering healthier understandings of sexuality is evident in her workshops, research, and public speaking, making her a transformative force in sexual health education. *IG: njasminej/Venmo: JetSettingJasmine/ PayPal:* njasminej@icloud.com

Dylan Kapit (they/them), MA is a white, queer, transmasculine, autistic sex educator. Their background is in special education, with a focus on working with the autistic community. Dylan developed an Autistic Sex Education training that they lead at conferences and for educators nationwide. Dylan's life dream is to write a queer and trans inclusive sex education curriculum for autistic young people, a project they are incredibly excited to be working on now. *Venmo: dkapit94*

Dr. Roger Kuhn (he/him) is a Poarch Creek Two-Spirit Indigiqueer soma-cultural sex therapist, sexuality educator, writer, activist, and musician. Roger's work explores the concepts of decolonizing and unsettling sexuality and focuses on the way culture impacts and informs our bodily experiences. He is a community organizer of the Bay Area American Indian Two-Spirit powwow, and a board member of the Two-Spirit & Native LGBTQ+ Center for Equity. His first book, Somacultural Liberation, is available in both paperback and audio. His music can be streamed on all digital platforms. www.rogerkuhn.com

Aubri Lancaster (Bri/she) BA², CSE is an independent AASECT and ANTE UP! Certified Sexuality Educator, conducting workshops and training for clinicians and sexuality professionals since 2021 and in-home adult toy parties since 2003. As a Greyromantic Asexual person Aubri has lived experience and a connection to the Asexual and Aromantic communities that provides a unique perspective on the issues facing the changing landscape of sexuality and orientation today. AceSexEducation.com/*PayPal: aubrilancaster/ Venmo: Aubri-Lancaster*

Dr. Bianca I. Laureano is an award-winning educator, curriculum writer, and sexologist. She is a co-foundress of the Women of Color Sexual Health Network, the SPM Disability Justice Fund a 501(c)(3) nonprofit fiscal sponsor for disability justice initiatives led by disabled global majority/BIPOC, and in 2017 founded ANTE UP! a virtual freedom school. She has written several curricula and led the curriculum development for the award-winning Netflix film *Crip Camp* and PBS documentary *I Didn't See You There*, both guided by disability justice principles. She is an AASECT certified sexuality educator and supervisor and was awarded an honorary doctorate from the California Institute for Integral Studies for her work in expanding the US sexuality field. Bianca is the editor of *The People's Book of Human Sexuality: Expanding the Sexology Archive* (2023), was part of the Black Mamas Matter Alliance inaugural Black Materna Health Incubator Hub pilot program offering a five-part series on Disability Justice for birth workers, and has been an abortion doula for over a decade. BiancaLaureano.com *and ANTE UP! at* www.AnteUpPD.com

Dirty Lola (She/Her) is an award-winning sex edutainer, speaker, and self-proclaimed dildo slinger. Known for her live sex ed Q&A show, *Sex Ed A Go-Go,* and as a Sexpert on the Emmy Nominated Netflix docuseries *The Principles of Pleasure,* Lola has spent over a decade working to end the stigma and shame surrounding sex and sexuality while sharing her discoveries with polyamory and kink. Lola is an instructor for Everyone Deserves Sex Ed and is on the board of the Youth Sexpert Program. She has brought her unique flavor of sex ed to numerous sexual wellness brands and media outlets such as *New York Magazine, HBO,* and *Vice.* www.dirtylola.co/*Venmo: Dlola/PayPal:* DirtyLola69@yahoo.com/*Cash App: LolaSEAGG*

Anne Mauro (she/her) is a licensed couples and family therapist, American Association of Sexuality Educators, Counselors, and Therapist (AASECT) certified sex therapist, sexuality educator, sex therapy supervisor, and American Association of Marriage and Family Therapy (AAMFT) clinical supervisor. Her private practice is nestled in the interwebs on the unceded territory of the Coast Salish peoples in Washington State. She has two publications: *More Than Ebony and Ivory: Complexities of sex therapy with interracial couples,* can be found in *An Intersectional Approach to Sex Therapy: Centering the lives of indigenous, racialized, and people of color* and *The Colonization of Black Sexualities: A clinical guide to relearning and healing.* www.annemauro.com/ *IG: iamannemauro*

Midori (美登里) (she/her) is an educator, artist, and irritant to banality. She teaches, coaches, and consults on alternative sexuality, BDSM, Shibari cultural competency, and empowerment.

Originally from Japan and shaped by 90s San Francisco safer sex activist circles, Midori brings a multicultural and holistic approach to kink, BDSM, and consent education. Founder of Rope Dojo (2003), ForteFemme Women's Intensive (2004), and Consent Dojo (2020), she is also Co-director of Education for Kink Informed Certification through the Sexual Health Alliance. Midori collaborates with mental health professionals, academic institutions, and intimacy coordinators, advising on BDSM and consent. She authored *The Seductive Art of Japanese Bondage,* the first English instructional book on Shibari and contributed a chapter on BDSM and women of the Asian diaspora in *An Intersectional Approach to Sex Therapy.* Her work is featured in numerous articles, columns, and instructional books. planetmidori.com/*Venmo: PlanetMidori/PayPal: PayPlanetMidori/Zelle:* ask@planetmidori.com

Alysha Oorjitham has a Bachelor of Science in Occupational Therapy (Honors), works with a focus on celebrating diverse sexual identities and LGBTQIA+ exploration, and advocates tirelessly for accessible sex and relationship education for people with disability. She is currently pursuing a graduate diploma in sexology, further expanding her expertise and insight into human sexuality. Alysha is passionate about comprehensive sex education that is trauma informed due to its value in harm prevention, promoting understanding, inclusivity, and empowerment in all aspects of sexual health. Alysha enjoys utilizing her OT skills to promote equity and pleasure for all, including assisting people with disability to find sexual aids tailored to their unique preferences and functional needs. *IG: sexiselfcare_/PayPal: alyshaoorjitham*

Dr. Alecia Rodriguez is in private practice, holding licensure in Florida, Colorado, Virginia, and Utah and provides clinical mental health services and marital, couples, and family therapy. She also coordinates mental health services for Miami-Dade County Public schools, including support of LGBTQ+ youth. Dr. Rodriguez offers lectures and workshops on subjects such as adolescent sexuality and working with justice-involved families and provides a range of therapeutic services, including sex therapy and treatment for juvenile and adult sex offenders. She has completed advanced training in clinical trauma, child abuse and neglect, adoption competency, gaming addiction, and autism spectrum disorder. *IG: theuniquetherapist/PayPal: UniqueTherapy*

Yael R. Rosenstock Gonzalez (she/her/ella), aka YaeltheSexGeek, is a pleasure activist who centers identity and social positioning work, values self-exploration, and promotes intentional practice as a vehicle for desired shifts. Through her company Sex Positive You, Yael offers support in finding pleasurable, joyful, and positive experiences with self and sex. This includes connecting to embodied pleasure and pleasure techniques, improving confidence and self-worth, increasing emotional, physical, and sexual intimacy with partners, developing communication skills, setting and respecting boundaries, improving one's relationship with their body, and more. Yael is a sex researcher, educator, coach, and consultant. She is a certified Authentic Consent Facilitator, EroSomatic Touch Practitioner, Sex Doula, a 2023 Scholars of Sexology Scholar with the Kinsey Institute, and the author of *An Introguide to a Sex Positive You: Lessons, Tales, and Tips.* www.sexpositiveyou.com/*Zelle:* info.kvibrations@gmail.com/*PayPal:* yael.gonzalez.rosenstock@gmail.com/*Venmo: yael-rosenstock/Cash App: yaelrosenstock/Google Pay:* yaelthesexgeek@gmail.com

Arc Telos Saint Amour (they/them) is a neurodivergent, queer and trans, Two-Spirit, gender non-conforming person of Mexican Indigenous descent (Coahuiltecan), and a victim/survivor of childhood abandonment, trauma, and abuse. This lived and living experience has led them to a deep belief in Native Indigenous animism, radical empathy, and the power of holistic affirmation and self-agency. Professionally, Arc Telos spent over ten years as a business developer opening start-ups and working with established organizations to expand into new territories all over the US. Following this, Arc Telos spent another ten years active in the non-profit field, working with organizations throughout Chicago, New York, Vermont, California, and Michigan centering Justice, Equity, Diversity, and Inclusion (JEDI) practices and using trauma-informed and intersectionality based frameworks. They are currently a national speaker/facilitator, the Executive Director of Youth MOVE National, and the owner/founder of Arc Telos Consulting. www.arctelosconsulting.com/*Venmo: arctelossaintamour/Cash App: ARCTELOS*

Danielle Simpson-Baker (she/her) is a licensed marriage and family therapist (FL) and a board certified sexologist (American Board of Sexology). Danielle earned her master's in marriage and family therapy from UCF in 2021 and is currently working towards a certificate in sex therapy. She also runs a sex-positive Instagram page (@thesexpottherapist) that has garnered almost 24,000 followers since its inception in 2019; with that following, Danielle started a virtual sexual wellness clinic called Sex(pot) Therapy, LLC (sexpottherapyllc.com; instagram.com/*sexpottherapyllc*). Danielle hopes to provide sex therapy, coaching, and consulting, as well as a host of sexual wellness products for every person's needs! *IG: thesexpottherapist/Cash App: sexpottherapyllc/PayPal:* thesexpottherapist@gmail.com/*Zelle:* dsb2015@aol.com

Hannah Smith (she/her) is an occupational therapist living and working on the land of the Noongar people in Western Australia. Hannah works with people across the lifespan with a broad range of disabilities and needs in community settings. On beginning her work in the disability field, Hannah was confronted with the critical need for more accessible education. Following this, providing education and coaching to clients, families, and other professionals to facilitate access to sexual healthcare, sexuality, intimacy, and safe, positive relationships become a large portion of her daily clinical work. This lead Hannah to become deeply passionate about the capacity for all relationships and sexuality educators to improve the health and well-being of others and to facilitate joy through access to such a valued and meaningful occupation. This is a passion she continues to serve through facilitating workshops, training, and consultation to professional and community organizations and contributing to the development and distribution of sexuality and relationship education resources. *PayPal: thespookyot*

Delia Sosa (they/them) is a medical student living in the midwestern US, a transgender and intersex advocate, and an LGBTQIA2+ educator. Delia's research focuses on the incorporation of LGBTQIA2+ health into phase I undergraduate medical education curricula, providing continuing education to clinicians and researchers regarding the care of intersex patients, and obstetric and gynecologic care received by transgender and intersex patients. They are Associate Executive Director of the national Medical Student Pride Alliance, a former member of the GLMA Health Professionals in Training

Curricular Reform Committee, and a Point Foundation BIPOC scholar. Delia has co-authored policy within the American Medical Association to strengthen protection for gender-affirming care across the United States, as well as policy within their State Medical Association to prevent unnecessary surgeries on intersex youth and infants. Delia spends their free time creating educational resources and social media educational tools for healthcare providers and staff on how to care for LGBTQIA2+ patients. They have been recognized for their work by The Latino Medical Student Association, Tufts University School of Medicine, *Them* magazine, NBC News, *USA Today*, and Yahoo! *IG: enbydelia/Venmo: Delia-Sosa/PayPal:* deliasosa1@gmail.com

Marla Renee Stewart (she/her) is an award-winning sexologist, sexual strategist, and author who has been running her sexuality education company, Velvet Lips Sex Education, for 15 years and co-founded the Sex Down South Conference, which has been running for ten years. Highly sought-after, Marla developed the Be Sexcessful Business Coaching Program to help new entrepreneurs who have adult brands to excel by providing the foundations they need that are often missing in sexuality education curriculum. Her methods have helped multiple entrepreneurs go above and beyond the six-figure mark by navigating social media and marketing, brand development, and expanding upon their financial literacy. www.marlareneestewart.com/*Zelle:* marla@velvetlipssexed.com/*Venmo: @Marla-Stewart/PayPal: VelvetLips/Cash App: VelvetLips*

Hilary F. Towle (she/her) has dedicated her career to working at the intersection of health and education in the US and around the globe, addressing public health disparities by increasing access to sexual and reproductive health information. Hilary hails from North Carolina where she was raised in values of social justice and began her career in safe abortion access work. Currently, she oversees the development, facilitation, and expansion of research-based professional education opportunities for sex educators nationwide as Associate Director of Professional Education & Training at Planned Parenthood League of Massachusetts (PPLM), including training and supporting educators in implementing the PPLM-authored, evidence-based program *Get Real: Comprehensive Sex Education That Works*. She holds a BA in sociology from Meredith College and a master's in education from the Harvard Graduate School of Education. Hilary is passionate about the transformative power of comprehensive sexuality education and strives to make it accessible to all people. *Please consider making donations to the following organizations, led by and/or serving communities experiencing marginalization by institutional -isms, specifically racism, homophobia, transphobia, ableism, and sexism. SisterSong:* www.SisterSong.net, *National LGBTQ Task Force:* www.thetaskforce.org *or American Association of People with Disabilities:* www.aapd.com

Quinn Vermillion (she/her) uses her degree in human sexuality education from Widener University to increase access to inclusive, sex-positive education. Her background in Deaf education motivates her to create lessons that are accessible to learners outside of a mainstream classroom. She currently works at Planned Parenthood of Delaware as the Disabilities Program Coordinator, teaching high quality sex education to individuals with IDD, their families, and professionals who serve them. *Consider making a donation to: Planned Parenthood of Delaware:* www.plannedparenthood. org/planned-parenthood-delaware, *Planned Parenthood Southwest Ohio Region:* www.plannedparenthood.org/planned-parenthood-southwest-ohio *or SIECUS Sex Ed for Social Change:* www.siecus.org/donate

Sonja Vitow (she/they) is a writer, educator, and PhD student at the Center for Human Sexuality Studies at Widener University. They have been teaching in K-12 schools for over a decade, and hold an MEd in Human Sexuality Education from Widener University as well as an MFA in Creative Writing from Emerson College. Sonja serves as Professional Development Coordinator at Planned Parenthood Southeastern PA, working to bring comprehensive sex education that empowers children, guardians, and educators to the Greater Philadelphia area. They are a support group facilitator at the Gender and Sexuality Clinic at the Children's Hospital of Philadelphia, where they lead support groups for trans and gender-nonconforming teens and their families. Sonja spends evenings as a post-abortion support counselor for Exhale Pro-Voice. They are also the Director of Educational Consultation at FUSE Compassionate Consulting, LLC., a private sex ed consulting firm, as well as an occasional contributor to Slate.com's "How to Do It" sex advice column. They are currently working on writing children's books that encourage communication about difficult topics between children and their safe adults. Their short fiction and poetry can be found at sonjavitow.com.

Isabella Weber, MPH (she/her) is Vice President of Education & Training at Planned Parenthood of Delaware, which provides comprehensive sex education and professional training to over 5,000 people annually in Delaware and neighboring states. She has been a sex educator since 2010 and is a certified trainer for multiple age levels of Our Whole Lives, a faith-based, comprehensive sex education program. Her specialty is in sex education for people with intellectual and developmental disabilities and authored the curriculum *You're in Charge: A Customizable Sex and Relationships Education Program for Self-Advocates with IDD.* She has a master's degree in public health from the University of Michigan. *Consider making a donation to: Planned Parenthood of Delaware:* www.plannedparenthood.org/planned-parenthood-delaware, *Planned Parenthood Southwest Ohio Region:* www.plannedparenthood.org/ planned-parenthood-southwest-ohio *or SIECUS Sex Ed for Social Change:* www.siecus.org/donate

Steph Zapata is a well-seasoned, nationally recognized, award-winning, NuyoRican sexuality educator and space creator. They have become a long-term catalyst for change within sexuality education through their radically intentional approaches that call out systems of oppression and call in individuals and community to disrupt and reimagine what can be. Their work focuses on collective liberation tactics through innovative and honest sex ed that creates space for the whole self and the whole truth. Steph is a self-titled Unprofessional Professional who offers no apology for the disruption of white supremacy through the joy of decolonial sexuality education. Learn more about their consulting/training services + The S.L.A.M. Conference at stephaniespeakshere.com/*IG: RiseWSteph/PayPal: StephanieSpeaksHere@ gmail.com/Venmo: StephanieSpeaksHere/Cash App: StephanieSpeaksHere*

Preface

Our Process

As co-editors, we bring together a wealth of diverse experiences in sex and sexuality education, having delivered comprehensive and critical sex education to audiences that include creating public literature, providing individual consultations, facilitating small and large group workshops, and delivering presentations to packed auditoriums. From our varied regions, diverse backgrounds, and social locations, we enrich our collaborative work, working to ensure a multifaceted and inclusive approach while conceptualizing this book.

For several months, before a callout to contributors and within the limitations of this book, we discussed what are important sections to include and what critical, current, and future topics we see as foundational to address. We wanted to develop this book thoughtfully serving as a resource as an extension or compliment to current practices as well as challenging unrecognized bias and oppression in critical pedagogy and praxis.

Contributor Acknowledgments

We recognize and value that the seen and unseen leaders in sex education are deeply embedded in their communities beyond professional roles, delivering sex education in ways that challenge traditional teaching methods. Despite their contributions and broad impact, many sex educators are on the ground, volunteers, or work within underfunded organizations often facing low pay and limited opportunities for advancement and have experienced exclusion due to cultural stigma and systemic and interpersonal discrimination.

Acknowledging the challenges that contributors may face, we do not take for granted the in-kind token appreciations they receive for their contributing work. For full transparency, we as editors receive only a nominal fraction of sales, which is then divided equally among us. In light of this, we sought thoughtful ways for contributors to receive broader compensation beyond under a dozen free thank you books from the publishers. We strongly encourage readers to not only acknowledge contributors in their references but also to honor their chapter contributions through their contact links provided in the contributors' section. How you choose to acknowledge their contributions is at your discretion. We encourage consideration of the lived realities of many of our contributing authors.

Considerations and Limitations of This Book

Our intention is to offer an array of topics common in the field of sex education. Regionally and culturally we recognize that sex education extends beyond sexual behaviors and encompasses an ecology of human sexuality. When we say "sex education" or "sex educators" it is meant to be expansive beyond sexual acts and expressions keeping in mind the impacts of settler colonization on human sexuality, systemic and interpersonal discrimination, social determinants that impact sexual health and wellness, laws and policies that are an affront to sexual self-agency and self-determination, and all other aspects that inform human sexuality. That said, we recognize that even in our attempt to address as many areas as possible some gaps may remain, in both the subject matter that was included and nuance with which these topics could be discussed. As you read we invite your grace in perspective and look forward to the ways future volumes of this book will evolve.

Fundamental Concepts and Critical Developments in Sex Education

Intersectional and Trauma-Informed Approaches

Fundamental Concepts and Critical Developments in Sex Education: Intersectional and Trauma-Informed Approaches is a collection of sex and sexuality topics that offer emerging and experienced sex educators contemporary critical pedagogical considerations and foundational principles for developing and delivering topics in sex education.

Through their extensive experience as sex educators, authors for each section intend to demonstrate how they deliver sex education considering principles of decolonization, trauma-informed applications, inclusion and accessibility, and intersectionality and equity supported by offering practical applications, examples, and scenarios and concluding with introspective questions for further consideration.

Fundamental Concepts and Critical Developments in Sex Education: Intersectional and Trauma-Informed Approaches is an essential resource for sex educators across various sectors and educational settings. It equips educators with the knowledge and tools needed to address diverse student needs and foster equitable, inclusive, and respectful learning environments. By integrating these approaches, sex educators can better support learners holistically in both traditional and nontraditional learning environments.

Additional resources for each chapter can be downloaded via Routledge.

Introduction

Emerging sexuality educators often describe their desire to enter the profession for a plethora of reasons including:

- Sexuality education was lacking in their youth
- Information provided was driven by a combination of abstinence, avoidance, or fear and shame-based approaches
- Lived and lifelong both positive and negative experiences informed their career paths
- Developmentally normative sexual behavior is pathologized as a risk factor

DOI: 10.4324/9781032615479-1

Sexuality educators encompass both professionals and non-professionals; drawing from a richness of backgrounds and experiences, they play pivotal roles across a multitude of sectors, contributing uniquely to the advancement of sexual health and wellness.

In the realm of education, the development and delivery of comprehensive sex education curriculums is crucial to foster understanding and informed decision-making among learners of all ages. Within healthcare, sex educators collaborate with medical professionals to integrate sexual health into overall well-being, ensuring patients receive holistic care.

In the mental health and wellness industry, they design programs that promote healthier approaches to sexuality and relationships, enhancing individuals' and communities' quality of life. Their work in science and research is crucial, as they engage in studies that shed light on sexual behaviors, health outcomes, and the impact of societal norms, informing evidence-based practices and policies. Sex educators who are in counseling and therapy sectors integrate their expertise as they provide critical knowledge, resources, and support to individuals, couples, and relationships navigating sexual health challenges and relationship dynamics.

Sexuality educators also thrive in coaching and enrichment roles, offering personalized guidance encouraging individuals expansiveness when it comes to experiencing pleasure, fluidity of identities, and shifts in lifestyle circumstances. Sex educators' influence extends into the arts, where they use creative expression to explore and communicate complex themes related to the intersections of culture and sexuality. Sex education entrepreneurs innovate and bring new products, services, and technologies that enhance sexual health and well-being.

In all these sectors and beyond, sex educators are united by their commitment to fostering a more informed society and where sexual well-being is recognized as a fundamental aspect of human life.

Gaps in Critical, Trauma-Informed, Inclusive, and Accessible Sex Education

For many sex educators, the eagerness, enthusiasm, and hopeful outcomes of "doing" sex ed can supersede critical pedagogical deliveries that are comprehensive, inclusive, and accessible. This combined with the realities of restrictive policies and legislation renders status quo practices in sex education. As noted by Elia and Tokunaga (2015), "sexuality education within these parameters is mostly heteronormative, sex negative, ableist, and discriminatory, and in consequence deleterious."

A common reality for many sex educators housed in underfunded organizations and agencies is they are often left to their own devices, to know and understand the content and deliver information that is palpable and understandable to their diverse audiences. Sex education topics that discuss or contain sexual violence;

center communities that remain invisibilized, stigmatized, and oppressed; and address topics that challenge community standards and cultural norms require a trauma-informed, intersectional, inclusive, and accessible approach, especially given that learning theory includes experiential and interactive individual and group exercises.

Professional and personal development opportunities towards becoming a sexuality educator may offer a broad landscape of sexual development, diverse sexualities, and sexual practices; however, critical issues and more nuanced considerations are often excluded.

To address the critical praxis gaps in progressive sex-positive sexuality education, in combination with trauma-informed application while facilitating developmentally appropriate learning theory, this book contains the fundamentals of being a trauma-informed, equitable, inclusive, anti-oppressive, and accessible sex and sexuality educator.

What We Envision

We envision this book as a resource for emerging and experienced sexuality educators. Chapter contributions will fall under the following sections:

- PART I. Informing our values and attitudes as sexuality educators
- PART II. Critical approaches and lenses from which to view when providing sex education
- PART III. Key information, research and continuous learning
- PART IV. Critical skills and considerations for increasing impact and inclusivity
- PART V. Navigating the business and limitations of sex education

Importance of Critical Pedagogy in Sex Education

Intention doesn't necessarily equate to impact.

As sex educators our goal is not only to deliver content but to employ an understanding that our content relevant and to acknowledge that learners learn differently and those differences come from an array of systemic factors.

This is where critical pedagogy is essential in sex education as it promotes inclusivity, reflection, and empowerment while at the same time recognizing systemic, societal, and cultural influences in the development and delivery of curricula. Critical pedagogy ensures the curriculum acknowledges and respects human diversity, histories, and experiences of intersectionality. It encourages learners to question societal norms, encouraging critical thinking to analyze information, question sources, and form their own informed opinions, leading to more educated decisions about their sexual health and relationships. This empowerment also enhances their ability to advocate for their own needs and boundaries, promoting autonomy in navigating relationships and sexual encounters respectfully and ethically.

Understanding power dynamics and challenging oppressive practices are crucial components of critical pedagogy; this is inclusive of the power dynamics in the settings and environments where sex educators are positioned.

It helps learners to recognize and understand the power structures in sexual relationships and societal attitudes towards sex, fostering more equitable and consensual interactions. Additionally, it equips learners with the tools to identify and challenge oppressive practices and beliefs such as sexism, queer and transphobia, ableism, racism, ageism, ethnocentrism, and erotophobia. The reflective and dialogic approach of critical pedagogy encourages open discussions about sex, breaking down taboos and stigma to create a more honest and open learning environment. It promotes continuous reflection on personal beliefs and experiences, allowing learners to evolve in their understanding of sexuality and relationships and by extension shift cultural understandings of human sexuality.

Conclusion and Visions

Overarchingly, the outcome of comprehensive sex education expands well beyond behavioral interventions that avoid sexually transmitted infections and unplanned pregnancy as well as the enhancement of pleasure as many contemporary sex educators posit. The impact of sex education dismantles all oppressive systemic structures unburdening and liberating individuals, their families, and communities with a return or revisioning of what it means to truly be an authentic person in their sexuality; their humanness.

As editors, we acknowledge the brilliance from the contributing authors contained in this book and we invited additional visionaries in our field to share their philosophies, values, dreams, and hopes with the following question:

When you imagine the impact that sex ed can have on the liberation of all people, what does that look like?

Here is what they've shared:

Anne Mauro, MFT, LMFT, DHS, AASECT certified sex therapist, sexuality educator, CST and AAMFT supervisor, published author, and speaker

Resistance is the gateway to liberation. It shouldn't be feared, but expected. Pulling us backwards with every step forward, in sex education, we live in resistance. Systemic barriers, oppressive structures, colonial ideologies, societal norms, religious beliefs, political agendas, laws and policy, censorship, stigmatization, pathologization, and misinformation are a constant tug at our liberation. Through studying historical trends in the backlash against sex education you will find many of our professional pioneers and elders have paid a price, either personally or professionally, to build the foundation that we stand on now. With the significant systemic resistance, the backlash and opposition is, oftentimes, coupled with advancements in the field. This violence and discrimination has tried many weary sexuality educators. Liberation, in the context of sex education, means coming prepared and armed for pushback. This includes practicing radical self and communal love. Your sustainability in the field may be dependent on healing the professional wounds inflicted upon you and us. Present and past. For our liberation, you must rest, tend to your body, and spirit. Arm yourself with mentors, colleagues, supervisors, and personal kinships that can carry you when you become weary. To be good ancestors to those that come after you in our field, you must continue to make progress for our collective liberation.

Steph Zapata, Award-Winning Educator, Speaker, Somatic Explorer & Space Creator

The liberation of all people can be found and felt in the sexuality education you choose to create and offer. In part, to decolonize is to give land back. Our intentionally inclusive sex education has the power to give communities their power back, to help learners return to the home within. We get to birth a world (classroom, event, etc.) where each person is given the tools to develop and nurture a compassionate relationship with themselves and those around them. One may see sex ed as just that, but I encourage you to engage your childlike-ever-expanding imagination to view the lessons you offer as self-advocacy through intentional development of self. Liberation is actualizable through complex, intentional, honest education that affirms the full human experience. We will not gatekeep and assume sovereignty over the identities, stories, and bodies of our learners any longer. It's time to give back.

Roger Kuhn (Poarch Creek), PhD, LMFT, CST

When I dream of liberation, I see a present that is illuminated by the past, and a future that prioritizes abundance. From our past we learn what was and what now is, our present teaches us what is working and where further understanding is needed, and our future is where we continue to imagine what is possible. This requires both a learning and an unlearning, and neither is a linear process, for education is not a one-size-fits-all problem-solving solution.

Liberation is also inherently tied to land and the bodies on the land. Sex education must also include how the practices of naming gender, sexual orientation, and sexual behaviors, were intricately linked to a specific and limited understanding of the broad umbrella of sexuality regarding culture.

When you control someone's culture and force them to assimilate to another culture, you control their liberation. When we say decolonize and unsettle sexuality, we are speaking directly to the systematic infiltration of colonial ideology on Indigenous sexuality, and more broadly the sexuality of all peoples who have been oppressed by colonial forces.

Jennifer Driver, Senior Director of Reproductive Rights, State Innovation Exchange

Tattered textbooks, overburdened high school coaches, and 25 teenagers struggling to come into their own: that's what I remember about sex education growing up. Reflecting on it today, I ponder how my sexual identity might have evolved differently had my early education focused on agency and pleasure, rather than scaring and shaming those who were already sexually active.

I realize that what I craved back then was a lesson in Reproductive Justice, the Black-woman conceptualized framework advanced in 1994. Reproductive Justice expands upon reproductive rights by emphasizing the intersectionality of various social justice issues, including race, class, gender identity, sexual orientation, disability, and socioeconomic status. An RJ-oriented sex ed approach empowers young people to build foundations for sexual freedom and joy.

Sex education in the United States has been stifled by our inability to be imaginative, and continues to perpetuate the past harms and traumas of adults who did not receive the fullness of what sex education can be. It's past time that we lean into the possibilities of all the richness that sex education has to offer.

Kai Cheng Thom, MSc, Certified Somatic Sex Educator, Certified Jungian Life Coach, and Certified Professional Coach

At the core of sex education is the potential to affirm that all bodies are inherently deserving of dignity, intimacy, and pleasure. Truly liberatory sex education goes far beyond teaching contraceptive methods and the prevention of STIs (both worthy goals) and offers us collective opportunities to develop embodied somatic intelligence as a society.

Through liberatory sex education, we can unwind traumatic social conditioning around body image, race, gender, ability, and more. We can open the possibility of developing empowered choice and voice in intimate situations and beyond. We can envision a world that has evolved beyond colonial, sexual, and gendered violence. In other words, sex education is a means through which we can start to build a society that is safer, more just, and more life-giving.

Bianca I. Laureano, PhD, MA[2], CSE, CSES

Collective liberation requires collective access and interdependence. As more disabled people are birthed or become disabled, in a world where climate chaos, pandemics, increased plastics in our food, lack of healthcare, transmission of airborne viruses (to name a few–and all being classic forms of eugenics), collective access and being led by those most impacted is the only sustainable way to survive.

Disability Justice has ten principles – the last two being collective liberation and access. To move there together, white disabled people need to get out of the way and stop taking up so much space! This includes white queer and trans, working class, disabled people too, as many view disability as a social construction. Disability is also a social *reality,* where we move together yet not with white people leading the way; as history has demonstrated, they collectively and individually leave so many of us behind – on purpose, especially our children and elders. Collective liberation and access cannot and will not be from a settler colonial imperialist lens. It will be through diasporic Indigenous and Black queer and trans disabled people's leadership. For those who forget, Black people are indigenous to Africa! There is an ethics of care, a model that requires a divestment from the legacy of white supremacist colorist cisheteropatriarchy. That means it won't only be the democratic-voting, salaried Black queer, degreed, disabled person in the lead. They too will know their place, have a succession plan, and move out of the way.

Imagining a world where we are moving in a culture of consent; where there is no expected way to have a body, radical acceptance guides the collective, and our bodyminds, hearts and souls follow. A commitment to cross-disability solidarity and cross-movement organizing is the only path forward, where the reproductive justice movement finally begins to withdraw from ableist ideologies and practices. Where I (and other Black disabled people) no longer have to remind people that ableism is anti-Black, non-disabled people understand that asking us what our disabilities are is considered a consent violation, and where a collective intergenerational community-based curriculum for disabled people learning about sex, math, history, languages, and geography becomes the expectation, because we are all disabled.

Our commonly cited disabled white and light skinned Asian disabled scholars will know their roles too, not have to be reminded by us, and know that moving out of the way means divesting from colorist model minority myths. The misuse and cultural appropriation of Black feminist linguistic gifts–such as intersectionality, engaged pedagogy, and abolition–will cease! And any attempt to discuss or "decolonize" anything will always already have a land back grounding that does not separate from Indigenous knowledge.

It's not only what a future *looks* like, it is a more sensual experience, not invested in using or privileging one sense (vision) over all others. What the future smells, sounds, feels, looks, and tastes like is a full bodymind experience. This requires more than a theory in the flesh; it is a theory of the *bodymindsoul* and abundance. A revolutionary love approach. It is a rehumanizing of ourselves for ourselves and a transforming of trauma.

How to Read This Book

When approaching *Fundamental Concepts and Critical Developments in Sex Education: Intersectional and Trauma Informed Approaches* there are no expectations on how to read this book. It is not meant to be read in a linear way but rather treated as a versatile resource and a source of shared knowledge. We encourage readers to use the book as one of many methods to critically evaluate incorporating continuous assessment, reflection, and refinement of praxis and pedagogical approaches.

Reference

Elia, J., & Tokunaga, J. (2015). Sexuality education: Implications for health, equity, and social justice in the United States. *Health Education, 115*, 105–120. https://doi.org/10.1108/HE-01-2014-0001

Part I

Informing Our Values and Attitudes as Sexuality Educators

1 The Great Pushback

Why Social Justice Is CompSexEd

Mariotta Gary-Smith

Key Terms

- **Comprehensive Sex Education (CSE):** a teaching approach that enables young people to advocate for and protect their health, well-being, and dignity by providing a toolkit of knowledge and skills. It provides medically accurate and age-appropriate information about sexuality and sexual/reproductive health. This supports the exercise of full bodily autonomy, which requires the right to make choices about one's body AND the information to make choices in a meaningful way. These ideals are based on human rights principles that advance gender equity and the rights and empowerment of young people.
- **Reproductive Justice:** the human right to maintain personal bodily autonomy, to have or not have children, and to parent the child we do have in sage and sustainable communities.
- **White Supremacy (WS):** a form of racism centered upon the belief that white people are superior to people of other racial backgrounds and that whites should politically, economically, and socially dominate non-whites. While often associated with violence perpetrated by the KKK and other white supremacist groups, it also describes a political ideology and systemic oppression that perpetuates and maintains the social, political, historical and/or industrial white domination.
- **Intersectionality:** a term coined in 1989 by Kimberlé Williams Crenshaw, PhD; and is the study of overlapping or intersecting social identities and related systems of oppression, domination, or discrimination. This approach has been largely advanced by women of color, who clearly state that classifications such as gender, race, class, and others cannot be examined in isolation from one another; instead, they interact and intersect in individuals' lives, in society, in social systems, and are mutually constitutive.

One of my foundational beliefs is that the delivery and practices of comprehensive sex education (CSE) must be challenged AND changed to reflect the needs for each person who receives it. As a Black woman/femme sexuality

DOI: 10.4324/9781032615479-3

educator, I am responsible for the information I share, as much as how I share it (Gary-Smith & Hunte, 2024). I'm also accountable for how I engage conversations around other historically impacted identities and communities. Teaching CSE requires that the various perspectives of many communities be considered. From LGBTQAI2S+, to the Disability community, Immigrant/Refugee communities, language access, and community literacy; these are all valuable perspectives that deserve full space within the information being shared.

While research studies and other academic offerings can support what I've stated – which is important – I will offer some personal context on why CSE matters and how to potentially negotiate any pushback that may come from engaging in a comprehensive social justice framework.

First, my experience is informed and defined as a Black person – which is how the world first defines and interacts with me. My personal/lived experience and my work as a sexologist/sexuality educator is grounded there. I'm unapologetic about my lens being intentionally centered on Black and Black, Indigenous and People of Color (BIPoC) folks and communities (Flowers, 2016). During my career, I've had pushback from various places and have been successful in creating more brave spaces for people to learn, live, and love themselves, their cultures, and communities.

This chapter will also offer ways to use knowledge, compassion, and insight as part of using a justice lens as a primary component of CSE and not the afterthought. Hopefully, there are a few tools here to support your ability to curate spaces, opportunities to learn and share information about sexuality, how folks have the right to be safe and honored for their personhood and others in their communities, and how to celebrate their identities, cultural heritage, relationships, wisdom, and knowledge as part of their learning experience.

My first sex ed lesson (in school) happened in the seventh grade. This lesson was made up of an old film that promoted archaic stereotypes of women and what they were supposed to do (housework, raising children, and volunteering in their spare time). There wasn't any specific information about bodily functions, no medical terms for body parts, nothing about identity or expression, feelings, and pleasures. And absolutely no discussion about sexual engagement or encounters. This 30-minute black and white film raised more questions than gave answers.

In today's society, sexuality education is vast and varied, with many ways to access all kinds of information. From YouTube to Reddit to TikTok, there are so many avenues to find information, and what's also true is there's a lot of misinformation available, which can lead to harmful and inaccurate learning. In this chapter, I'll share how I see the reproductive justice (RJ) framework as a core component of CSE and some ways to engage and navigate pushback if and when it presents itself. I'll also discuss how I use CSE as a foundation to normalize the perspectives of other communities and how a multi-layered and expansive approach in CSE actually uplifts and supports diverse communities, their members, the people they love, and how they live (Gary-Smith et al., 2022).

Pushback #1: Racism

To start, let's take a high-level overview of the impact of White Supremacy on RJ movement spaces. Many examples exist that document the harm and trauma to historically impacted communities that have forever shaped the landscape of the movement. Two historically significant ones for me are (1) using enslaved African folks for medical experimentation and (2) the history of Indian boarding schools. Both of these experiences have continued ripple impacts across multiple systems and outcomes for each of these communities and their members.[1,2]

These histories of harm and erasure have left indelible imprints on how health care is accessed and offered, the importance of informed consent, and bodily autonomy – issues that are still deeply personal and valid today. I've experienced people telling me in my learning spaces that these moments and their lingering impacts are "not the fault of ancestors" and/or that "Black people always make a big deal of something that happened in the past." One way I redirect their energy and comments is to ask them to consider how they have a personal stake in those experiences. I suggest reading materials, like *Medical Apartheid* by Harriet Washington or the Reproductive Justice Timeline (Gary-Smith et al., 2022), along with a firm yet gentle nudge for them to find themselves in these moments. Meeting people with proof can move some folks into reflection.

Then, there's the overturning of *Roe v. Wade*, which was the law for 50 years. It was removed by the now conservative US Supreme Court in 2023. This watershed moment of removing access to reproductive health care has directly contributed to increased interstate travel for people seeking abortion care, as well as increasing the level of danger for RJ advocates, abortion providers/educators, and health care workers from "law abiding citizens" who want to protect the unborn. With these personal and seemingly polarizing moments, I try to engage from a simple question: "is this moment and decision yours? How are you going to impact this decision to make the life of the person better? What are you willing to sacrifice in order for your desired outcome to win?" (Christian, 2021). Here, the resurgence of historical tropes about BIPoC folks and Immigrant/Refugee communities of color are given air, and it's important to interrupt those backlash flashpoints.

Pushback #2: Language

In 2023, there's been a wave of more conservative ideologies and policies that focus on dismantling equity gains for BIPoC communities and LGBTQAI2S+ spaces. One example is the recent anti-critical race theory (CRT) movement – a response to the growing number of Black people in positions of power/decision-making and the call for multi-racial/-cultural coalitions in various organizations and spaces. To me, this was the knee jerk reaction to the racial uprising that swept through the US urban cities in 2020 after the murders of George Floyd and Breonna Taylor. CRT was part of the context where these conversations were grounded, and this included the sexuality profession.

In late 2022, the pushback was that "CRT made White people feel bad," with emphasis that teaching the truths of the genocide of Indigenous and Native communities and American chattel slavery would no longer be tolerated. There's a straight line of connection from these claims to the recent removal of DEI programming across the nation, notably in higher education and government. Some US states and local school boards have voted in policies that disallow the gathering/recognition of Black Lives Matter (BLM), Gay, Lesbian, Straight Education Student Network (GLSEN), and other ally-centered student groups in schools, while removing members from those local school boards who supported them.

For me, these situations are very personal. As a Black sexologist/sexuality educator, it can still be difficult to hear that BLM is a dangerous movement or that my presence in the profession is problematic. In these moments, I remain firm in reminding folks – as participants in my learning spaces and beyond – that they don't get to define or tell me what my experience of them is. It's important to center my own safety (whatever way it needs to be) and that I'm the expert in this/that moment. And, they also have the ability to not participate. You have the right to not be disrespected, to not feel unsafe, and to hold these boundaries as part of your agreement practices for who/where and how you work. These considerations can be non-negotiables.

Pushback #3: Gender Roles

Finally, let's consider the lingering impacts of White Supremacy on gender roles and presentation standards. The perpetuation of Eurocentric gender roles is limiting and binary, including archaic and flawed concepts of beauty ideals. There are multiple studies that speak to the long-lasting impacts of the Eurocentric concepts of beauty: lighter skin (closer to White), longer and straighter hair, more narrow and slender features and body types, height, able-bodied – these ideals have been promoted and elevated as the standard to emulate. It's unrealistic and dishonors what other cultural communities see and embody as attractive to them.

I often talk about how the perception of attractiveness is a full spectrum across all identities. How people function in practices of beauty and adornment can be as far ranging as the roles that people hold in relationships. Using outdated concepts of attractiveness and roles in relationships doesn't support my way of teaching or engagement on this. Being able to speak to the impact of archaic and harmful beliefs as they're continuously promoted and perpetuated in updated packaging is important for teaching critical thinking skills. It's important for us to practice discernment as much as we teach it.

Consider the recent "TradMom" (traditional Mom/Mother) concept, which centers traditional binary gender roles for women as a "reclaiming of what is right"; that caretaking is part of a "woman's place" in the world. This repackaging of an outdated and harmful idea that values women only for their appearance, ability to manage a household, and caretake others requires us to be mindful. We must teach people how to consume media in a responsible and intentional manner. Critical thinking allows for information to be consumed and sifted through, with realistic options for an optimal outcome as part of a decision-making process.

Being able to provide CSE that's accessible, transparent, and welcoming matters even more. Reaching communities where they're at means having an expansive approach, which includes the curricula that's used and broadening who is teaching. If you're not well versed in a community or concept/practice, do some research. Ask questions of your trusted colleagues to find out who the subject matter expert is. And, when it comes to BIPoC and other historically impacted communities, it's time to retire the excuse of "I don't know anyone." Between social media and more grassroots, community focused organizations, there are opportunities to connect with some amazing folks and information (Dixon et al., 2021).

Next is knowing who you're talking/teaching to. The phrase "know your audience" hits differently when considering the diverse and expansive communities that sexuality education reaches. As a Black sexuality professional, I'm accountable for how I show up with consumers/participants in my learning spaces. My approach should shift if I'm working with youth, elders, providing support to a LGBTQAI2S+ space, or in a spiritual/faith space. If it's an all-Black space, I'm still responsible to ensure that what I offer is relevant, easily understood, and accessible (learning, hearing, printouts, etc.).

Being in culturally specific spaces can provide a different sense of community, because of a general experience that connects everyone. The information and instructors should reflect the communities and their members that are being served. Black sexuality educators working in mostly Black or all Black spaces makes a difference, as well as using materials that have clear and plain language, along with media that reflect/look like the folks they're working with are vital. If we're about a multi-racial, multi-diverse welcoming learning experience, we are responsible to expand our own resource circle and networks. There are many organizations, affinity groups, and influencers that can provide guidance on ways of strengthening the connections among the profession.

Personally, I've been privileged to provide sexuality education in Black-centered spaces. I've had folks share how much my presence as their sexuality educator made a difference to them, that seeing Black bodies as part of the learning materials (print, media, etc.) honored their own personhood – and lessened the sting of not being reflected from a past experience. We each deserve to have ourselves reflected back as an integrated part of our knowledge process and be able to determine the best use of the information given with someone who shares a similar lived experience. CSE provides a strong foundation to build important life skills that support strong decision-making for optimal life outcomes.

A Call Up to Action

So after all that, you might be saying, "okay, that's great. But what's next?" This is such an important question – and a call up to action. Let's start on the larger end of the spectrum: sex education programs, education departments/school districts, and sex educators themselves need to understand the impact of the curricula/materials that are being used. For example, if these materials weaponize the sexuality of BIPoC folks and don't acknowledge intersectionality (as it relates to racialized folks) as a key component, it fails BIPoC folks who seek out sex ed, as well as BIPoC educators who teach. There must be an active practice of reviewing sexuality education provisions and/or plans that adhere to a comprehensive lens of inclusion and equity across multiple communities as it relates to social justice. We must develop a collective knowledge base of understanding and language that highlights how using archaic and outdated stereotypes of historically impacted groups (i.e. BIPoC, LGBTQAI+, Disability, Immigrant/Refugee, etc.) is harmful within CSE, to the participants and the practitioners.

Even within the academic and professional spaces, there is a need and desire to see a more diverse representation across the board – sexuality professionals, justice advocates, leaders in RH/RJ organizations – that are reflective of the communities that are being served. A strong network of allies should also be part of this work, where folks who support these diverse voices model how to engage and uplift as part of this collective. Being able to understand how to support a movement without being the center of the movement allows for growth and new ideas to be shared and adapted to what is needed in the moment (Sex Education Collaborative, 2022).

For example, honor the wisdom that historically impacted communities have to inform lessons and curricula – and be bold in the engagement practices to make this happen. The practice of letting communities tell you what they need and how they would like to access information should be the foundation of what is written, reviewed, and offered. Lived experience is just as valuable as any social scientific study that tells us what we already know. When these steps are taken, the best options for change are centered – which could also lead to better policies and practices becoming instituted as the standard instead of an option.

Another offering is to utilize an anti-racist/RJ framework as a core part of human sexuality programming and/or curricula. This requires a reconsideration of the old way of doing business and who the business will be done with. There has to be a commitment to ensuring that the most impacted are being centered from beginning to end and to prepare for changes and redirection as part of the process. This isn't easy, as it means that what has been done for so long has to be undone, unlearned, and replaced with something new. There may be a shift in power and decision-making and the focus points may shift. It has been done before and can be again. It's crucial to make changes that lead to new consistent habits and to hold ourselves and each other accountable in our justice practices in CSE.

And, as part of this relearning, we as sexuality professionals have our part to do as well. We're just as impacted by WS in our profession and we need to do our own work to ensure that we are acting from a place of alignment in our intent and desired impact. Being accountable to the people we work with/for requires the ability to take constructive feedback in a way that improves and builds upon our work. This doesn't mean that you should allow someone to be disrespectful to you or your work – not at all. Make sure that your personal ethics and boundaries are honored as part of this process, and clearly state how you want to receive your feedback. But be aware that we all have biases and beliefs that will be challenged.

Backlash is a part of my experience as a sexuality professional and equity practitioner, and being able to navigate it in a way that honors my safety and values is very important. Maintain a sense of clarity about what you will and will not tolerate in the spaces you facilitate, and if needed, have another person present to support you if/as you see fit. As a sexuality professional who subscribes to a justice centered foundation for the work I do, it's important to know how to navigate pushback, because it's going to come. There will be someone who will challenge your work, your knowledge, even your presence in the space. Being able to respond and to manage yourself in the midst of it is key.

Introspective Questions for Consideration

- What does comprehensive sex ed look like for/to YOU? What are some important pieces of information you'd want to see as part of a lesson plan or conversation?
- What kind of sexuality educator would you have wanted when you first learned about sex/sexuality?
- Why is it important to consider the lived experiences of BIPoC folks as part of sexuality education? And what about BIPoC sexuality educators and their experiences as they teach? What other communities should sexuality educators consider as part of their comprehensive sexuality education teaching?
- How do you approach the topic of sexuality with folks in your life now? Is there anything you've learned in this chapter that may be helpful to support that conversation?

Notes

1 The history of using the "fear of the uncontrolled" when it comes to BIPoC communities and reproductive rights/justice is well documented. Some well used examples include the hypersexualization of Black people as part of the "criminalization" around sexuality; the fear of the "browning of America" that targets growing Latino/e communities and the manipulation of this "fear" are recycled racial tropes that are frequently used to whip up the fear of White communities.

2 From this, there are direct connections to so many things: Jim Crow laws, the anti-Immigrant movements, connection points to various policies and policing of racialized bodies and communities. And looking beyond that social construct, we can also see the history of using disrespectful caricatures of LGBTQAI+ folks as promiscuous and dangerous as part of former HIV/AIDS education campaigns and the forced sterilization of disabled folks without their consent.

References

Christian, K. (2021). *Let's talk bodily autonomy: What is it and why do we need it?* Retrieved August 2021, from www.thegoodtrade.com/features/reclaiming-body-autonomy-for-women

Dixon, R., Gilbert, T., Soto, M., Gathings, J., & DiPonio, S. (2021). *Centering racial justice in sex education: Strategies for engaging professionals and young people.* Sex Education Collaborative White Paper. www.sexeducationcollaborative.org.

Flowers, S. C. (2016). *Perceptions of fidelity and adaptation in evidence-informed interventions by women of color sexuality health educators.* CUNY Academic Works. http://academicworks.cuny.edu/gc_etds/1586

Gary-Smith, M., Alves, C. L., Founding Members, WoCSHN (Women of Color Sexual Health Network), Harley, C., Doyle, G., & SIECUS: Sex Ed for Social Change. (2022). *Sex, race, and politics in the U.S.: A call to action to address racial justice in sexuality education.* SIECUS. https://siecus.org/wp-content/uploads/2022/06/2022-Racial-Justice-Resource.pdf

Gary-Smith, M., & Hunte, R. (2024). *Protected care as our liberatory pleasure practice: A sit-down with 2 Black femmes/women.* Pressbooks. https://pressbooks.pub/sexualitysocialjustice/chapter/protected-care-as-our-liberatory-pleasure-practice/

Sex Education Collaborative. (2022, February 28). *Comprehensive means intersectional: Moving sex education forward.* Retrieved September 17, 2024, from https://sexeducationcollaborative.org/comprehensive-means-intersectional

2 From Values-Based to Values-Neutral

The Pedagogical Power of Transparency

Anne Hodder-Shipp

Key Terms

- **Belief Systems:** assumptions, ideas, and expectations that we make about life, society, ourselves, and others so we can better understand it all. Some treat their belief systems as universal "truths." Belief systems often inform laws, rules, and regulations.
- **Constructs:** ideas, theories, or concepts that are subjective and often based on belief systems rather than verifiable experiences or factual information.
- **Norms:** cultural standards or rules within certain groups, peoples, or cultures that are considered typical or expected; often misrepresented as universal to all peoples and cultures and used as a tool of oppression by those who hold the most power.
- **Values:** guiding principles, personal beliefs, standards, or rules that we use to make decisions and live a life that we believe is "right" or valid.
- **Values-based Sex Education:** curricula or pedagogy that espouses specific beliefs, standards, or rules without explicitly identifying them, usually with the intention to influence or change students' feelings, beliefs, or choices.
- **Values-neutral Sex Education:** curricula or pedagogy that explicitly identifies the beliefs, standards, or rules present, usually in order to acknowledge the impact of values on human sexuality and identity development while encouraging students to identify their own.

Values motivate our behaviors and guide our decision-making – from how we express ourselves and decide which parts to keep private, to the relationships we prioritize and the ones we choose never to explore. Values are not innate, however, and are constantly learned, unlearned, and relearned throughout our lives, which also means they are inevitably fluid.

The values we may have held in childhood – that cursing or swearing is offensive; that we must always eat our vegetables; to treat others as we'd like to be treated – likely transformed as we entered adolescence – cursing or swearing is fun; eat what sounds good; treat others as they'd like to be treated – and were

DOI: 10.4324/9781032615479-4

exposed to ideas, communities, cultures, history, environments, and people different from the ones we grew up with.

Our assortment of "values teachers" begins in childhood and diversify exponentially in adolescence and early adulthood, as we have experiences, build friendships, consume multimedia, engage with systems and authority, and receive education from the various institutions (e.g., schools, religious groups, community leaders) we have access to.

In the US, institutions have often weaponized values as a tool of white supremacy, colonization, conservatism, and systemic oppression. Since it was first introduced in the early 1900s, school-based sex education has been one of the most successful methods of doing this with young and other marginalized people, often doing so in the name of "public health" (Porreca, 2019).

Some of the earliest advocacy for formal sex education programming came out of the so-called social hygiene movement of the early 20th century, in which physicians attempted to reduce "sexual problems" like STIs by showing students explicit and sensationalized imagery. Though that might sound unexpectedly "progressive" for its time, their curriculum was largely informed by eugenics – the scientifically inaccurate assumption that some human beings are inherently more valuable than others and that the human race could be "improved" by preventing the "unfit" – specifically disabled, Black, Indigenous, Eastern European immigrant, mentally and chronically ill, and impoverished people – from having children (National Human Genome Research Institute, n.d.).

As will be explored in this chapter, values-based sex education initiatives – including ones that may have appeared or been described as liberal or sex-positive – have been historically linked to harmful and dehumanizing movements that kept powerful social, religious, and political interests in mind rather than the edification of students and youth (Porreca, 2019).

Though values-based sex education has caused harm, even when provided with positive intent, values-free sex education is not the solution because values – learning about them, exploring them, defining them – are a core part of sexual identity and development. Sex ed curricula must include discussion and representation of values because they have a significant lifelong impact on our decision-making, relationship-building, cultural and community connection, and learning and growth processes. (This is, itself, a value!)

Instead of values-based or values-free, this chapter will describe and present the importance of *values-neutral sex education*: teaching the significance and relevance of values to human sexuality while explicitly acknowledging the values present in the curriculum used or held by the educator. A form of harm reduction, this transparency makes space for critical discussion of values while also encouraging students to identify and explore their own without undue influence.

Contemporary Sex Ed Values in the United States

The most recognizable example of values-based sex education in the US today is abstinence-based, which uses curricula that upholds choosing *not* to have sex as the best or only way to maintain sexual health. This form of sex ed was first introduced at the start of the Reagan administration in response to curricula developed during the Sexual Revolution, which promoted values related to pleasure and equity, and normalized sexual experimentation among youth and outside of marriage. With the Adolescent Family Life Act of 1981, abstinence-based sex ed (ABSE) emphasizing values like "chastity" and "self-discipline" began receiving millions in federal funding and became standard in public and private schools (SIECUS, 2019).

From then, ABSE remained funded and upheld by every presidency, save a short stint from 2010–2012 during the Obama administration (Hopkins Tanne, 2009). During those years, funds were redirected to comprehensive sex education that was geared towards being "evidence-based." While not strictly promoting abstinence and without explicitly stating as much, funded curricula during this time was also values-based, with the goal of pushing students to delay having sex until early adulthood (i.e. abstinence) (Jeffries et al., 2010) and promoting contraceptives to prevent pregnancy – predominantly heteronormative, cisnormative ideals and representations of sex, relationships, and sexual risk.

Federal funding for ABSE returned after 2012 and, as of this publishing, continues to thrive in US schools thanks to its successful rebrand as "sexual risk avoidance" (Boyer, 2023). This is despite empirical data suggesting that ABSE fails to prevent teens from having sex, neglects LGBTQ students, promotes heterosexist and racist stereotypes, and may contribute to increasing teen pregnancy and STI rates (Bordogna et al., 2022; Fox et al., 2019; Goldfarb & Lieberman, 2021; Guttmacher Institute, 2023; Heels, 2019; Hoefer & Hoefer, 2017; Lederer, 2017; Santelli et al., 2017; SIECUS, 2023; Stanger-Hall & Hall, 2011).

This means it is often up to sex educators who commit themselves to practicing values-neutrality to identify the values within the curricula they have been given. This can be challenging not just because of how prevalent values-based sex education is, but also because they are not always easy to recognize. Even progressive, comprehensive sex ed curricula designed to be inclusive, accurate, and empowering is laden with values that are not explicitly named.

Identifying and Neutralizing Values: Considering Language

When attempting to identify the values inherent to a curriculum, look for:

- "Should" statements, like "Sex should be saved for someone special," "teens should listen to their parents," or "abortion should be a last resort."

- Moral absolutes, like "Always wear a condom," "watching porn is wrong," or "fantasizing about other people is never OK."
- Language or perspectives that are specifically aligned with religious values, like "sacred," "premarital sex," "sex is for reproduction," "losing virginity," or "same-sex attraction is unnatural."
- Binary or ableist language, like "good/bad," "smart/stupid," "right/wrong," "normal/abnormal," "natural/unnatural," or "healthy/unhealthy."
- All-or-nothing language, like "If it's not an enthusiastic yes, then it's a no," "if you feel nervous, then you are not ready to have sex," or "everyone is curious about sex."
- Scare tactics, like "your doctor will be able to tell if you have had sex," "masturbating too much can cause erectile dysfunction," or "wearing revealing clothing invites sexual assault."
- Inaccurate or generalized medical information, like "PreP is for gay men," "birth control regulates periods," "only women can get pregnant," or referring to assigned sex at birth as "biological sex."
- Exclusively negative consequences of sexual behavior, like using explicit imagery of severely infected genitals, "teen pregnancy ruins lives," or describing HIV and STIs as "deadly."
- Exclusion or misrepresentation of gender and sexual orientation, like only referencing "men and women" or "boys and girls," describing gender as a "spectrum," or calling non-heterosexual non-cisgender people "sexual minorities."
- Exclusion or misrepresentation of disability, like having no imagery of physically disabled people, stating consent must be "enthusiastic" or "a verbal yes," or discussing body "functions" and "dysfunctions."
- Heteronormative language and points of view, like "foreplay," referring to sex as "penetration" or "intercourse," calling anal sex "gay sex," or having an LGBTQ section separate from the rest of the curriculum.
- Cisnormative language or points of view, like "kids are too young to understand gender," "men, women, and other genders," conflating gender expectations with biological traits, or only referencing gender affirming care in the context of being transgender.
- Racist or sexist stereotypes represented as factual, like "Boys are naturally more sexual," "Black or Latinx teens are more sexually active," or "Girls naturally mature faster."

Something else sex educators can do is modify their language to demonstrate a more values-neutral approach to discussing sexuality. Table 2.1 shares some examples:

Table 2.1 Language using values-neutral approaches

Instead of:	Try:
Premarital sex, underage sex	Sex, youth sexuality
The best kind of sex is safe sex.	All kinds of sex can come with risks, but we can help reduce them by learning about and using safer sex tools like condoms, birth control, and open communication.
It is dangerous for teens to watch porn.	It is common for teens to accidentally see or intentionally look for porn online, and they might feel shame, discomfort, or curiosity about it. Having a trusted adult to talk to can help them better understand that porn is entertainment for adults and not accurate representations of sex.
Everyone masturbates, masturbation is normal/natural.	Most people masturbate or try masturbating at some point, but it's not something everyone enjoys, wants, or has to do.
Sex is something that two people do when they're in love.	People have sex for many reasons, and some people use it as a way to feel connected or express love to each other.
Safe sex	Safer sex
Losing virginity, giving it up	First-time sex, sexual debut
Your body is a temple.	We did not choose the bodies we live in, and some of us have to take extra steps to feel comfortable, safe, or neutral about them. There are lots of ways to take care of them.
Foreplay is essential.	Sex can feel more pleasurable and comfortable by spending time building arousal in our bodies, especially before having vaginal or anal sex.
Don't have sex unless you're on birth control.	Safer sex methods like birth control can help prevent pregnancy when having penis-in-vagina sex, but they won't prevent STIs. Using birth control along with condoms can help prevent both.
If it's not a hell yes, then it's a hell no.	Everyone's "yes" looks and sounds different, so if you aren't sure, stop what you're doing and check in. "Maybe" or "I don't know" means no in that moment.
Gender is a spectrum.	Gender is like a galaxy and has no limits.
Men and women are naturally different.	All people are naturally different.

Values-neutral sex education also must include instruction and discussion of values and the role they play in our lives. The following is an example of a visual and scripting from a curriculum I was trained in by Planned Parenthood Los Angeles to teach ninth graders in LA County (Planned Parenthood Los Angeles,

2016–2017). I have since modified it to better suit the approach I take with my students and clients.

> Sexuality is a fluid part of human identity that plays a key role in how we feel about ourselves, the world, and our relationship with others. It is self-defined and determined by what we know and feel comfortable with. Sexuality is not defined by our actions, relationships, or other people. It is also not permanent. Our sexuality is informed and influenced by four components: Our feelings, values, behaviors, and bodies. Each is important on its own, but they are in

Chart 1: Four Components of Sexuality

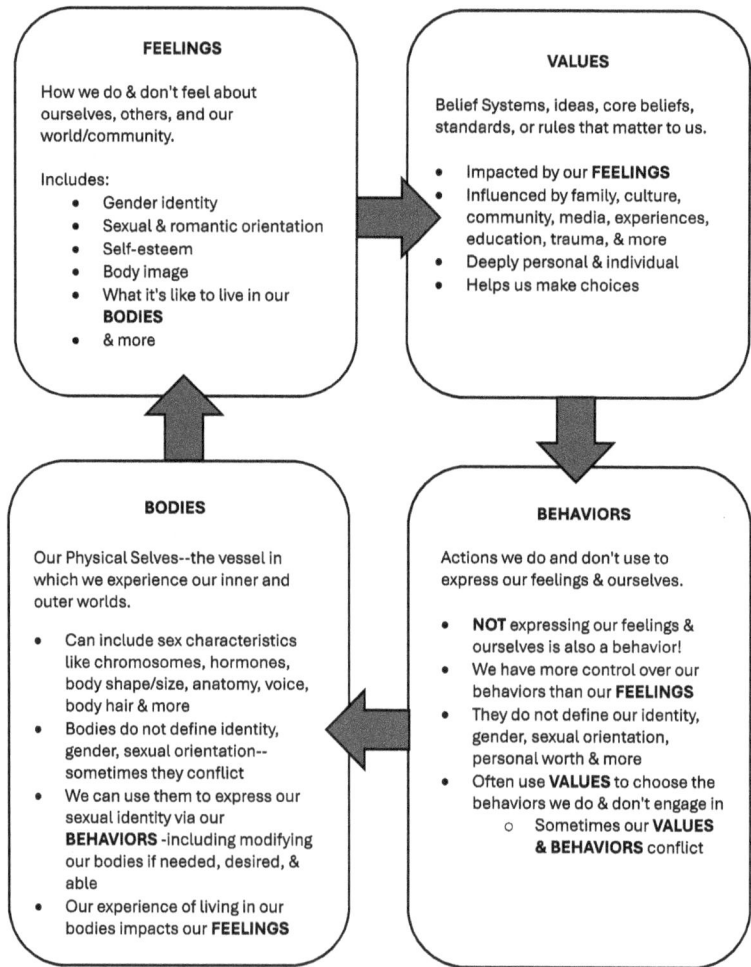

FEELINGS

How we do & don't feel about ourselves, others, and our world/community.

Includes:

- Gender identity
- Sexual & romantic orientation
- Self-esteem
- Body image
- What it's like to live in our **BODIES**
- & more

VALUES

Belief Systems, ideas, core beliefs, standards, or rules that matter to us.

- Impacted by our **FEELINGS**
- Influenced by family, culture, community, media, experiences, education, trauma, & more
- Deeply personal & individual
- Helps us make choices

BODIES

Our Physical Selves--the vessel in which we experience our inner and outer worlds.

- Can include sex characteristics like chromosomes, hormones, body shape/size, anatomy, voice, body hair & more
- Bodies do not define identity, gender, sexual orientation-- sometimes they conflict
- We can use them to express our sexual identity via our **BEHAVIORS** -including modifying our bodies if needed, desired, & able
- Our experience of living in our bodies impacts our **FEELINGS**

BEHAVIORS

Actions we do and don't use to express our feelings & ourselves.

- **NOT** expressing our feelings & ourselves is also a behavior!
- We have more control over our behaviors than our **FEELINGS**
- They do not define our identity, gender, sexual orientation, personal worth & more
- Often use **VALUES** to choose the behaviors we do & don't engage in
  - Sometimes our **VALUES & BEHAVIORS** conflict

Figure 2.1 Four Components of Sexuality

constant conversation with each other. Chart 1 represents the four components and how they interact with each other.

As can be seen in the chart, values can be named and discussed as an essential
part of sex education and development. What matters most when practicing
values-neutral pedagogy is recognizing how values are used, presented, and
incorporated into classroom discussion.

Additional Factors for Consideration and Approach

Because values-neutral sex ed is not the norm in the US, and few sex education
trainings center values-neutral pedagogy, it can take time and effort for sex educators to get familiar and build comfort with it. Part of that work is a process of
unlearning constructs, norms, and standards related to sexuality and pedagogy
that center dominant perspectives, values, and belief systems. All of these have
been inevitably informed by white supremacy, patriarchy, capitalism, and other
systems of oppression, which do not make space for the expansiveness of being
human. The unlearning process also involves compassionate exploration and
investigation of our own values and belief systems, including recognizing if/
how they influence the way we teach.

I like to use the analogy of a garden to describe this process: I have a garden
bed that looks lush and full of an eclectic variety of plants and living things.
I am able to use it, enjoy it, and benefit from what I have been cultivating over
the years; part of the care process for my garden, however, involves weeding.
Weeding can be difficult for many reasons, including:

- I can only remove what I know to look for
- I only know what I have been told or taught, read, heard about, or had access to
- Some weeds are difficult to recognize because they look like all the other plants
- I might keep some plants even though someone else planted them
- I might keep some plants just because they've always been there
- Some plants are actually invasive and need to be removed
- Some look healthy, but their roots are rotting
- Some weeds are only weeds because that's what people call them
- Weeding, pruning, replanting, and cleanup takes time and energy
- I cannot guarantee that weeds won't grow back or that the garden does not, in
  fact, prefer the weeds I desire to pull
- The process is messy and sometimes looks worse before it gets better
- I need to know when to ask for help, and where and whom to go to for it

In this analogy, the plants and weeds represent our values, constructs, knowledge, and information. They all live together and relate to each other, and they
aren't all good/bad/right/wrong, but they do need to be looked at and evaluated over time in case changes need to be made. Like many things related to

sexuality, values are fluid and can change over time as we learn, grow, have experiences, build community, start and end relationships, and more. As educators, we need to practice and be prepared to do this just like we want our students and clients to.

Introspective Questions for Consideration

- Did anything in this chapter make you feel uncomfortable, defensive, resistant? Or excited, inspired, affirmed? Why or why not?
- What did you learn or observe about yourself and/or your values by reading this chapter?
- What would you add, remove, or change in this chapter?
- How would you explain the difference between values-based and values-neutral sex ed to someone who hasn't read this book?
- How does your sexual identity and experience inform the way you learn, teach, and engage with students?
- What are your personal values? What are your professional values? Where/how do they overlap?
- What do you see as the benefits of evaluating what values may be present in your and others' sex education work? What is "in it for you"?
- Whose comfort do you prioritize when you teach? Why? Where is there room for adjustment or change?
- What behaviors might you start, stop, or continue as a result of reading this chapter?

References

Bordogna, A. L., Coyle, A. C., Nallamothu, R., Manko, A. L., & Yen, R. W. (2022). Comprehensive sexuality education to reduce pregnancy and STIs in adolescents in the United States: A systematic review and meta-analysis. *American Journal of Sexuality Education, 18*(1), 39–83. https://doi.org/10.21203/rs.3.rs-764336/v1

Boyer, J. (2023, July 20). *New name, same harm: Rebranding of federal abstinence-only programs.* Guttmacher Institute. https://www.guttmacher.org/gpr/2018/02/new-name-same-harm-rebranding-federal-abstinence-only-programs

Cheedalla, A., Moreau, C., & Burke, A. E. (2020). Sex education and contraceptive use of adolescent and young adult females in the United States: An analysis of the National Survey of Family Growth 2011–2017. *Contracept X, 2,* 100048. https://doi.org/10.1016/j.conx.2020.100048

Fox, A. M., Himmelstein, G., Khalid, H., & Howell, E. A. (2019). Funding for abstinence-only education and adolescent pregnancy prevention: Does state ideology affect outcomes? *American Journal of Public Health, 109*(3), 497–504. https://doi.org/10.2105/AJPH.2018.304896

Goldfarb, E. S., & Lieberman, L. D. (2021). Three decades of research: The case for comprehensive sex education. *Journal of Adolescent Health, 68*(1), 13–27. https://doi.org/10.1016/j.jadohealth.2020.07.036

Guttmacher Institute. (2023, July 18). *Federally funded abstinence-only programs: Harmful and ineffective.* https://www.guttmacher.org/fact-sheet/abstinence-only-programs

Heels, S. W. (2019). The impact of abstinence-only sex education programs in the United States on adolescent sexual outcomes. *Perspectives*, *11*, Article 3. https://scholars.unh.edu/perspectives/vol11/iss1/3

Hoefer, S. E., & Hoefer, R. (2017). Worth the wait? The consequences of abstinence-only sex education for marginalized students. *American Journal of Sexuality Education*, *12*(3), 257–276. https://doi.org/10.1080/15546128.2017.1359802

Hopkins Tanne, J. (2009). Obama's budget changes sex education funding from abstinence-only to comprehensive education. *BMJ*, *338*. https://doi.org/10.1136/bmj.b2008

Jeffries, W. L., Dodge, B., Bandiera, F. C., & Reece, M. (2010). Beyond abstinence-only: Relationships between abstinence education and comprehensive topic instruction. *Sex Education: Sexuality, Society and Learning*, *10*(2), 171–185. https://doi.org/10.1080/14681811003666317

Lederer, A. (2017, August 1). Why the use of scare tactics to promote sexual health for Youth may backfire. *Scholars Strategy Network*. https://scholars.org/contribution/why-use-scare-tactics-promote-sexual-health-youth-may-backfire

National Human Genome Research Institute. (n.d.). *Eugenics and scientific racism*. https://www.genome.gov/about-genomics/fact-sheets/Eugenics-and-Scientific-Racism

PlannedParenthood Los Angeles. (2016–2017). *PPLA High School Curriculum 2016–17*. https://www.plannedparenthood.org/planned-parenthood-los-angeles/local-education-training/classroom-education

Porreca, S. I. (2019, September). *Birth control, sex education, and eugenic feminism: The peculiar activism of women physicians*. Drexel University. https://drexel.edu/legacy-center/blog/overview/2019/september/birth-control-sex-education-and-eugenic-feminism-the-peculiar-activism-of-women-physicians

Santelli, J. S., Kantor, L. M., Grilo, S. A., Heck, C. J., Rogers, J., & Ott, M. A. (2017). Abstinence-only-until-marriage policies and programs: An updated position paper of the Society for Adolescent Health and Medicine. *Journal of Adolescent Health*, *61*(3), 273–280. https://doi.org/10.1016/j.jadohealth.2017.06.001

SIECUS. (2019). *A history of AOUM funding*. https://siecus.org/wp-content/uploads/2019/05/AOUM-Funding-History-Report-5.2019.pdf

SIECUS. (2023). (rep.). *Federal funding overview: Fiscal year 2023*. SIECUS. https://siecus.org/wp-content/uploads/2023/12/SIECUS-Federal-Funding-Overview-FY-2023-Alternate-Cover-8.pdf

Stanger-Hall, K. F., & Hall, D. W. (2011). Abstinence-only education and teen pregnancy rates: Why we need comprehensive sex education in the U.S. *PLoS One*, *6*(10), e24658. https://doi.org/10.1371/journal.pone.0024658

3 Centering Safety and Resilience Through Trauma-Informed Approaches

Kirsten M. deFur

Key Terms

- **Safety:** feeling comfortable being your authentic self and speaking your truth. Safety is grounded in trust and respect and is characterized by an absence of fear.
- **Resilient Zone:** when our mind and body are in a state of well-being; we can manage our thoughts and feelings; we have the best capacity for flexibility and adaptability in mind, body and spirit (Miller-Karas, 2023).
- **Trauma:** "trauma results from an event, series of events, or set of circumstances that is experienced by an individual as physically or emotionally harmful or threatening and that has lasting adverse effects on the individual's functioning and physical, social, emotional, or spiritual well-being" (SAMHSA's Trauma and Justice Strategic Initiative, 2014, p. 7).
- **Trauma Response:** the way someone reacts to trauma at any point following their experience.
- **Trauma-informed Approach:** a program, organization, or system "realizes the widespread impact of trauma and understands potential paths for recovery; recognizes the signs and symptoms of trauma in clients, families, staff, and others involved with the system; and responds by fully integrating knowledge about trauma into policies, procedures, and practices, and seeks to actively resist re-traumatization" (SAMHSA's Trauma and Justice Strategic Initiative, 2014, p. 9).

The term 'trauma' was traditionally associated with veterans and assault survivors until the landmark Adverse Childhood Experiences (ACES) study in 1998 (National Center for Injury Prevention and Control, 2019). This study showed that 61% of adults in the United States had at least one adverse childhood experience, with long-lasting impacts on health outcomes. Since then, it's widely accepted that trauma is nearly universal. Sexuality educators need to approach participants, colleagues, and parents assuming they've experienced at least one traumatic event.

DOI: 10.4324/9781032615479-5

Sexuality educators are called to cultivate spaces where participants feel valued and seen as their full selves. To achieve this, sexuality educators need to establish and actively maintain a sense of safety in their educational spaces. This necessitates a deep, foundational understanding of trauma, intersectionality, educator positionality, and the implementation of trauma-informed approaches in all aspects of program delivery – from conceptualization to follow-up. By integrating this knowledge into their pedagogical practices, sexuality educators work to establish sensitivity to the diverse experiences and histories of their participants, fostering a more inclusive and safer learning environment.

Society's roots in trauma are deep and multifaceted. Historical events like wars, colonization, and systemic injustices have inflicted lasting scars on collective consciousness. Societal structures perpetuate cycles of trauma through poverty, discrimination, and violence, exacerbating individual and systemic wounds. These traumas shape behaviors, beliefs, and interactions, impacting mental health, relationships, and social justice.

We must view trauma through a lens of intersectionality. Trauma exists within the personal and social contexts of individuals, influenced by intersecting identities such as race, socioeconomic status, gender identity, sexual orientation, ability, religion, and body size. How someone experiences trauma, the effects it has on them and even that they experienced a traumatic event is intertwined with who they are and what that means relative to privilege and discrimination. An intersectional lens asks us to consider elements such as vulnerability to trauma, what support is available for survivors, access to resources, stigma, and acceptance of abusive behaviors within the context of marginalization, systemic racism, systems of oppression and historical trauma. A survivor is not only a survivor of trauma – their multiple identities all play a part.

Organized by the 4 Rs of SAMHSA's guidance for a trauma-informed approach, Realize, Recognize, Respond and Resist Re-Traumatization, this chapter provides foundational information about trauma, trauma responses, and how those responses can occur in sexuality education. This chapter presents seven trauma-informed, safety-first approaches and describes scenarios that may undermine the goal of centering safety. Readers are encouraged to reflect on their own beliefs and responses to situations related to trauma-informed sexuality education.

**Readers are encouraged to practice self-care as they engage with the chapter content. Some elements may evoke strong emotional reactions. Readers can take their time with each section of the chapter, talk with a trusted colleague or friend, and/or reach out to a professional for support.

*R*ealize the Impact of Trauma

Trauma encompasses single events, series of events, or experiences with deep, long-lasting impact. It's not just what happens but also how it's experienced and its aftermath.

Trauma can be categorized in several ways:

- *Acute-Situational Trauma* refers to a single overwhelming event. For example, a car accident, natural disaster, invasive medical procedure, or an incident of sexual assault.
- *Toxic/Chronic Stress* results from exposure to stressful life events over a prolonged time period. For example, discrimination, body shaming, gender-based bullying, or abusive parenting.
- *Complex Trauma* refers to exposure to multiple traumatic events/conditions in the absence of stable and nurturing caregiving. For example, chronic abuse at the hands of caregivers, chronic sssssneglect, emotional abuse, or repeated physical violence.
- *Historical Trauma* refers to multigenerational trauma experienced by a specific cultural, racial, or ethnic group related to major events and oppressive acts of human design. For example, acts of genocide, the effects of colonization, tribalism, dispossession or dislocation, pathologization of sexual orientation or gender identity.
- *Intergenerational Trauma* refers to multigenerational trauma that can be transferred from generation to generation and caregiver to child through complex psychological and physiological mechanisms within the family. For example, a parent that experiences trauma and has difficulty attaching to their child, creating the possibility for the child to be more vulnerable to trauma.

Trauma types can intersect, affecting individuals on multiple levels. Research indicates trauma's impact on the autonomic nervous system (ANS), which is crucial for self-regulation and resilience (Van der Kolk, 2014). Trauma survivors may find themselves chronically "stuck" outside their resilient zone, experiencing heightened survival responses. These responses include social engagement, fight-flight-freeze, or collapse/shutdown.

- *Social engagement responses* encompass seeking attachment or attention; pleasing and appeasing (known as the "fawn" response); and tending/befriending.
- *Sympathetic nervous system responses* encompass fighting, fleeing, or freezing
- *Parasympathetic nervous system responses* include collapse/shutdown (going limp, slowing breathing, dissociation) (National Institute for the Clinical Application of Behavioral Medicine)

For trauma survivors, the goal is to be able to regulate responses and move forward while also acknowledging the past. It's not about forgetting or returning to pre-trauma states. The focus is on staying within the resilient zone during daily life. Healing varies for each person; many rely on trusted support from professionals and loved ones. In fact, connection to others is one of the most meaningful ways survivors tap into their own healing and resilience (Calhoun et al., 2022). Sexuality education, providing safe and supportive spaces, can facilitate such healing connections.

Recognize Trauma Responses

Trauma elicits varied responses that can evolve over time, occurring within or outside one's resilient zone. Individuals may exhibit one or multiple responses at any moment. It's crucial for sexuality educators to discern behaviors that could signal trauma responses. Common responses include:

> *Behavioral* – changes to eating, sleeping, or movement; verbal reactions such as using an aggressive tone; difficulty setting/maintaining boundaries; hypervigilance; re-experiencing/flashbacks.
> *Emotional* – experiencing intense emotions such as anger, sadness, anxiety; difficulty regulating emotions; showing little or no emotion; minimizing; difficulty trusting.
> *Intellectual* – increased/decreased interest in work/education; difficulty processing information; challenges remembering things related to trauma correctly or in order.
> *Spiritual* – increased/decreased interest in spirituality or religion.
> *Social* – withdrawal from friends/family; dependence on others.

*This is not an all-inclusive list.
   Trauma survivors may or may not recognize their responses as trauma-related and may or may not seek support. Their reactions can be surprising to both themselves and others.

How Do Trauma Responses Show Up in Sexuality Education?

Participant behaviors – participants may exhibit high engagement as a social response or withdraw entirely as a flight or freeze response. Boundary issues and challenges with honoring group agreements may also arise.
   Participant reactions to others – another participant or the educator says or does something that initiates a trauma response.
   Educator responses – an educator can experience their own trauma response or have a reaction to the responses of others.

Example: Rey, an enthusiastic sexuality educator, leads a group of engaged teens in a brainstorm about characteristics of healthy and unhealthy relationships. During the discussion, Tyler's offhand comment, "Isn't

> it obvious? How could anyone not know that's unhealthy?" creates a sudden chill in the room. Jesse, who was actively participating, withdraws and leaves. Unsure how to respond, Rey continues with minimal participation. Rey feels defeated and the participants feel disappointed.

This example highlights various possible trauma responses: Tyler's comment, Jesse's withdrawal, the discomfort of other participants, and the educator's sense of defeat. Each reaction could stem from trauma.

When faced with behavioral outbursts, inappropriate comments, or shutdowns, educators may be tempted to think or say, "What's wrong with you?" However, this places blame on the individual. Instead, shift to, "What happened?" Understanding the context leading to the response and showing compassion for someone's lived experience is key. Educators *can* address unacceptable behavior while maintaining boundaries and group agreements. The following section outlines seven approaches to center safety and support participants in staying within their resilient zone, even during difficult conversations.

Respond and Resist Re-Traumatization

Sexuality educators don't need to be trauma experts, but they must proactively adopt trauma-informed approaches to reduce the risk of re-traumatization and enhance feelings of safety.

Seven Trauma-Informed, Safety-First Approaches for Sexuality Educators

1. Center Safety
2. Show Compassion
3. Be Aware of Physical Space
4. Consider Visuals
5. Use Language of Accountability
6. Remain Transparent
7. Be Prepared

---

1. **Center Safety** – Adopt a "safety first" principle – considering both physical and emotional safety. While feeling 100% safe may be unrealistic – especially for those with lived experiences of trauma – educators can help participants feel safe *enough* to be vulnerable, learn, and think about real-life application

of concepts. Acknowledge that learning can sometimes be uncomfortable. And ensure that no one is pushed beyond their resilient zone. When someone does something in conflict with group agreements – which may be a trauma response – it is the educators' responsibility to name it and bring the group back to the agreements. Always provide an opt-out option, especially for activities involving scenarios or role plays. Give clear instructions using multiple communication methods. Use language of safety, for example, "I want everyone to feel as safe as possible doing this activity – I will read the instructions aloud."

2. **Show Compassion** – lead with compassion and empathy – seeking to understand other perspectives without jumping to conclusions or telling/finishing someone's story. Lean into curiosity and avoid expressing judgement. Be mindful of scenarios and role plays that have someone play the part of being victimized or playing an aspect of someone's identity. If someone discloses a traumatic experience, express gratitude for sharing, define your role, and provide appropriate resources (see approach #7, Be Prepared).

3. **Be Aware of Physical Space** – Educators should assess the physical environment of the program to mitigate potential reminders of trauma, as the space could evoke trauma or re-traumatize someone. This includes considering proximity to exits, seating arrangements, educator-participant positioning, restroom accessibility, ambient noise, scents, and dietary options. Some individuals may need visibility of exits or prefer more personal space. During the registration process, ask about safety and/or sensory accommodations. Offer diverse seating options and avoid overly institutional lighting, opting for softer, more comfortable illumination if possible. Make sure safety measures for entering and exiting the building and using the restroom are in place. Ensure a gender-neutral restroom is available and inform all participants. Provide tactile and sensory objects or activities like stress balls or coloring pages to help ground participants within their resilient zone.

4. **Consider Visuals** – Bring attention to images and videos that could be re-traumatizing. Preview content from the participant's perspective, considering their potential reactions. Before showing any visual material, tell participants what to expect – how long it is, if acts of violence/trauma/oppression are depicted, and/or potential emotional impact. Before initiating discussion, allow time for reflection after viewing.

5. **Use Language of Accountability** – Avoid language that blames survivors. Instead of asking "why," which can be blaming, use alternatives like "tell me more about . . .," "what happened," or "what led up to that situation." Remember, the responsibility for harm rests with the person committing it. Embrace the shift from "what's wrong with you" to "what happened" to promote understanding and compassion.

6. **Remain Transparent** – Inform (and remind) participants about confidentiality and reporting requirements, including mandatory reporting. Clearly

outline session topics in advance to avoid surprises, which can be retraumatizing for survivors. Re-traumatization can happen in response to any topic, not only topics explicitly related to trauma. Educators need to communicate their limitations and how they can offer support, especially in response to trauma disclosures.

7. **Be Prepared** – Be mentally and emotionally prepared for disclosures, which can occur during or after sessions (e.g., through an anonymous question box or email). A useful framework is:

   - Thank them for sharing – express gratitude, recognizing the strength and vulnerability required to discuss trauma
   - Define your role – clarify what you can and cannot do, and if applicable, remind them of reporting requirements
   - Provide resources/referrals – offer resources for additional support, and if requested, assist in connecting them with providers
   - Follow-up – check in later to offer support

Educators must be ready to provide resources for support that is beyond their scope, such as those for related to dating violence or sexual assault, suicidality, or psychosocial services like counseling or therapy.

There are several scenarios that could be re-traumatizing, diminish feelings of safety, or even evoke trauma:

- Role-playing exercises in pairs, with one person acting out a traumatic event or portraying a survivor. Pairs can make it hard for someone to opt-out/pass
- Insufficient video details, like duration or subject area. Videos have the potential to illicit strong emotions by showing lived experience. For instance, a video showing gender-based discrimination or sexual stereotypes may push someone out of their resilient zone or even be traumatizing
- Neglecting to address victim-blaming or judgmental comments, like implying that a survivor was responsible for an assault, criticizing the number of sexual partners, or using phrases that place people in an "other" category, as "those people." If unaddressed, participants may not feel supported or could feel harmed
- Surprising the group with a topic or not being clear about the purpose of an activity. When someone does not know what will be covered or why they are to do something, they cannot emotionally be prepared, which can increase the likelihood of re-traumatization
- Disclosing personal history with trauma. Educators may aim to illustrate the commonality of experiences by sharing their own, but this can risk shifting the focus away from participants. Additionally, participants' judgment of the educator could undermine the trust crucial for fostering a safe environment. While storytelling can be a powerful learning experience for others, educators need to be mindful of not oversharing

- Minimizing an experience of trauma or describing one type of trauma as less impactful than others. For example, "it was just emotional abuse" or "at least they didn't use physical violence" ("just" and "at least" are two words/phrases that often minimize). Educators need to avoid comparisons when discussing trauma

Engaging in activities in which participants enact losing support systems, hopes, and dreams and experiencing feelings of loss and depression without preparing the group and discussing the rationale. These activities could push individuals outside their resilient zone and illicit strong emotional reactions.

Self-Awareness

Sexuality educators need to practice self-awareness and engage in ongoing self-reflection of their direct or indirect experiences of trauma and trauma responses. Understanding personal experiences prepares educators to respond effectively to others' trauma responses *and* manage their own reactions. Educators should challenge their beliefs about trauma and trauma responses and shift from a blame-focused mentality to one of understanding and compassion.

They need to recognize what provokes them – behaviors, comments, or non-verbal expressions – and learn to respond without judgment. It's essential for educators to examine their anxieties about trauma and supporting survivors. Reflecting on what helps them feel safe and supported in their roles is crucial. Self-regulation tools like pausing, having participants discuss something amongst themselves to allow an educator time to collect themselves, and asking for help from another educator can help educators navigate their emotional reactions.

Additional Factors

Integrating trauma-informed approaches into sexuality education is fairly new. There is still work needed to ensure that educators are proactive about being trauma-informed and centering safety. That work means being vulnerable and open to input and courageousness in sharing feedback.

"Trauma-informed care" has become a buzzword in social service environments, often lacking full implementation despite good intentions. We need to examine all aspects of a program to assess:

- Will participants feel safe enough?
- Will survivors of trauma feel supported?
- Will the content be re-traumatizing?
- Will the educator respond with compassion?
- Will the group agreements be upheld?
- Will the educator feel supported?

Lastly, there is a growing conversation about moving from being *trauma-informed* to being *resilience-informed*. By emphasizing resilience and healing, survivors may feel more empowered on their healing journeys. Centering discussions around helping someone stay in their resilient zone can foster a sense of support and validation. We need to take steps to be trauma AND resilience informed to foster feelings of safety that inspire learning. It's essential to acknowledge the existence and profound impact of trauma while also recognizing that healing is possible, particularly through meaningful connections. Sexuality education can be one space for learning, connecting, and even healing for survivors, especially if we bring intention and attention to promoting safety.

Introspective Questions for Consideration

• How do you center safety?
• What helps you stay in your resilient zone as an educator? What pushes you out of it?
• What makes you anxious about discussing trauma?
• What might you say to someone who has experienced trauma?
• How will you bring an intersectional lens to trauma, resilience, and safety?

References

Calhoun, C. D., Stone, K. J., Cobb, A. R., Patterson, M. W., Danielson, C. K., & Bendezú, J. J. (2022). The role of social support in coping with psychological trauma: An integrated biopsychosocial model for posttraumatic stress recovery. *The Psychiatric quarterly*, *93*(4), 949–970.

Felitti, V., Anda, R., Nordenberg, D., Williamson, D., Spitz, A., Edwards, V., Koss, M., & Marks, J. (1998). Relationship of childhood abuse and household dysfunction to many of the leading causes of death in adults: The Adverse Childhood Experiences (ACE) study. *American Journal of Preventive Medicine*, *14*(4), 245–258. https://doi.org/10.1016/S0749-3797(98)00017-8

Miller-Karas, E. (2023). *Building resilience to trauma: The trauma and community resiliency models* (2nd ed.). Routledge.

National Center for Injury Prevention and Control. (2019). *Adverse Childhood Experiences (ACEs)* (CDC Vital Signs Nov. 2019). Centers for Disease Control and Prevention. https://www.cdc.gov/vitalsigns/aces/pdf/vs-1105-aces-H.pdf

National Institute for the Clinical Application of Behavioral Medicine. *How the nervous system responds to trauma*. Retrieved March 30, 2024, from https://www.nicabm.com/topic/trauma-responses/

SAMHSA's Trauma and Justice Strategic Initiative. (2014). *SAMHSA's concept of trauma and guidance for a trauma-informed approach*. Office of Policy and Innovation, Substance Abuse and Mental Health Services Administration.

Van der Kolk, B. (2014). *The body keeps the score: Brain, mind and body in the healing of trauma*. Penguin Books.

Part II

Critical Perspectives for Inclusive Sex Education

4 Embracing Professional Humility

Cultivating Dispositions and Reflective Practice in Sexuality Education

Tanya M. Bass

Key Terms

- **Professional Humility:** is a characteristic grounded in an accurate self-assessment, avoiding overly negative or positive views of oneself (Bass, 2021). It involves three key components: acknowledging what you do not know, recognizing what you cannot do, and understanding your motives, particularly for yourself (Mercurio, 2022). This trait is essential in professional practice as it encourages learners to remain open to new concepts, ideas, and information (Bass, 2021).
- **Dispositional Humility:** is the integration of self-confidence and humility within one's professional disposition, characterized by the attitudes, values, and beliefs expressed through both verbal and nonverbal behaviors during interactions with students, families, colleagues, and communities. This balanced trait enhances respectful and effective communication and fosters positive relational dynamics in professional settings. (Bass, 2021; Landrum, 2011).
- **Sexuality Educator Professional Disposition:** the attitudes, values, and beliefs demonstrated through both verbal and nonverbal behaviors while teaching sexuality topics, including comfort and capability in teaching sexuality topics (Bass, 2021).
- **Sexuality Educator Dispositional Humility:** is not likely to be exhibited noticeably but can be displayed by a willingness to learn from others and the ability to acknowledge shortcomings or mistakes (Bass, 2021).
- **Reflective Practices:** Reflective practice involves learning from experiences to understand oneself and one's teaching approach better. This process systematically reviews past lessons, helping educators connect different experiences to ensure learners achieve optimal progress (Finlay, 2008).

Sexuality education is a complex and dynamic field that requires educators to navigate sensitive topics with empathy, understanding, and professionalism. At the heart of effective sexuality education lies the disposition of the educator – the

DOI: 10.4324/9781032615479-7

attitudes, values, and beliefs that shape their interactions with learners, families, colleagues, and communities. This chapter explores the pivotal role of professional disposition in sexuality education, emphasizing the importance of cultivating humility and reflective practice to promote inclusive and trauma-informed teaching approaches.

Defined as the demonstration of attitudes, values, and beliefs through both verbal and nonverbal behaviors, professional disposition in sexuality education encompasses a broad spectrum of qualities. From empathy and cultural competence to a commitment to social justice and equity, the disposition of educators profoundly influences learning experiences. Understanding the significance of professional disposition is essential for educators as they create safe and supportive environments where learners feel valued and respected. Within the context of sexuality education, norming and naming privilege emerge as critical components of fostering inclusive learning environments and dispositional humility. By challenging assumptions and acknowledging the inherent power dynamics present in learning environments, sexuality educators can work towards promoting equity and social justice. This requires a willingness to engage in difficult conversations, confront biases, and embrace diverse perspectives internally and with learners. Intentional efforts to normalize conversations around privilege and intersectionality, sexuality educators can create spaces where all learners feel seen, heard, and affirmed.

Professional humility serves as the cornerstone of an effective professional disposition. Recognizing the limitations of one's knowledge and expertise, sexuality educators can embrace a mindset of continuous learning and growth. Reflective practice offers a framework for sexuality educators to critically examine their teaching approaches, identify areas for improvement, and adapt their practices to better meet the needs of their learners.

In this chapter, we explore the interconnectedness of professional disposition and reflective practice in sexuality education. Through an examination of these concepts, sexuality educators can develop the skills and mindset necessary to promote holistic well-being and empowerment among their learners. By fostering dispositional humility, sexuality educators can cultivate meaningful connections with learners and create transformative learning experiences that resonate well beyond the learning environment.

Embracing professional and dispositional humility in sexuality education: sexuality education is a profession in which assessing and maintaining a positive professional disposition is critical. A professional disposition encompasses the cumulation of behaviors a sexuality educator exhibits while interacting with learners, significantly influencing the learning environment. The impact of educational effectiveness rests in learner-educator interactions. For example, the language used in the learning environment or cultural references. Additionally, the nuances of possible behavioral exchanges and connections play a central role in learning. For sexuality educators, fostering a welcoming and inclusive disposition is crucial. Such a disposition encourages open dialogue with learners and helps build a trustworthy space where learners feel valued and respected. Deliberate cultivation and reflection on one's professional disposition is not merely beneficial but essential to maximize effectiveness and positively shape the educational journeys of learners.

Professional and Dispositional Humility Are Foundational Characteristics

Professional and dispositional humility are foundational to fostering an environment conducive to effective learning and respectful interactions, which is essential for teaching sex education. Humility has historical roots and a psychological context. The term humility is derived from the Latin word "humilis," meaning "from the earth" or "grounded," embodying qualities of modesty and a balanced perspective of one's importance (Stubbe, 2020). Similar to cultural humility, it requires introspection, assessment, reflection, and behavioral modification. Cultural humility involves engaging with others while aiming to respect their beliefs, customs, and values. It requires continuous self-reflection, self-evaluation, and a willingness to learn from others. In contrast to cultural competence, cultural humility emphasizes recognizing one's own implicit biases, developing self-awareness and interpersonal sensitivity, and valuing the complex aspects of each person, such as culture, gender, sexual identity, ethnicity, religion, and lifestyle. This approach supports learner-centered sexuality education (Stubbe, 2020).

Cultural and Dispositional Humility

While cultural and dispositional humility emphasizes the importance of self-awareness and respectful engagement with others, both concepts promote positive interpersonal interactions, encouraging individuals to approach relationships with an open mind, acknowledge personal limitations, and value the diverse attributes of those they interact with. Cultural humility aims to honor and respect the unique beliefs, customs, and values of others. In contrast, dispositional humility integrates confidence with humility to enhance communication and foster healthy relationships.

The primary distinction between the two lies in their focus and application. Cultural humility emphasizes continuous learning about cultural differences and implicit biases while fostering sensitivity to the multifaceted aspects of others, such as their gender, race, ethnicity, or sexual identity. It is particularly relevant in patient-centered care, where understanding and valuing these differences is crucial. Dispositional humility, on the other hand, is a personal trait encompassing attitudes, values, and behaviors that reflect confidence tempered with cultural humility. It applies broadly to professional settings and is crucial for effective communication and positive interactions with learners, families, colleagues, and communities. Cultural humility is more context specific; dispositional humility shapes one's overall demeanor and relational dynamics in all professional interactions.

Research on well-being and happiness emphasizes *humility as a critical character* trait (Exline & Geyer, 2004). As a component of "temperance," humility is a safeguard against excess and promotes a balanced evaluation of oneself. This psychological construct, deeply studied by psychologists like Tangney and others, include an accurate self-assessment of abilities and achievements, recognition of one's limitations, openness to new ideas and advice, and a perspective that keeps one's abilities in balance with the world at large (Tangney, 2000).

In the realm of professional humility, this translates to sexuality educators recognizing what they do not know, admitting their limitations, and understanding their true motives in their instruction (Bass, 2021; Mercurio, 2022). Professional humility is crucial in allowing sexuality educators to remain open to evolving concepts and information, which is particularly vital in a field that deals with sensitive and diverse subject matter, an area that is ever-evolving in itself.

Professional humility in sexuality education is not just beneficial but essential. It enables sexuality educators to maintain a grounded perspective on their work, fosters openness to continual learning, and supports the development of meaningful and transformative educational relationships. The integration of professional and dispositional humility within sexuality education underscores a commitment to ethical practice, lifelong learning, and the holistic well-being of learners. Professional humility allows sexuality educators to navigate complex social dynamics more effectively. This includes recognizing privilege and bias, challenging norms and stereotypes, and promoting inclusivity and diversity. Professional humility influences sexuality educator dispositional humility. This characteristic not only fosters a culture of openness to new concepts, ideas, and information but also enhances the sexuality educator's ability to connect with diverse learning communities.

Dispositional humility in sexuality educators is a balancing act between self-confidence and humility, which involves a stable and accepting self-concept that resists ego threats. It encompasses a clear and honest reflection on one's strengths and weaknesses, a focus on others rather than oneself, and a belief in the intrinsic value of all individuals. This form of humility is not self-deprecation but maintaining a realistic and optimistic self-view that fosters genuine interactions and learning experiences.

By integrating professional humility with dispositional humility – the balance of self-confidence and humility in one's professional interactions as defined by Landrum (2011) – sexuality educators can navigate the complexities of their role with greater efficacy and ethical awareness.

Moreover, sexuality educator dispositional humility involves demonstrating appropriate attitudes, values, and beliefs not only in verbal and nonverbal behaviors but also in the comfort and capability in teaching sexuality topics. Sexuality educator dispositional humility, though subtle, manifests in a willingness to learn from others and the ability to acknowledge shortcomings or mistakes and areas of growth.

Challenging Norms and Stereotypes

Humility in sexuality education also involves questioning and challenging prevailing norms and stereotypes. This type of engagement reflects an understanding that these norms are not merely academic or educational concepts but realities that affect learners' lives. Sexuality educators who embrace this aspect of humility are better equipped to foster a learning environment that encourages students to explore and express their identities safely and openly. This practice supports the dismantling of harmful stereotypes and promotes a broader understanding of human sexuality.

An essential aspect of professional humility involves recognizing, acknowledging one's privileges and inherent biases. Sexuality educators benefit from understanding how their backgrounds and experiences may shape their perspectives and potentially influence their teaching. By admitting to and reflecting on these aspects of identity, sexuality educators can mitigate their negative impact on the learning environment. This enhances self-awareness and can often deepen an educators' empathy towards the diverse experiences of their learners, paving the way for more equitable and sensitive educational practices. Power dynamics are multidimensional and common in educational systems, in research, and in the human service profession. They manifest in different forms and to different ends, but at the core of power is the capacity to influence or direct actions, behaviors, and decisions. Power dynamics are to be recognized, assessed, and shifted by sexuality educators.

Sexuality educators equipped with a grounded sense of professional and dispositional humility often actively recognize and reflect on their privileges and biases. This involves understanding how their unique backgrounds – racial, economic, gender, or sexual orientation – might influence the perspectives they bring to their teaching and potentially affect their interactions with students. Operating with professional humility allows sexuality educators to critically evaluate the curriculum and teaching methods, ensuring that these elements do not inadvertently reinforce existing social inequalities but contribute to a more inclusive and reflective educational experience. Acknowledging privilege is about understanding one's position in a broader social context and leveraging this awareness to support and elevate diverse voices within the learning environment.

Sexuality education is a multifaceted profession fostering character development, personal growth, and sexual interactions while also preventing harmful outcomes that can negatively impact an individual. The scope of sexuality education precedes and extends beyond adolescence, emphasizing the need for culturally relevant, inclusive, and sex-positive content accessible to individuals across all stages of life. It is especially critical for groups such as LGBTQIA+ individuals, people of color, and those with physical, intellectual, or developmental disabilities, among other marginalized identities. These communities require sex education that not only recognizes but also prioritizes their specific needs, ensuring that all learners receive the support and information necessary to lead safe, healthy, and fulfilling sexual lives.

Promoting inclusivity and diversity within sexuality education requires strategies rooted in humility. Educators can foster inclusivity by designing curriculum and learning experiences that reflect and respect all learners' diverse backgrounds and experiences. This includes using inclusive language, providing diverse examples and perspectives, and creating spaces where all voices are heard and valued. Moreover, ongoing professional development in cultural competence can help sexuality educators continually refine their approaches to teaching, ensuring they remain responsive to the evolving needs of their learners. These strategies make dispositional humility a practical tool for building a more inclusive and empowering educational environment. Reflective practices is a strategy that puts sexuality educator dispositional humility into action.

Critical Skills: Reflective Practice

Reflective practice in sexuality education is a structured approach that enables sexuality educators to learn from their experiences and gain a deeper understanding of themselves and their teaching methods. It involves critically reviewing one's comfort, ability, and teaching approaches to draw connections between previous experiences and future actions. This reflection is significant for challenging assumptions, reducing bias, evaluating responses to different classroom scenarios and dynamics, and identifying opportunities for improvement. By collaborating with peer professionals to share effective strategies and seek support, sexuality educators can better modify their teaching practices to meet diverse needs. Ultimately, this reflective approach ensures that teaching is aligned with learner needs and fosters an equitable, inclusive, and supportive environment.

Reflective practice is required in sex education because it allows sexuality educators to critically examine their teaching methodologies to reinforce effective strategies while recognizing areas for improvement. This intentional reflection helps maintain a positive and purposeful approach that enhances professional growth. It also helps sexuality educators navigate socio-cultural nuances, challenge biases, and create an inclusive environment that supports diverse learners in achieving better learning or behavioral outcomes. To implement reflective practice effectively, sexuality educators might wish to start by understanding their underlying beliefs and comfort levels in sexuality education. Before teaching, sexuality educators can outline their goals, instructional strategies, and potential challenges. For the reflective aspect, sexuality educators can gather evidence of their teaching effectiveness through learner feedback, peer observations, or self-evaluations. Afterward, they may critically analyze this evidence, considering what strategies worked well, which areas could be improved, and how biases may have influenced their teaching. This reflective cycle encourages sexuality educators to adapt their methods, engage in continuous learning through professional development.

Critical Learning Through Professional Development

One way to grow your sexuality educator professional disposition and dispositional humility is to participate in professional development. Professional development for sexuality educators involves training that enhances their academic knowledge and practical skills. It includes both formal academic preparation and specialized training provided by organizations that establish guidelines and standards. This training helps educators develop their professional disposition, which is closely linked to their comfort and capability in teaching various sexual health topics. Research by Clayton et al. (2018) demonstrates that professional preparation and development are crucial in increasing educators' comfort levels when addressing sensitive subjects. Ongoing professional development is vital for sexuality educators to improve their teaching skills and confidence. Studies show that recent training is associated with higher educator competence and confidence, leading to greater comfort and capability when discussing challenging topics like sexual orientation, race, culture, and masturbation. Such training also encourages educators to cultivate self-awareness, which Stayton (1998) emphasizes as essential for effective teaching. Despite high self-perceived comfort and capability, one study shows a moderate need for further professional development among sexuality educators. Addressing this gap could enhance their confidence in covering underrepresented topics, improving the quality and inclusivity of sexuality education programs.

Professional development can foster reflective practice and self-assessment. For example, in 2021 during a facilitated Sexual Attitude Reassessment (SAR), participants offered the following comments in their evaluations:

> *In the beginning of the SAR, I initially felt uncomfortable, as some of the material was different and contradictory to certain cultural and religious belief. . . . This training has challenged me to re-evaluate my own thinking and feelings, and empowered me in ways I didn't know I needed.*
>
> *We (sexuality professionals) think we do and know sex, but after this I realize I have so much more to learn about sex and myself.*
>
> *This training has helped me understand aspects of sexuality that I'm less familiar with and gain comfort and confidence with my own beliefs as well as an understanding and respect of those with different sexuality beliefs/ practices.*

> *I am still processing some of the experiences and feelings from the SAR content. It has made me rethink how we teach or do we teach others, including our own children about their own sexuality in a way that is healthy for future relationships.*

Embracing professional and dispositional humility involves a balanced perspective on one's abilities, acknowledging biases and cultivating an openness to continuous learning. Professional humility encourages sexuality educators to recognize their limitations while remaining receptive to evolving information in this sensitive and diverse field. Dispositional humility adds a layer of self-confidence tempered with acknowledging one's privileges and biases, promoting inclusivity and understanding in the classroom. Reflective practices further amplify these traits, enabling sexuality educators to critically assess themselves and their teaching strategies and adapt to the unique needs of diverse learners. By participating in ongoing professional development and continually refining their approaches, sexuality educators can cultivate a learning environment that is inclusive, empowering, and transformative, ultimately advancing the well-being of all participants.

Introspective Questions for Consideration

- How do my biases, privileges, and life experiences shape how I approach and teach sexuality education, and what steps can I take to minimize their impact on my learners?
- How can I cultivate a learning environment that encourages open dialogue and values my learners' diverse experiences and backgrounds?
- How do I reflect on my teaching practices to ensure that my educational approaches remain inclusive, up-to-date, and responsive to the evolving needs of my learners?
- What professional development opportunities can I pursue to develop my dispositional humility further and improve my understanding of culturally relevant and sex-positive teaching strategies?
- How can I better challenge harmful norms and stereotypes in my teaching to promote a more nuanced and empathetic understanding of human sexuality for my learners?

References

Bass, T. M. (2021). *Examining the professional disposition among community-based sexuality educators*. Widener University.

Clayton, H. B., Brener, N. D., Barrios, L. C., Jayne, P. E., & Everett Jones, S. (2018). Professional development on sexual health education is associated with coverage of sexual health topics. *Pedagogy in Health Promotion, 4*(2), 115–124. https://doi.org/10.1177/2373379917718562

Exline, J. J., & Geyer, A. L. (2004). Perceptions of humility: A preliminary study. *Self and Identity*, *3*(2), 95–114.

Finlay, L. (2008). *Reflecting on reflective practice. Practice-based professional learning paper*, *52*. The Open University.

Landrum, R. E. (2011). Measuring dispositional humility: A first approximation. *Psychological Reports*, *108*(1), 217–228. https://doi.org/10.2466/02.07.09.PR0.108.1.217-228

Mercurio, M. R. (2022). Priorities, professional humility, and communication in the setting of medical uncertainty. *Pediatrics*, *149*(6), e2022056737.

Stayton, W. (1998). A curriculum for training professionals in human sexuality using the sexual attitude restructuring (SAR) model. *Journal of Sex Education and Therapy*, *23*(1), 26–32. https://doi.org/10/1080/01614576.1998.11074203

Stubbe, D. E. (2020). Practicing cultural competence and cultural humility in the care of diverse patients. *Focus*, *18*(1), 49–51.

Tangney, J. P. (2000). Humility: Theoretical perspectives, empirical findings and directions for future research. *Journal of Social and Clinical Psychology*, *19*(1), 70–82.

5   Navigating the Emotional Landscape

Cultivating Emotional Literacy in Sex Education

Rachael E. Gibson

Emotions. They are part of the human experience. Whether we wear them on our sleeve or hide them in the deepest parts of ourselves, they are there. I once came across an old Yiddish saying, "Not to have felt pain is not to have been human." I have often thought of this phrase during my career as an educator, which spans nearly three decades. I've had students cry to me, asking, "Why don't my parents love me?", confess to having a miscarriage and putting the fetus in the trash, and boys tell me about their experiences of sexual assault. I have cried talking about sexual assault in class, walked in on kids (and teachers) having sex at school, seen teachers break down in front of young people, known young people who are sex workers, and witnessed teachers mocking trans students. The pain of the human experience abounds and is amplified within learning spaces. As educators, we are trained to remove our emotions from our teaching; that, however, is an impossible task, and I believe we do so to the detriment of our students and, ultimately, ourselves.

The best advice about teaching I ever received was about emotions. It was in an undergraduate education course; our professor implored us to remember that "We teach children, not content." She insisted that regardless of the subject we taught, our students' lives, experiences, and feelings were the most crucial thing to center. For many people, sex is emotional, but beyond the act of sex, emotions about our sexuality, our development, our bodies, and how we interact sexually and romantically with others (or not) holds deep emotions. These emotions can simultaneously be uplifting, shameful, empowering, engaging, terrifying, morose, morbid, hateful, and joyful. Our ability to identify these emotions in ourselves and others truly connects us with our students to create meaningful learning and growth in sex education.

Emotional Literacy and Intelligence

In recent years, emotional literacy and emotional intelligence have become the new "buzzwords" in educational spaces. This is especially true in sex education, as the very word "sex" elicits a wide variety of emotions from educators and learners alike.

DOI: 10.4324/9781032615479-8

Emotional literacy (EL) and emotional intelligence (EI) are often used interchangeably in the field. However, EL first came into academia to advance humanistic educational practices. In 1995, the term emotional intelligence broke into pop culture vernacular with the release of Daniel Goleman's book of the same title. While the definitions and words are consistently intermixed, revised, and modified, the basic definitions and tenets remain. Emotional intelligence is the ability to recognize our own emotions and the emotions of others, while emotional literacy is using this information to guide our thinking and behavior.

To be emotionally literate is to be able to handle emotions in a way that improves your personal power and improves the quality of life around you. Emotional literacy improves relationships, creates loving possibilities between people, makes co-operative work possible, and facilitates the feeling of community.

(Steiner, 2003)

The 4 C's of Emotional Intelligence and Literacy are Self-awareness, Social awareness, Self-management, and Relationship management. These four tenets are crucial if we genuinely want sex education that is inclusive and affirming of all identities. Figure 5.1 makes adaptations that include Goleman's Emotional Intelligence Quadrant along with the 4 C's of Emotional Intelligence and Literacy.

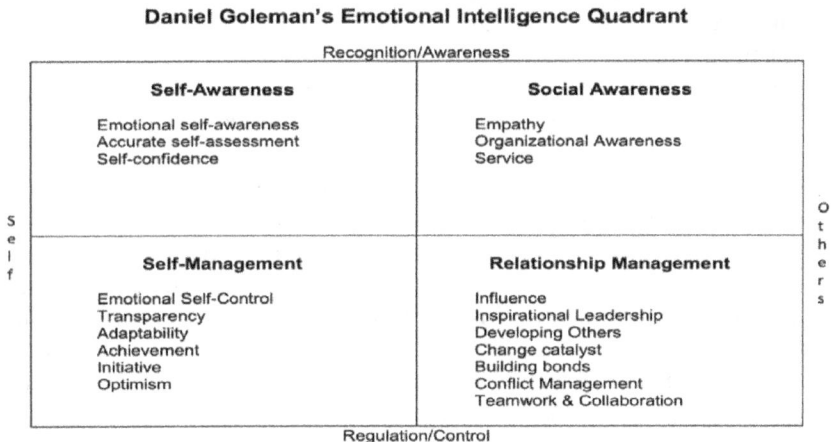

Daniel Goleman's Emotional Intelligence Quadrant

Recognition/Awareness

Self-Awareness	Social Awareness
Emotional self-awareness Accurate self-assessment Self-confidence	Empathy Organizational Awareness Service
Self-Management	**Relationship Management**
Emotional Self-Control Transparency Adaptability Achievement Initiative Optimism	Influence Inspirational Leadership Developing Others Change catalyst Building bonds Conflict Management Teamwork & Collaboration

(Self) (Others)

Regulation/Control

Figure 5.1 Daniel Goleman's Emotional Intelligence Quadrant

Note: *adapted from Ohio State University Extension; Goleman, D. (1998). Working with Emotional Intelligence. Goleman, D., Boyatzis, R., & McKee, A. (2002). *Primal leadership: Realizing the importance of emotional intelligence*. Harvard Business School Press.

Connectedness and Emotional Literacy in the Sex Ed Classroom

Sexuality education is (or at least should be) a place where learners can build their knowledge, attitudes, and skills for promotive sexual health behaviors and healthy sexuality. That said, teachers must also be trained to meet learners where they are academically, socially, and emotionally and modify pedagogy to create an inclusive, affirming, and socially just learning experience (Gibson, 2021). School connectedness is the "belief by students that adults and peers in the school care about their learning as well as about them as individuals" (CDC, 2009, p. 3). Thompson et al. (2006) explained that the overarching theory of connectedness is that students who have positive and prosocial interactions with teachers at school will have positive academic, physical, and social outcomes in the classroom and life in general.

Before we can teach our students to build their own emotional intelligence and literacy, we must ensure that we have done and continue to do that work ourselves. Dee (2004, 2005) explored how teacher identities can influence student outcomes using passive and active teacher effects. The first passive teacher effect, known as the role model effect, is "simply triggered by a teacher's racial, ethnic, or gender identity, not by explicit teacher behaviors. The presence of a demographically similar teacher raises a student's academic motivation and expectations" (Dee, 2005, p. 159). Stereotype threats, the second type of passive effect, explain that in situations where students perceive stereotypes, they may experience an apprehension that [slows] their academic achievement (Dee, 2005). Conversely, active teacher effects are defined by Dee (2004, 2005) as unintentional teacher biases based on prior expectations of and interactions with students – including how those biases affect their instructional practice.

Teachers' emotional intelligence influences their active effects (i.e., pedagogy/instruction), which then mitigates or enforces any present passive effects. Learners' perceptions of a teacher can impact their experience and learning; because of this, responsible sex educators must examine and reflect on their emotional intelligence and how it may create active and passive teacher effects in the classroom (Gibson, 2021). For example, within my career I have thought about the young Black boys in my class and wondered if I am truly making a connection or if they are ever (rightfully) thinking, "Here goes another white lady who doesn't know what she's talking about." Even if I have followed all the "rules" of culturally inclusive and responsive pedagogy, I will never truly understand what it feels like to be a young Black boy in New York City, which means a disconnect is possible. Within our careers, we may or may not have a choice in whom we teach sex education, and our students will rarely share all of our identities. What has been more critical for me then is to build my emotional intelligence, so that even if I do not understand, I can build relationships where students feel safe to learn regardless of our differences.

Emotional Literacy in Sex Education

Once you practice emotional intelligence and literacy for yourself, it begins to build a bridge for you and your students, an ebb and flow of crossing and retreating within vulnerability. In sexuality education, the KAB model is a common framework used in instructional design. The "K" is the knowledge or cognitive domain of education. We learn data, statistics, and other information in this learning sphere. In sex ed, this typically looks like learning the vocabulary of sexuality terms, memorizing the structure and function of sexual and reproductive anatomy, or revisiting the history of LGBTQ+ populations. The "A" is the affective domain of education, where our feelings are recognized and unpacked, or the awareness of issues is presented. In sex ed, this is often implemented through the Sexuality Attitudes Reassessment (SAR). The "B" is the behavioral domain, where learners are taught the skills for promotive sexual behaviors. This looks like learning how to correctly put on a condom, advocating for LGBTQ+ rights, or practicing asking for consent. We need all three learning domains to complete the arc of learning. For example, a lesson might start with the definition of consent, then move to understanding and believing that consent is essential, and finally, students practice asking for consent.

While emotional literacy is vital throughout the KAB model of instruction, it is especially essential in the "Affective" domain. It is crucial for teachers to use their emotional intelligence to build an affective pedagogical approach to sex education. Affective pedagogy may include giving positive feedback, creating an inclusive and affirming classroom management style, and having an overall welcoming teacher demeanor (Gibson, 2021). In addition, affective strategies may include exploring feelings, experiential learning cycles, reflecting on attitudes, and value clarification activities within a sex ed course. Expanding teacher affective domain strategies builds upon student-teacher relationships and trust, with students experiencing increased comfort in sex education. As students feel more comfortable in their learning spaces, they can grow beyond their comfort zone, increasing their emotional intelligence and literacy.

Supporting Students in Building Emotional Literacy

Using an affective model as part of the teacher's pedagogical practice supports this increase in students' emotional intelligence and literacy. Affective strategies can be as simple as leading a body scan before and after an activity or asking students to specifically name a feeling coming up for them from Plutchik's Wheel of Emotions (Plutchik & Kellerman, 1980). While they seem simple in nature, students in US educational contexts rarely have the space to examine emotions while learning, and these "simple" tasks lead to tremendous growth. Another affective learning strategy for a sex educator is the Experiential Learning Cycle. The Experiential Learning Cycle consists of the following layers: Experiencing,

Reflecting, Thinking, and Acting. When used in Sex Ed spaces, this might look like students hearing about how HIV has impacted the life of a person in real-time, then reflecting on what feelings, emotions, and biases arise within the student during the experience of a first-hand account. Next, a sex educator might facilitate a discussion that examines the theoretical (the "Knowledge") domain of HIV and its impact on society/communities as a whole. Finally, students will use what they have learned to guide their next steps; perhaps they become advocates for increasing public awareness of STI/sex stigma, they might change their actions/thoughts about PrEP, or they might modify their own behaviors.

Throughout the experiential learning process, students go through a specific experience that leads them through the following inquiry: "what is this? What does this mean to me? And now, what do I do with what I have learned?" Answering these questions supports the students' ability to recognize their own emotions, build awareness of the feelings of others, regulate and modify their emotions as needed, and use emotions to build relationships with others. This building of emotional literacy through the experiential learning cycle is how sexuality students can go beyond their comfort range to examine their biases and move towards understanding, acceptance, and advocacy of concepts in sexuality education.

Practicing Emotional Literacy Across Difference

For those of us in the profession with privileged identities, how we develop our emotional intelligence while working across differences is of pronounced and even fragile importance. The nuance of educating those who hold different identities than ourselves, especially as part of a group that holds immense power and privilege, is a lifelong journey filled with error, shame, vulnerability, and discomfort.

The Developmental Model of Intercultural Sensitivity (Bennett, 2017) explains a continuum of ways in which people experience, interpret, and interact across cultural differences. Moving from ethnocentric worldviews (denial, defensiveness, and minimization) to ethnorelative worldviews (acceptance, adaptation, and integration), the model is used as a reflection tool to support educators' more profound understanding of cross-cultural differences. This model is intrinsically linked to emotional intelligence within sexuality education, as one must reflect and recognize one's worldviews and privileges, and how one's ever-changing place on the continuum will affect one's pedagogy, both consciously and unconsciously.

Given the historical trauma that has been caused by some privileged communities towards others, it can be challenging for individuals within those communities – whether victimized or perpetrator – to feel safe having emotionally charged conversations with each other. I am an outsider to my students. I am an outsider to their cultures. I am a middle-aged white woman teaching in all-Black and Latine schools. No amount of education, multicultural socialization, or "being down" changes the way my students may perceive me. My words and actions have a different and significant impact than someone in their community. So often, as educators, we can get so wrapped up in our shame, discomfort, and embarrassment at being an outsider that we keep silent about our faux pas, impeding our development. Shame thrives in secrecy; I want other educators with privileged identities to acknowledge their mistakes so they can continue to learn and grow. We must remember that we don't get to self-identify as being cultural insiders; only the community we have integrated into can proclaim that. Even if you are not white, there will be moments when you hold a privileged identity in your teaching that must be interrogated. Emotional intelligence and emotional literacy are ways that can support us in growing and connecting with our students who hold marginalized identities.

As I continue to grow in my career, I often ask myself, is this working? Is what I am doing making a difference? Why am I doing this work? How can I, someone so different from my students' communities, actually make authentic connections and culturally responsive lessons without being performative? Some would argue that education by nature is a performance. However, to do this work well, specifically in sex education, we must continuously reflect, interrogate, change, and humble ourselves. I recognize that my sheer presence will be activating for some, and I won't be able to make connections no matter what I do. That is when we must move back to let others do their work meaningfully without jealousy or spite. We must continue working through those feelings when they arise, building our emotional intelligence for ourselves and those we support.

For sex education to be a place where learners build their knowledge, attitudes, and skills for promotive sexual health behaviors and increased emotional intelligence, teachers must be prepared to teach the course effectively. This preparation takes time and must focus on building personal and professional emotional intelligence and literacy. An intersectional teacher training approach (Flowers, 2016, 2018) that addresses identity and emotional literacy in its pedagogical strategy building is the most effective way to increase students' positive experiences in sexuality education classes, leading to an increase in their own emotional intelligence and literacy.

Reflection Questions for Consideration

- Would you say emotional intelligence and literacy are important in sex education? Why or why not?
- What might an emotionally literate sex ed learning experience look, sound, and feel like to you? Your students? Observers?
- In what ways might your identities support or be a barrier to developing your students' emotional literacy? What strategies can you develop to bridge the

barrier/gap in your own emotional intelligence when it comes to working across differences in your sex ed practice?
- What tools can you build into your instructional practice today to develop emotional literacy among your students?
- What steps can you take to support expanding your emotional intelligence as an educator? How about your emotional literacy?

References

Bennett, M. (2017). Development model of intercultural sensitivity. In Y. Kim (Ed.), *International encyclopedia of intercultural communication*. Wiley.

Centers for Disease Control and Prevention. (2009). *School connectedness: Strategies for increasing protective factors among youth*. U.S. Department of Health and Human Services. https://doi.org/10.1037/e568202009-001

Dee, T. S. (2004). Teachers, race and student achievement in a randomized experiment. *Review of Economics and Statistics*, *86*(1), 195–210. https://doi.org/10.1162/0034 65304323023750

Dee, T. S. (2005). A teacher like me: Does race, ethnicity, or gender matter? *The American Economic Review*, *95*(2), 158–165. https://doi.org/10.1257/000282805774670446

Flowers, S. (2018). Enacting our multidimensional power: Black women sex educators demonstrate the value of an intersectional sexuality education framework. *Meridians*, *16*(2), 308–325. https://doi.org/10.2979/meridians.16.2.11

Flowers, S. C. (2016). *Perceptions of fidelity and adaptation in evidence-informed interventions by women of color sexuality health educators*. CUNY Academic Works. https://academicworks.cuny.edu/gc_etds/1586

Gibson, R. E. (2021). *Learner experiences of teacher gender: Associations among gender and comfort in the sexuality education classroom* (Order No. 28417370). ProQuest Dissertations & Theses A&I. (2528080184). http://0-search.proquest.com.libcat. widener.edu/dissertations-theses/learner-experiences-teacher-gender-associations/docview/2528080184/se-2?accountid=29103

Goleman, D. (1998). *Working with emotional intelligence*. Bantam Books.

Goleman, D., Boyatzis, R., & McKee, A. (2002). *Primal leadership: Realizing the importance of emotional intelligence*. Harvard Business School Press.

Plutchik, R., & Kellerman, H. (1980). *Emotion, theory, research, and experience: Theory, research and experience*. Academic Press. https://doi.org/10.0125587031

Steiner, C. (2003). *Emotional literacy: Intelligence with a heart* (2nd ed.). Personhood Press.

Thompson, D. R., Iachan, R., Overpeck, M., Ross, J. G., & Gross, L. A. (2006). School connectedness in the health behavior in school-aged children study: The role of student, school and school neighborhood characteristics. *Journal of School Health*, *76*, 379–386. https://doi.org/10.1111/j.1746-1561.2006.00129.xsss

Part III

Key Information, Research, and Continuous Learning

6 Deconstructing Desirability

Sexual Racism in Focus

Aydrelle Collins

Content Warning: this chapter makes mention (with some detail in two instances) of historical bodily and sexual trauma experienced by African people in the United States and Europe. Please practice self-care in reading it as you need.

Key Terms

- **Sexual Racism:** refers to the discrimination and prejudice in sexual and romantic contexts based on racial or ethnic identity. It involves the marginalization and exclusion of individuals from certain racial groups due to stereotypes and biases about their race, which impacts their desirability and experiences in intimate relationships (Dumas, 2016).
- **Anti-Blackness:** a specific form of racism that involves the devaluation, discrimination, and exclusion of people of African descent. It is characterized by negative stereotypes and systemic practices that marginalize and oppress Black individuals and perpetuate racial inequalities (Dumas, 2016).
- **Fetishization:** the act of making something – or, in this case, someone – an object of sexual desire based on limited features about them – in this case, presumptions about their skin color and/or racial background.
- **Colorism:** a form of discrimination based on skin color, where lighter skin tones are often favored over darker ones within the same racial or ethnic group. This bias can influence social, economic, and interpersonal interactions, affecting perceptions of beauty and desirability (Hunter, 2007).
- **Intersectionality:** a framework developed by Kimberlé Crenshaw that examines how various social identities, such as race, gender, sexuality, and class, intersect to create overlapping systems of discrimination and privilege. It helps understand how multiple forms of oppression can impact individuals differently and simultaneously (Crenshaw, 1989).
- **Fatphobia:** systemic prejudice and discrimination against individuals with larger bodies; originally used against African slaves in the United States during the Trans-Atlantic Slave Trade.

DOI: 10.4324/9781032615479-10

- **Texturism:** discrimination based on hair texture, particularly within racial and ethnic communities. It involves the preferential treatment of certain hair textures (e.g., straight or wavy) over others (e.g., kinky or coily), often rooted in Eurocentric beauty standards (Mathews, 2013).

Sexual racism refers to discrimination or bias exhibited within the realm of intimate relationships based on racial preferences. It is a multifaceted phenomenon that operates at the intersection of race, gender, and sexuality, shaping the dynamics of attraction and desire. While often subtle and implicit, sexual racism can have profound implications for individuals and communities, perpetuating inequality and exclusion in the pursuit of love and intimacy. Understanding sexual racism is paramount for sexual health professionals in navigating the complexities of intimate relationships and promoting inclusivity and equity in their practice. By examining how racial biases manifest in sexual preferences, educators can better support individuals in challenging and dismantling these biases.

This chapter unpacks the topic of sexual racism by first outlining several historical factors that have played a role in establishing the matrix through which it exists today. From there, it will delve into white racial folklore theory to provide a framework for understanding how racism is used to rationalize bias in selecting sexual partners. White racial folklore theory also explains why discriminating against a potential sexual partner based on race is not a preference but rather sexual racism. The chapter will conclude with special considerations and concrete steps that educators can use to examine their own biases and facilitate productive conversations about sexual racism.

One of the main takeaways from this chapter is a clear understanding of what sexual racism entails and how our learners' sexual preferences can be rooted in these ideals. By recognizing the ways that societal norms and stereotypes shape our perceptions of attractiveness and desirability, sexual health professionals can work towards creating more inclusive and affirming spaces for all individuals, regardless of their racial background. As foundational practice, sex educators need to be equipped with the knowledge and skills to address sexual racism in their practice. This includes fostering critical awareness among their clients, challenging harmful stereotypes, and advocating for systemic change to dismantle the structures that perpetuate racial inequalities in intimate relationships.

A Brief History of White Supremacy and Racism

White supremacy, deeply ingrained in Western societies, has historically perpetuated racial hierarchies and systems of oppression (Bonilla-Silva, 2019). From colonial conquests to chattel slavery and Jim Crow segregation, the ideology of racial superiority has been systematically enforced, shaping societal norms and structures (Anderson, 2017). In early

American colonial life, racial hierarchies and prejudices were evident in the ways colonists viewed Native Americans and Africans. Native peoples were often portrayed through the lens of "sexual savagery," a dehumanizing stereotype that justified their subjugation and exploitation. Colonists depicted Native Americans as sexually wild and untamed, which was used to rationalize their displacement and mistreatment (Smith, 2015). For example, colonial narratives frequently described Indigenous peoples as living in a state of sexual barbarism, reinforcing a worldview that justified violent colonial practices (Smith, 2015).

Similarly, Africans were subjected to deeply racist stereotypes that depicted them as hypersexual and dangerous. One extreme example of this is the obsessive focus on the genitalia of Black men, which fueled fears of Black male sexuality as a threat to white women. Stark historical illustration of this can be seen in the 1893 lynching of Henry Smith in Paris, Texas, an African American man falsely accused of assaulting a white girl. During the lynching, Smith was subjected to horrific public torture, including the mutilation and burning of his genitalia. Postcards of the lynching were also sold, serving as a chilling reminder of the commonality of racial terror used to underscore everyday American life. These commonalities reflect the deep-seated anxiety and racialized myths many whites had about Black bodies (Wells, 1893).

Genital objectification was not limited to men at this time; the colonial-era fascination with Sara Baartman, a Khoikhoi woman exhibited in Europe as the "Hottentot Venus" during her lifetime, exemplifies the objectification and dehumanization perpetuated against Black AFAB bodies as well. Baartman was paraded as an exotic curiosity, and her body was dissected posthumously, reflecting a deep-seated racial obsession with Black physicality; her mistreatment is particularly significant because it laid the groundwork for enduring stereotypes that portray Black women's bodies as hypersexual and otherworldly, perpetuating harmful myths that continue to affect how Black women are perceived and treated today (Crais & Scully, 2009).

Colonialist notions of colorism also played a role in historical racial attitudes. During slavery, lighter-skinned Black individuals – most often the product of white slaveowners raping their darker-skinned slaves – were typically deemed more attractive and given slightly better treatment than their darker-skinned counterparts. This preference was institutionalized in practices such as lighter-skinned slaves being assigned domestic roles with less physical labor, while darker-skinned slaves were subjected to harsher fieldwork. The pervasive belief that lighter skin was inherently more desirable not only reinforced hierarchies within Black and other colonized communities but also perpetuates systemic racism and societal perceptions and treatment within these same communities today. This colorist preference was a means to divide and control enslaved people, reinforcing the idea that Blackness, particularly darker Blackness, was inherently undesirable (Hunter, 2007).

Sexualized racism did not end with slavery, continuing through into the Jim Crow era with egregious events like the gang rape of Recy Taylor in 1944, the murder of Emmett Till in 1955, and the Tuskegee Syphillis Study, which lasted between 1932 and 1972. Racial stereotypes and biases continue even through the present day, influencing individual preferences and choices in dating and sexual interactions (Bonilla-Silva, 2019; Hughey, 2010a). Public figures like Michelle Obama and Serena Williams have faced racially charged criticisms about their appearances, with both being subjected to derogatory comments that attempt to dehumanize and masculinize them. And in the media, dating shows like *The Bachelor* often portray a predominantly white cast, with contestants of color frequently being eliminated early, or being typecast as physically and/or socially inappropriate. The sum total of these behaviors reflect unchecked biases that Black people are sexually improper and in need of wholesale sterilization and/or extermination, as well as implicit biases regarding the sexual rightness and purity of lightness/whiteness. These events reflect several of countless ways that sexual racism has been socially codified.

Application of White Racial Folklore Theory in Understanding Sexual Racism

White racial folklore theory, proposed by William B. Harvey in his foundational work "The Imprint of White Folklore upon America" (1992), posits that racial stereotypes and prejudices are deeply ingrained in cultural narratives, shaping individual preferences and behaviors. In contemporary dating dynamics, Harvey suggests that these ingrained beliefs manifest in the construction of racial hierarchies and the valorization of whiteness. As a result, he asserts that individuals, both consciously and unconsciously, eventually begin to internalize these narratives, leading to the justification of discriminatory behavior in partner selection. For instance, a study by Feliciano et al. (2009) revealed that Black men and women faced significant racial bias in online dating, with Black women being rated as less desirable compared to women of other racial backgrounds. Research conducted by Callander et al. (2015) on the racial preferences of users on online dating platforms found that individuals of Asian descent were often subjected to stereotypes associating them with submissiveness and exoticism. Similarly, Asian men may face emasculation and desexualization due to stereotypes portraying them as submissive or unmanly (Lundquist & Lin, 2015). In studies by Lundquist and Lin (2015) and Yancey (2009), college students of diverse backgrounds often reported seeking partners within their own racial group while still expressing overwhelming preferences still for white individuals.

White racial folklore theory provides a robust framework for understanding the rationalization and perpetuation of racial biases in modern-day dating. By illuminating the ways that cultural narratives shape individual perceptions of attractiveness and desirability, this theory underscores the urgent need for critical examination and effort to dismantle race-based prejudices in intimate relationships.

Distinguishing Between Preference and Sexual Racism

It is essential to recognize that people of color can possess diverse physical attributes, including height, hair color, and eye color. For example, a Black person may be tall, while another may be short; an Asian person may have blonde hair, while another may have brown eyes. The only commonality among people of color is that they have been explicitly racialized, which is why racial discrimination in dating cannot be justified as a mere preference (Cohen, 2018). Racial preferences in dating mirror societal stereotypes and hierarchies, perpetuating exclusion and discrimination. These preferences are not just personal choices but reflections of deeper systemic biases and historical prejudices ingrained in society.

Understanding the Significance of Anti-Blackness

An understanding of sexual racism is not complete without a clear understanding of the related yet separate phenomenon of Anti-Blackness, the specific exclusion and discrimination lobbied against people of African descent. This form of bias manifests in social, economic, and political discrimination, as well as in the perpetuation of negative stereotypes and the devaluation of Black lives (Dumas, 2016). What is perhaps most significant to recognize about Anti-Blackness is how it often runs concurrently with White Supremacy, such that even non-white groups may simultaneously pursue whiteness in their dating relationships while actively working to avoid Blackness and Black people. Indeed, Black people and other people of color are not immune to perpetuating anti-Blackness. Consequently, this internalization can lead to prejudiced attitudes and discriminatory behaviors towards Black people, even within communities of color or among Black people themselves (Pyke, 2010). Recognizing this phenomenon is crucial for addressing and mitigating the effects of racial biases within and across communities.

White racial folklore theory also helps elucidate how anti-Black prejudices are perpetuated and internalized among non-Black people of color. For example, within many Latino communities, there can be a preference for lighter skin tones, where darker-skinned individuals are viewed as less desirable or worthy

(Moreno Figueroa, 2013). Similarly, in Asian communities, there can be an expressed tendency of some to distance themselves from Black people, due to stereotypes that associate Blackness with criminality or poverty (Bonilla-Silva, 2019). A study on online dating found that Asian and Latino individuals were less likely to express interest in Black individuals compared to other racial groups, demonstrating a clear pattern of exclusion based on race (McGrath et al., 2016). Within Black communities, there can be internalized colorism where lighter-skinned individuals are often preferred over those with darker skin (Keith et al., 2010; Mathews, 2013). This dynamic is especially pronounced in romantic relationships, where lighter-skinned women are often preferred, even by Black men, due to societal ideals of beauty shaped by white-dominant standards. Colorism not only affects self-esteem but also leads to disparities in areas like marriage, income, and education (Hochschild & Weaver, 2007; Saperstein & Penner, 2012). In extreme cases, phenomena like the "Passport Bros" trend involve Black men encouraging other Black men to seek relationships with non-Black women, often from other countries, under the belief that these women are more desirable and submissive compared to Black women (Curry, 2020). This movement not only reinforces harmful stereotypes about Black women being less desirable partners, but also perpetuates misogyny against other women of color who are subsequently fetishized by these biases. These instances of anti-Blackness illustrate how deeply ingrained racial biases can affect intimate relationships, reinforcing the need for a critical examination and active dismantling of these prejudices within all communities.

The Impact of Sexual Racism in Interracial Relationships

Sexual racism can manifest in interracial relationships, even among individuals who have well-meaning intentions. For instance, when White women profess a preference for only dating Black men or other men of color, these patterns of attraction may be rooted in fetishization if not properly interrogated, rather than genuine respect and appreciation. Choosing partners under the notion, for example, that Black men are presumably more sexually potent or physically dominant reduces them to a racial stereotype not only eclipses them as a complete individual in the offending partner's mind but sets both partners up for potential stress and disappointment in the instance that their projections are not fulfilled. Relationships built on fetishization can create or perpetuate imbalances of power, where one person – usually the person of color – feels valued only for their physical attributes or their ability to fulfill a specific sexual fantasy, rather than for who they are as a person (Callander et al., 2015).

For couples where one or both partners have not addressed their potential internal biases, the relationship may suffer from a lack of genuine emotional connection and mutual respect. For example, a white-presenting Latino person who refuses to date an Afro-Latino person, citing racist stereotypes or tropes, may be reflecting internalized racism and self-hatred. This mindset can lead to toxic dynamics within relationships, where one partner's humanity underneath their racial identity is devalued or dismissed. These individuals may additionally reinforce societal racial hierarchies by seeking validation or worth through relationships with individuals from other racial groups, rather than addressing and dismantling their internalized prejudices (Pyke, 2010). It is crucial for individuals in interracial relationships to engage in deep self-reflection and actively work to unlearn these biases, ensuring that their attraction and connections to each other are based on genuine respect, love, and equity.

Implementing Intersectional Pedagogy to Address Sexual Racism in Sex Education

When addressing sexual racism in the sex education classroom, it's essential for educators to go beyond recognizing the issue and actively implement pedagogical strategies that foster a more inclusive and intersectional learning environment. Here are a few concrete strategies that educators can use:

Incorporate Diverse Perspectives and Materials: one of the first steps in operationalizing an intersectional approach is to integrate diverse voices and experiences into the curriculum. This means using educational materials – such as readings, videos, and case studies – that highlight the sexual experiences of people from different racial and ethnic backgrounds, as well as those with intersecting identities (e.g., LGBTQ+ people of color, disabled people of color). By doing so, educators can provide students with a context for considering show sexual racism manifests in within relationships and the impact it has on various communities.

Facilitate Critical Discussions on Media Representation: educators can create activities where students critically analyze how race, gender, and sexuality are portrayed in media and popular culture. For instance, students could examine how racialized sexual stereotypes are perpetuated in music videos, movies, or advertisements. Educators can guide discussions that explore how these representations contribute to sexual racism and shape societal attitudes towards different racial and ethnic groups. Encouraging students to reflect on their own media consumption and its influence on their perceptions of race and sexuality can help them recognize and challenge internalized biases.

Use Case Studies and Role-playing: to help students understand the real-world implications of sexual racism, educators can use case studies or role-playing exercises. For example, a case study might involve a scenario where a person of color faces discrimination on a dating app due to their race. Students can discuss the emotional and psychological impact of such experiences and consider how intersectional identities might compound these effects. Role-playing activities can also be effective, as they allow students to step into the shoes of individuals who experience sexual racism, fostering empathy and a deeper understanding of the complexities involved.

Create a Safe and Open Learning Environment: it's crucial for educators to establish a classroom environment where students feel safe to share their experiences and perspectives. This can be done by setting clear guidelines for respectful dialogue and by actively listening to and validating students' contributions. Educators should be well-read enough to at least name instances of racism or discrimination that arise during discussions, using them as teachable moments to reinforce the importance of intersectionality and divestment from racist ideals.

Encourage Self-reflection and Personal Growth: Educators can assign reflective exercises that prompt students to examine their own biases and the ways in that they might contribute to sexual racism. For example, students could answer prompts discussing how their racial and cultural backgrounds have influenced their attitudes towards sex and relationships. These reflections can be shared in small groups or in a larger class discussion, allowing students to learn from each other's experiences and perspectives. (NOTE: assignments like these should mirror the personal work educators themselves do to increase their understanding of – and capacity to address – these topics.)

By implementing these strategies, sex educators can move beyond simply acknowledging the existence of sexual racism to actively challenging it in the classroom. Through an intersectional approach, educators can help students develop a more nuanced understanding of how race and other social identities intersect to shape sexual experiences and relationships, ultimately fostering a more inclusive and equitable society.

Special Considerations: Fatphobia and Texturism in Sexual Racism

When discussing sexual racism, it's crucial to understand how fatphobia and texturism intersect with racial biases, particularly in the context of relationships. These forms of discrimination, often rooted in societal standards of beauty, play a significant role in shaping perceptions of desirability and can deeply impact individuals' sexual identities and experiences.

Understanding Fatphobia in Relationships

Fatphobia refers to the systemic prejudice and discrimination against individuals with larger bodies. This bias affects many aspects of life, including relationships, where societal norms often prioritize thinner bodies as more desirable (Sassler & Miller, 2018). Within communities of color, particularly among Black women, fatphobia is compounded by racial stereotypes that depict Black women as inherently "larger" or "less feminine," contributing to the devaluation of their bodies (Strange, 2020). This double standard is evident in popular culture, where Black women's curves are sometimes fetishized in rap lyrics celebrating "big booty" but stigmatized in everyday contexts, leading to exclusion and discrimination in dating (Strings, 2019). For a deeper understanding of fatphobia, consult *Fearing the Black Body* by Sabrina Strings (2020) and *The Body is Not an Apology* by Sonya Renee Taylor (2018).

Understanding Texturism in Relationships

Texturism is the preference for looser, straighter hair textures over tightly coiled or kinky hair. This bias is particularly salient for Black individuals, whose natural hair textures have historically been deemed "unprofessional," "unattractive," or "unmanageable" (Gibson, 2022). Such biases not only affect how Black individuals are perceived in broader society but also impact how they are viewed in intimate relationships. References to "good hair" in rap music reflect these societal preferences and reinforce the idea that straighter hair is more desirable (Davis, 2021).

Texturism influences how individuals express themselves sexually, affecting their self-esteem and interactions with partners. For further exploration of texturism, *Cocoa Butter and Hair Grease* by Dr. Donna Oriowo (2021) is a valuable resource, along with cultural commentary on the legacy of hair discrimination.

In essence, this chapter serves as a call to action for sexual health professionals to confront sexual racism head-on, acknowledging its existence, understanding its mechanisms, and actively working towards a future where love and intimacy are truly colorblind. Understanding sexual racism is paramount for sexual health professionals in navigating the complexities of intimate relationships and promoting inclusivity and equity in their practice. By examining how racial biases manifest in sexual preferences, educators can better support individuals in challenging and dismantling these biases, fostering healthier and more equitable relationships. Through education, advocacy, and allyship, we can create a more equitable and inclusive world where everyone has the opportunity to experience love and intimacy free from discrimination and prejudice.

Introspective Questions for Consideration

- How does my own racial identity and lived experiences shape my understanding of sexual racism, and how can I leverage this awareness to foster more inclusive and equitable learning environments?
- What biases or assumptions do I hold about racial preferences and sexual attraction, and how can I actively challenge and unlearn these beliefs in my practice?
- How can I center the voices and experiences of marginalized communities, particularly BIPOC individuals, in my sexuality education curriculum and discussions on sexual racism?

- What strategies can I implement to create safe and affirming spaces for dialogue and reflection on the intersectionality of race, gender, sexuality, and other social identities within intimate relationships?
- How can I advocate for systemic change within educational institutions and communities to address sexual racism and promote diversity, equity, and inclusion in sexuality education?

References

Anderson, C. (2017). *White rage: The unspoken truth of our racial divide*. Bloomsbury Publishing.

Bonilla-Silva, E. (2019). *Racism without racists: Color-blind racism and the persistence of racial inequality in America*. Rowman & Littlefield.

Callander, R., Newman, C., & Holt, M. (2015). Is sexual racism really racism? Distinguishing attitudes toward sexual racism and generic racism among gay and bisexual men. *Archives of Sexual Behavior, 44*(7), 1991–2000.

Cohen, L. (2018). Addressing sexual racism in the LGBTQ community: A social work approach. In *LGBTQ people and social work: Intersectional and political analyses* (pp. 151–171). Palgrave Macmillan.

Crais, C., & Scully, P. (2009). *Sara Baartman and the Hottentot venus: A ghost story and a biography*. Princeton University Press.

Crenshaw, K. (1989). Demarginalizing the intersection of race and sex: A black feminist critique of antidiscrimination doctrine, feminist theory and antiracist politics. *University of Chicago Legal Forum*, 139–167.

Curry, T. (2020). Exposing the "Passport Bros": A study on the intersection of race, masculinity, and sexuality in the African American community. *Journal of Black Sexuality and Relationships, 6*(2), 67–85.

Davis, K. (2021). The cultural impact of rap lyrics on beauty standards. *Journal of Contemporary Music Studies, 45*(2), 78–90.

Dumas, M. J. (2016). Against the dark: Antiblackness in education policy and discourse. *Theory Into Practice, 55*(1), 11–19.

Feliciano, C., Robnett, B., & Komaie, G. (2009). Gendered racial exclusion among white internet daters. *Social Science Research, 38*(1), 39–54.

Gibson, J. (2022). Texturism and its impact on black identity. *Ethnic Studies Review, 25*(3), 122–135.

Harvey, W. B. (1992). The imprint of white folklore upon America. *Quarterly Journal of Speech, 78*(4), 443–450.

Hochschild, J. L., & Weaver, V. M. (2007). The skin color paradox and the American racial order. *Social Forces, 86*(2), 643–670. https://doi.org/10.1093/sf/86.2.643

Hughey, M. W. (2010a). The (dis)similarities of white racial identities: The conceptual framework of "hegemonic whiteness". *Ethnic and Racial Studies, 33*(8), 1289–1309.

Hughey, M. W. (2010b). The white savior film and reviewers' reception. *Symbolic Interaction, 33*(3), 475–496.

Hunter, M. (2007). The persistent problem of colorism: Skin tone, status, and inequality. *Sociology Compass, 1*(1), 237–254.

Keith, V. M., Lincoln, K. D., Taylor, R. J., & Jackson, J. S. (2010). Discriminatory experiences and psychological distress: The case of African Americans. *Race and Social Problems, 2*(2), 75–91. https://doi.org/10.1007/s12552-010-9029.z

Lundquist, J. H., & Lin, K. (2015). Is love (color) blind? The economy of race among gay and straight daters. *Social Forces, 93*(4), 1423–1449.

Mathews, J. (2013). Light-skinned privilege in the workplace: An exploration of skin color stratification in African American women. *Race, Gender & Class, 20*(1–2), 139–153.

McGrath, A. R., Pryce, J. M., & Johnson, K. D. (2016). Online dating preferences and racial prejudice: Distinct effects of bias and familiarity in four minority groups. *Journal of Social and Personal Relationships, 33*(3), 367–383.

Moreno Figueroa, M. G. (2013). Displaced looks: The lived experience of beauty and racism. *Feminist Theory, 14*(2), 137–152.

Pyke, K. (2010). What is internalized racial oppression and why don't we study it? Acknowledging racism's hidden injuries. *Sociological Perspectives, 53*(4), 551–572.

Saperstein, A., & Penner, A. M. (2012). Racial fluidity and inequality in the United States. *American Journal of Sociology, 118*(3), 676–727. https://doi.org/10.1086/667722

Sassler, S., & Miller, A. (2018). The impact of fatphobia on dating and relationships. *Sociology of Body and Self, 11*(1), 45–60.

Smith, A. (2015). *Conquest: Sexual violence and American Indian genocide*. Duke University Press.

Strange, M. (2020). Fatphobia and racialized beauty standards. *Journal of Race and Gender Studies, 14*(2), 98–114.

Strings, S. (2019). *Fearing the black body: The racial origins of fat phobia*. NYU Press.

Wells, I. B. (1893). *The red record: Tabulated statistics and alleged causes of lynchings in the United States*. Arno Press.

Yancey, G. (2009). Experiencing racism: Differences in the experiences of whites married to blacks and non-black racial minorities. *Journal of Comparative Family Studies, 40*(1), 35–52.

7 Contemporary and Nuanced Approaches to Teaching Consent

Sonja Vitow

Key Terms

- **Consent:** freely given permission or participation in an agreed-upon circumstance between one or more individuals (or individual(s) and an institution) in which all individuals' boundaries are upheld and personal autonomy is respected.
- **Deficit Ideology:** a framework that that puts blame on individuals instead of inequitable systems.
- **Trauma-informed Education:** a teaching practice that centers the existence and impact of trauma on students and prioritizes mitigating harm and preventing retraumatization.
- **Traumatic Invalidation:** a process by which a person becomes traumatized through the invalidation of their lived experience.

Consent Education in the United States Today

In 2024 there are only 13 states that require some form of consent education in K–12 schools (SIECUS, 2022). There is no mutually-agreed-upon definition of consent used across states, and neither is there consensus on the goals of teaching it, or evidence about how effectively it's being taught. Most states' sex ed requirements defer to legal definitions of consent, focusing only on the judicial consequences of breaching sexual consent and ignoring the myriad other ways that issues of consent show up in our society. The majority of consent education programs in the United States are provided to college students (Willis et al., 2019), despite the fact that many people do not attend college and will never receive that education. As nearly 70% of all reported victims of sexual assault are minors (Snyder, 2000), it is clear that consent education needs to begin well before college age in order to protect our most vulnerable community members: children.

When we talk about teaching consent, most people immediately think of sexual consent. But that's like teaching a child multivariable calculus without first

DOI: 10.4324/9781032615479-11

teaching them to count, and while denying the existence of any other need for math. We must teach consent early and habitually and not make sexual consent our starting point. A meaningful understanding of sexual consent hinges on a meaningful understanding of consent as it applies to daily life, including the sociopolitical context in which that daily life occurs.

Trauma-Informed Consent Education

In order to be effective, consent education must be trauma-informed, or we run the risk of traumatizing – or, in many cases, *re*traumatizing – our students. Currently, many of the prominent guidelines for teaching consent education center their pedagogy around the legal definition of consent (SIECUS, 2022). An important part of teaching consent through a trauma-informed framework is divorcing the curriculum from the legal definition of consent. The United States Criminal Justice System is a system of punishment, oppression, and harm; it is antithetical to notions of healthy relationships, personal boundaries, and bodily autonomy, the themes that should be at the center of consent education. When we evoke criminal justice-based ideals within the consent education classroom, we reinforce behavioral expectations that are rooted in suppression and isolation of oneself against others, versus establishing relationship-building skills based on respect, choice, mutual care, and protection. These latter aspects are not typically granted to communities of color by the Criminal Justice System or to other groups that are also impacted by their policies, including LGBTQ+ people and those living in poverty.

If an educator prioritizes all aspects of consent in the classroom but does not do so through an anti-racist, anti-oppressive framework, they will continue to perpetuate harm and cause new trauma. As writer, educator, and activist Dr. Dena Simmons put it,

> Why teach relationship skills if the lessons do not reflect on the interpersonal conflicts that result from racism? Why discuss self- and social awareness without considering power and privilege, even if that means examining controversial topics like white supremacy?
>
> (Simmons, 2019)

By prioritizing conversations about racism, homophobia, and other intersections of oppression in our society, we are modeling to our students the sorts of conversations that are important to be having with one another. We are encouraging them to build healthier, stronger relationships, to advocate for themselves, and to think critically about their roles in society. We are not just teaching them to have safer sexual interactions but how to recognize injustice and fight for the autonomy of themselves and others in a society that does not prioritize their health, happiness, or safety.

As consent educators, we are in a sensitive but important position; done poorly, consent education has the potential to reinforce the existing white supremacist systems of oppression on which our nation's schools are founded. Done inclusively, through a trauma-informed lens that acknowledges systemic injustice and prioritizes our students' rights to bodily autonomy, consent education has the power to be revolutionary, by helping them steadily work to undo those systems. Students are too infrequently reminded of their rights as human beings and are too frequently invalidated when they point out the injustices they face in society, including at school. In order to fully teach consent through anti-oppressive, intersectional, trauma-informed lenses, we must acknowledge that schools are not consensual environments. We must be willing to have challenging conversations, to examine our own relationship with power in the classroom and to engage with how institutional racism and other systems of oppression impact our ability to live in society in a consensual way.

Contemporary and Nuanced Approaches to Teaching Consent

Trauma-Informed Consent Education and Deficit Ideology

Currently, consent education is steeped in *deficit ideology*, the perspective that individuals (and not the inequitable systems in which they exist) are at fault for inequitable outcomes. It focuses on individual behavior as having the sole responsibility for change and legality, ignoring the ways that racism and systemic oppression has contributed to our understanding of consent – who is allowed to consent, what consent looks like, and when we are allowed to exercise it (Mayes et al., 2022). Current practices also ignore how these harmful systems frequently utilize the concept of consent as a weapon to surveil or punish BIPOC individuals in the name of protecting their white counterparts, as well as how these systems can impact a person's ability to give consent or comply to the consent standards being taught (Mayes et al., 2022). Most current consent education practices aim to foster healthy relationships and to give students the tools to have difficult conversations with one another while failing to interact with navigating racism, misogyny, homophobia, ableism, or any other system of oppression in interpersonal conflicts. These are failures of the current system that do not align with trauma-informed practices and are ineffective at adequately preparing students to think critically about these issues.

Consent education that does not acknowledge the realities of students' oppressive experiences in their own schools is not trauma-informed, and contributes to the trauma these students are experiencing. An important aspect of trauma-informed education is understanding *traumatic invalidation,* or the trauma that occurs when an individual's environment is not set up to support them, sending the message that something about their existence is wrong, weird, or a problem (Cardona et al., 2022). It is not our job to provide education that reinforces the status quo; as consent educators, we must acknowledge that schools are not consensual environments, that our students do not attend willingly, and that they are often endangered through disciplinary tactics meant to regulate perceived unruly behavior versus helping students feel safe and supported. Consent educators are most effective when we're prioritizing our students' personhood, bodily autonomy, and boundaries, and we must do this through a framework of honesty, antiracism, and social justice, or we are simply continuing to replicate the traumatizing systems that do so much harm.

Antiracist Considerations in Consent Education

A primary consideration for consent educators is to identify and recognize their own positionality – its strengths and limitations – and to work to identify how it is influencing their teaching. It is important to model to students that different people have different perspectives on many issues regarding consent, boundaries, and relationships, and that their own community's values are important information when formulating their own. Similarly, consent educators must work to not uphold a deficit ideology when interacting with students or discussing issues of consent but to ask what societal or institutional conditions contributed to the situation at hand.

This can be challenging when there is a conflict that puts educators at odds with colleagues or the school that employs them, but the priority should be validating the student's experience and supporting them. By making themselves safe adults for students to confide in, consent educators are likely to hear more about injustices in the school and among their colleagues. Suppose several BIPOC students tell their consent educator they feel they are being graded more harshly than their white peers due to their race in English class. Even if the consent educator has exclusively positive experiences with the English teacher, it is their job to listen to their students, validate the likelihood of their experience, and help them advocate for antiracist grading practices. Similarly, if students approach their consent educator regarding misogynist and/or racist double standards being used to enforce dress codes at their school, it is the educator's job to validate the students' experience of those policies, help them name the systems of oppression at work, and to help them advocate for change within the school.

One of the best things we can do as consent educators is help our students develop the skills to be critical thinkers who understand how to contextualize the world around them, to be able to identify white supremacy in all its forms and push back against it. In our lesson planning and consideration of our physical classroom space, it is imperative for consent educators to use language, messaging, and imagery that is inclusive of many identities and experiences. In our curriculum and demeanor, we must prioritize inclusion and celebration of our students' many identities, preemptively empowering them and educating everyone in the class holistically, not just reacting to the damage when we see harm occurring. Example consent scenarios and discussions should feature a full range of racial, sexual, and gender identities, normalize experiences of people of different religions, classes, and abilities, and examine how power is impacted by intersectionality. As consent educators, we have the opportunity to instill habits of mind that ask students to assess their own positionality and to examine how power impacts interactions all around us, interpersonally, institutionally, and societally; to teach them to ask questions like:

> How does a person's race/religion/immigration status/social status impact how their negotiations of consent are perceived by those with differing privilege from them?
> How does a person's sexuality/gender/disability/body type/hair texture impact their access to bodily autonomy in the workplace?

Consent education has the power to be transformative, to help students make important connections that are vital to their health and well-being as well as their understanding of society. In order to reach students meaningfully, consent educators must model an ethos of trauma-informed, antiracist education that validates student experiences and pushes us all closer to a more just world.

Modeling Consent and Creating a More Consensual Learning Environment

As educators, we know that the single most effective teaching tool in our classroom is ourselves (Bandura, 1969). We use modeling to teach everything from throwing a softball to public speaking to solving math problems. We know that modeling is one of the most effective ways to teach just about anything, so how do we expect to teach consent meaningfully when we aren't modeling consent to our students by making our classrooms as autonomous as possible?

When we're talking about consent, we are always talking about power. So it only makes sense to teach consent in an environment that acknowledges the most visible power imbalance in the classroom: that between the teacher and students. It is hypocritical to teach consent education in a nonconsensual environment, and ignoring that dynamic detracts from our trustworthiness as educators. As teachers, it is important that we acknowledge that schools are not consensual spaces, and the injustices in school settings come at the intersection of (and reflect) many other systems of oppression in our society. Schools are environments that most students do not attend willingly, where many students feel unsafe, and where students are often misled about their own goals, needs, and desires (Stearns, 2022).

Because of this, it is important that we return as much of our students' autonomy to them as possible, prioritizing making the classroom a more consensual space. Centering their voices gives them more control over their learning and serves as a powerful message to them that their experience is an important focus of the class. One way to set that tone is to facilitate students in generating group expectations for themselves and their classmates, but also their instructor. By showing students that their teacher actively seeks their input in how the class will be run, and by encouraging them to consider what they want and need to feel supported and to learn, we are demonstrating that their voices are important to us and empowering them to advocate for how they should be treated at school. It legitimizes their right to be treated the way they deserve to be treated and teaches them to identify and interrogate people and institutions who don't treat them with respect.

For these reasons, it is especially important that consent educators fulfill the promises we set up in our classrooms. For example, if we invite students to create community norms for engagement, we must recognize ourselves as part of the community by adhering to them as well. It can be challenging to apologize to anyone, including students, when we transgress a boundary, but it is urgent that we model humility and community care when this happens. If we don't acknowledge when we have wronged a student, we are contributing to the traumatic invalidation that they face daily, and worse, invalidating their experience as someone who is supposed to be a safe adult. It is the job of the consent educator to empower their students in gaining autonomy, not impeding it.

In a consensual classroom space, students should have the right to pass, especially when discussing topics that are potentially triggering. In consent education this is especially important, as the topic of consent itself can be triggering to some students. The right to pass means that students have the right to avoid answering a question, to take a break, and to choose who they work with. As teachers, we don't always have a full understanding of the social dynamics in our classroom. Knowing that our students are complicated individuals who have complex relationships with one another means acknowledging that they are the experts of their own experience. If a student is made to work with another student who acts harmfully towards them, we are perpetuating more trauma by enforcing the partnership.

Additional Factors for Consideration

It is controversial to suggest that schools are not consensual environments, and that the people whose job it is to nurture and protect children often perpetuate the same systems of harm that do so much damage outside of the walls of the school. Consent educators are carrying a heavy load; we must be willing to examine consent on three levels: student to student interactions; teacher to student interactions; and institution to teacher and student interactions. We are tasked with teaching students how to treat one another while being mindful of our own power in the classroom dynamic, as well as the limitations our academic institution imposes on our own ability to give consent and grant it to our students.

We must juggle these interrelating parts while also being mindful of the way the relationship between the carceral system and the education system impact the autonomy of both teachers and learners. This work is nuanced, complex, and faces a lot of opposition, but it is work that is integral in providing students with a thorough, meaningful understanding of consent.

Paul Gorski and Katy Swalwell wrote, "Transformative equity's key task is not to help people overcome a barrier while we ignore the barrier itself" (Gorski & Swalwell, 2023). It is not effective consent education to provide white-washed lessons that teach students to be polite to one another while over-looking and perpetuating systemic injustice. Similarly, it is not effective consent education to teach in an institution that denies students' bodily autonomy without acknowledging those injustices. For many, it is risky to acknowledge the shortcomings of our workplaces, especially in a society that centers our livelihood and health care on our employment; however, If we do not validate the harm our students witness and experience, we run the risk of setting them up for future traumatization, and we demonstrate that the harm done to them doesn't warrant attention or change. Consent educators are in the joyous, empowering, justice-forward position to validate young people as they develop their understanding of systems-level thinking, of what they want to contribute to society, and what they deserve to receive.

Introspective Questions for Consideration

- What are some ways the power imbalance between myself and my students is visible in the classroom?
- What is my relationship to power, authority, and control in the classroom?
- How did I arrive at those relationships, and how does my identity influence them?
- How do I use the power that I have in ways that might be harmful to my students? Are there areas/ways I could relinquish some power and control in my classroom and return autonomy back to my students?

References

Bandura, A., Blahard, E. B., & Ritter, B. (1969). Relative efficacy of desensitization and modeling approaches for inducing behavioral, affective, and attitudinal changes. *Journal of Personality and Social Psychology, 13*(3), 173–199. https://doi.org/10.1037/h0028276

Cardona, N. D., Madigan, R. J., & Sauer-Zavala, S. (2022). How minority stress becomes traumatic invalidation: An emotion-focused conceptualization of minority stress in sexual and gender minority people. *Clinical Psychology: Science and Practice, 29*(2), 185–195. https://doi.org/10.1037/cps0000054

Gorski, P., & Swalwell, K. (2023). *Fix injustice, not kids and other principles for transformative equity leadership.* ASCD. https://www.ascd.org/books/fix-injustice-not-kids

Mayes, R. D., Pianta, R., Oglesby, A., & Zyromski, B. (2022). Principles of antiracist social emotional justice learning. *Theory into Practice, 61*(2), 178–187. https://doi.org/10.1080/00405841.2022.2036063

SIECUS. (2022). *Sex Ed state law and policy chart.* SIECUS. https://siecus.org/wp-content/uploads/2021/09/2022-Sex-Ed-State-Law-and-Policy-Chart.pdf

Simmons, D. (2019). Why we can't afford whitewashed social-emotional learning. In *Education update*. ASCD. https://www.ascd.org/el/articles/why-we-cant-afford-whitewashed-social-emotional-learning

Snyder, H. N. (2000). *Sexual assault of young children as reported to law enforcement: Victim, incident, and offender characteristics: A statistical report using data from the National Incident-Based Reporting System.* U.S. Department of Justice, Office of Justice Programs, Bureau of Justice Statistics.

Stearns, C. (2022). *Consent in the childhood classroom: Centering student voices across early years and elementary education.* Routledge.

Willis, M., Jozkowski, K. N., & Read, J. (2019). Sexual consent in K-12 sex education: An analysis of current health education standards in the United States. *Sex Education, 19*(2), 226–236. https://doi.org/10.1080/14681811.2018.1510769

8 Re-Teaching Contraception

LaShay Harvey

Key Terms

- **Contraception:** "individual choice, safe methods, as well as abortions when necessary" Angela Davis (1981).
- **Political:** of, relating to, or concerned with formal and informal policy, public affairs, the State, government, or citizens.
- **Black Girls:** used to identify those people who have experienced a racialized girlhood and continue to visit that developmental stage for answers to their current life. Current language may identify this person as a person of color and cisgender.
- **Freedom:** the state of being that allows one to make decisions about their life without the limitations or impositions of another.
- **Black Girl Reproductive Intelligence:** an intervention that honors that the decision to use birth control (or not) as part of a larger reproductive process.

Contraception in the United States, since at least 1973 and at most 1662,[1] has become both synonymous and intertwined with concepts of freedom. Having various expressions and definitions across time, freedom generally leads one to be released of, by, or from what is deemed oppressive. In modern contexts, contraception is viewed as an applied expression of the desire(s) for reproductive freedom. For decades, contraceptives were seen as a "private matter," growing ever more "public" in recent years. Each subsequent step towards "public interest" and away from "private matter" brings a new phrase into the media – family planning, birth control, "the pill," contraception, reproductive technology, etc. Each new phrase communicates something about the way modern society interprets a "non-political, individual choice" to have, or not to have, children. That is to say, an assumption of what is "good" and "right" becomes a large part of the analysis of someone's choice to use contraception. This includes what is, and can be, written, spoken, discussed, legislated, executed, and judged regarding who can/should/ought/will/wouldn't/won't reproduce. *Contrary to these narratives of freedom and choice and their attendant ideologies, which*

DOI: 10.4324/9781032615479-12

includes text and subtext, contraception has always been political because it is attached to and in relationship with the State/The State. Given that so many Black girls' and women's reproductive lives have been controlled by the State since at least 1662, it is impossible to have an informed conversation about contraception and, by extension, modern reproductive technologies, without knowing about the lived experiences of Black girls and women.

Knowing Contraception

On June 24, 2022 the United States Supreme Court overturned *Roe v. Wade*, in the *Dobbs v. Jackson Women's Health Organization* decision, ending the right of its citizens to have Federal access to abortion. Although many parts of American society were charged up by the decision, most individuals, no matter what side(s) they agreed with, "knew" this was going to happen. Maybe it was from years of fighting matches between Democrats and Republicans that were bound to explode one day, or from leaked confidential papers in May of 2022. Either way, people seemed to "know" something was going to happen to Roe.

Sexuality educators, direct service providers, and historians can never say the road to contraceptive access has been an easy one. Conflict and clashes are common in almost any discussion about the rights of reproduction, particularly and specifically women's[2] ability to, or not to, reproduce. The history record reflects several of these such scenarios.[3] This is in part due to the way a person, group of people, or a society uses reproductive frameworks to decide when, how, and by whom children will be born and raised in their community.

When one is asked to name the histories of reproduction and contraception in America, images of the eugenics movement may come to mind. Perhaps stories of forcing Black women to breed during slavery, followed by sterilizations of Black women, the "feeble-minded,"[4] and the poor, back-alley abortions before *Roe v. Wade*, and birth control pill experiments on Puerto Rican women, young African-American girls, and women and girls of the Global South. These historical reflections, while technically diverse, all have fundamental questions at their core: "who is allowed to have the children? When? Where? And how? For what purpose? And at what cost?" The appropriateness, and perhaps utility, of these questions functions differently if you are asking them about a woman of color or about a white woman, independent of their social class (Jackson et al., 2016). This is because it is impossible to discuss the evolution of contraception without considering the subjects of race, class, gender, nationality, age, and sexual orientation, at the same time.

It is important to note that women have probably wanted to control their fertility since the beginning of time given the amount of knowledge available on herbal abortifacients across all cultures,[5] from ancient times to the present. The decision by a woman not to have children has routinely been critiqued by society since at least the 1800s, when American feminists made the loud call for "voluntary motherhood."[6] At that time it was seen as ridiculous and outrageous that a woman could make the decision to deny her husband sex. A century later, in the mid-to late 1900s, the idea of "voluntary motherhood" had evolved to become a foundational element of the Women's Liberation Movement. However, at the forefront of each socio-cultural wave about contraception was that of white women's desires to negotiate their reproductive lives. Absent were the voices of Black, Puerto Rican, Chicana, and Indigenous/First Nation women. This does not mean that white women's desires to live full lives without domestic responsibility should be dismissed. Rather, it is to say that the conversation on the "positive" uses of contraception (e.g. contraception is a "smart woman's" decision) have been attributed to white women and the "negative" uses of contraception have been attributed to women of color (e.g. contraception is the "only way for you to escape poverty").[7] This long-standing paradox in contraceptive stories creates a social tension that invites people to again lean in on the questions noted earlier: who is allowed to have the children? When? Where? And how? For what purpose? And at what cost?

Birth Control – An Ideological History

Since its early days, birth control has been seen as a vehicle to further the goals and aspirations of wealthy white women and has been attributed to white women's liberation from reproductive oppression. This cannot be understated. And yet, it is also paradoxical[8] when considering Black American women's fight for liberation from the same oppression. Black American women have been "aborting themselves since the earliest days of slavery" (Davis, 1981) because their self-determination would not allow them to birth children into "a world of interminable forced labors, where chains and flogging and sexual abuse for women were the everyday conditions of life" (Davis, 1981, p. 204). Professor Angela Davis goes on to say that this phenomenon was well documented by southern slave doctors who thought (while representing "the State's" interests) enslaved Black women were "possessed of" a secret knowledge that allowed them to abort their pregnancies. While wealthy white women were seeking birth control as a way to live a more fully actualized life, Black enslaved women were seeking abortion as an "act[s] of desperation" and not yet an ode to freedom (Davis, 1981, p. 205).

It is of no surprise then, that in the years following the Civil War, newly freed Black women continued to practice herbal contraceptive methods[9] given that the fate of the Negro was highly unstable. However, somewhere between the First and Second World Wars a new discourse began taking shape. On the one hand, there was the Black intelligentsia that felt birth control was but one well-intentioned step towards advancing the social status of the newly emancipated Negro. On the other hand, there were also Black nationalists who felt birth control was nothing short of State-sanctioned race suicide. And supporting these two positions were the always-ready eugenicists who felt, especially during the Depression era, that it was best to limit the fertility (at this time by sterilization) of any person who may need to rely on the State for any current or future social support.

Reproductive Politics in the Present

It is precisely this story about who the State will and won't support that makes the need for birth control one that the State must use to promote its own survival, not one based on personal or collective freedom. Now, essential questions such as, "who among you has enough money to have children?" becomes the measure used by the State en masse. You only need to look at the current and historic landscape of reproductive technology to see the evolution of this political contraceptive consciousness. First, think about the number of women who made the choice to use long-acting reversible contraception in the time between when Donald Trump was elected president in November 2016 and his policy that gave publicly traded companies exemption from providing birth control to their employees if that company had a moral or religious objection to birth control, first outlined in the Affordable Care Act of 2010 (NPR, 2016). As a sexuality professor at the time, at least 12 women shared with me that they had chosen an IUD or implant because they "just didn't know how this birth control thing [was] going to work out."

Next, consider the reproductive landscape in Alabama at the moment. In early 2024, the Alabama State Supreme Court ruled that frozen embryos created during IVF procedures and stored for future use could be considered children. While I do believe sexuality educators should deeply study this case, I invite educators to consider how Alabama, or any other state, may use this policy for its own political advantage. The year before the IVF ruling, in early 2023, Alabama became the state known for building the most expensive private prison in the history of the United States with a record price tag of $1 billion. The way private prisons make money in America is to encourage these prisons to stay populated – with mostly poor people and people of color – meaning they are paid for every prisoner and now have a vested interest in maintaining, or increasing, mass incarceration.[10] The profit structure of private prisons is also one where they are often built in rural towns, with small populations that are in desperate need of economic development. For example, after a 4,000-bed private prison is built in a town whose population is 1,000, that town now has a population of almost 5,000 and is now eligible to receive state funding due to its increase in population. That same town of 1,000 would not have been eligible for state funding before the population increase, that is, the construction of the prison (Lawrence & Travis, 2004). If Alabama now considers all embryos in the state children, wouldn't that mean they may potentially be able to claim eligibility for State services to match this "population boom"?

Black Girl Reproductive Intelligence – a Framework in Practice

So, what can (sexuality) educators do with all of this?

I attempt to answer that question by inviting the exploration of the sexuality education intervention Black Girl Reproductive Intelligence (Harvey, 2020). Most theories on sexuality that comment on the process of gaining knowledge are often rooted in and organized by Western ideals that praise intellectual rigor while dismissing mythical, spiritual, and experiential ways of interpreting the world – that is, Indigenous ways of knowing. This educational intervention does something different by beginning with a bold premise: ***Black girls and young women hold an intelligence throughout and about their reproductive lives that exists before and extends beyond just the intellectual.*** Indigenous ways of knowing are those pedagogical approaches to learning that place a premium on the process over the outcome (Pember, 2008). **Black Girl Reproductive Intelligence** (Illustration 8.1) paints this picture in the following ways:

1. Black girls actively and passively engage a combination of at least four Indigenous ways of knowing – experiential, spiritual, mythic, intellectual – during their girlhood, prior to a reproductive event (e.g. first blood, first kiss, first consensual sexual experience, first pregnancy, first experience with contraception, etc.).

   - **Experiential**: the knowing/knowledge that resides inside the body.
   - **Spiritual**: those encounters where one senses they have experienced/are experiencing something outside of themselves.
   - **Mythic**: knowings about the world and ourselves expressed in art, music, story, and dreams. Expression of important truths held by entire cultures or people.
   - **Intellectual**: ability to recognize patterns and make generalizations; the ability to analyze.

2. Immediately following a reproductive event, Black girls enter a decision-making process that could last less than one minute or 20+ years.
3. With the information she has gained from her Indigenous ways of knowing and her lived experiences, she makes a sensual/sexual/contraceptive decision.
4. As an adult she is presented with the opportunity to reflect, as we all are, on the decisions she's made during her girlhood. And this time she has the privilege of seeing those decisions through her understanding of her own reproductive intelligences – experiential, spiritual, intellectual, mythical – that have existed, in raw and refined ways, since her girlhood.

As a way to imagine what Black Girl Reproductive Intelligence looks like activated in a classroom, let's consider language. When female-identified individuals talk about the first time they had consensual sex many of them

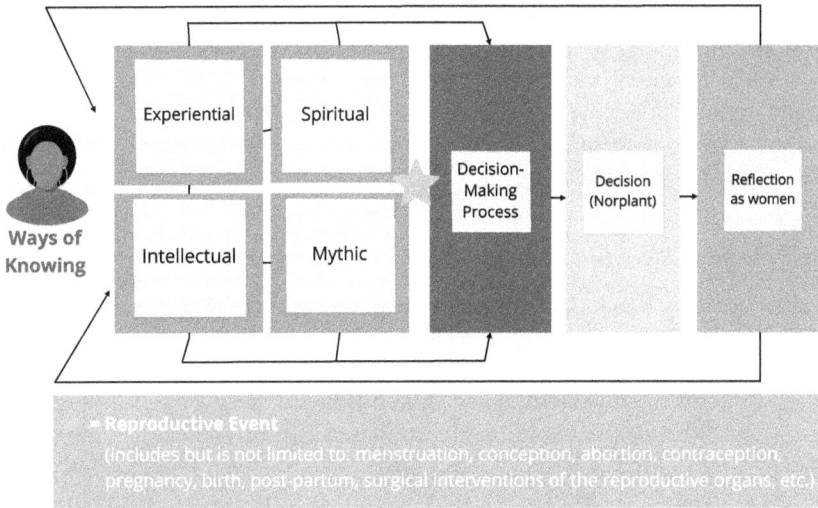

Illustration 8.1 Black Girl Reproductive Intelligence
Source: illustration by the author (Harvey, 2020).

will say, "when I lost my virginity" or "I lost my virginity at 16," as if their virginity was something they had given no thought to and one day it just up and disappeared between the cushions on the sofa. In actuality, most girls have been in a long relationship with their virginity; they have considered the ways they would like to share it with another person (Mythic Knowing), what it might feel like when they share this experience, consensually, with another person (Experiential, Spiritual Knowing), and are often consumed by the behaviors of the person they shared their virginity with, following that first consensual experience (Intellectual Knowing). Now, consider most teenage pregnancy prevention curricula: the emphasis is mostly on the intellectual experience of sex – yet, more specifically, its potential adverse outcomes (i.e. what may happen statistically after you have sex). So little, if any, of the curriculum acknowledges all that a Black girl may actually know before experiencing a reproductive event. What might the classroom conversation look like if the sexuality educator believed that *Black girls and young women hold an intelligence throughout and about their reproductive lives that exists before and extends beyond just the intellectual?* This is what a consideration of Black Girl Reproductive Intelligence allows to be included in regular classroom discourse.

I remember working as a peer educator in undergrad in the early aughts and thinking that the presentations we did on birth control were so boring. They had no sparkle to them. This is because our education and training on contraception rarely involves real depth. We mostly receive a regurgitation of "taken for granted" ideals (e.g., birth control is good for everyone). As a sexuality educator, one has to be willing to ask themselves, "am I ready to dig deeper into everything I believe to be true?" Regularly asking that simple yet profound, question is the perfect way to support the weight of change that may come on the other side of such a question.

Implications of Black Girl Reproductive Intelligence in Practice

For educators, Black Girl Reproductive Intelligence imagines that if the broad contraception questions – What do Black girls and women know about contraception?

How do they know what they know? How do they make sense of this knowing? What decisions do they make based on this knowing? – are asked at any point during and about Black girls' and women's reproductive lives; a specific and specialized body of information is produced. Accordingly, a specialized method of analyzing, understanding, and appreciating Black girls' and women's contraceptive lived experiences is necessary. That is to say, if sexuality educators, practitioners, and historians apply Indigenous ways of knowing to the reasons Black girls and women use – or don't use – birth control a more nuanced understanding of the decision-making that happens over the course of their entire reproductive life occurs.

Operationalizing Black Girl Reproductive Intelligence as a practice is meant to help usher in the spiritual elements of our work as sexologists – which is also about bringing educators and learners back to their own sexual and sensual intuition. The spiritual elements of our work are often overlooked by the field because there is a common assumption made that "spiritual" is the same as "religious." And connecting the spiritual and the sexual offends many people. This applied practice of Black Girl Reproductive Intelligence is also meant to support educators in their work to help learners reconnect with themselves. It is important to note here the author's belief that if sexuality educators and practitioners subscribe to a separation of the physical, emotional, and spiritual self, they are missing the fundamental mark of quality sexuality education. Because when the field of sexuality education fosters a politic of separation between these elements of self it creates an environment fertile for narrative(s) that promote, for example, external "political" reproductive technologies over internal reproductive intelligences.

Introspective Questions for Consideration

- Is a decision to use birth control that is based on the political climate or in response to a policy mandate a choice that is made freely?
- What implications do you think the current landscape of US reproductive politics have for future conversations about citizenship, "access" to resources, and reproductive technologies?

- Do you believe that Black girls and young women hold an intelligence throughout and about their reproductive lives that exists before and extends beyond just the intellectual? What evidence or belief do you base your answer on?
- How do you answer the questions: who is allowed to have children? When? Where? And how? For what purpose? And at what cost?
- In what ways, if any, might your answers to Question #4 impact the freedom of those you wish to teach?

Notes

1 See Virginia's enactment of hereditary slavery law by the General Assembly in 1662.
2 While I understand the expansive concept of gender, my choice to use the word "woman" is my attempt to honor my personal foremothers and forefathers in the work that I do. In this case, consider the term an altar offering and not a term of offense.
3 For research on the subject of reproductive history, consider Harriet Washington's (2008) *Medical Apartheid*, Dorothy Roberts' (1997) *Killing the Black Body*, and Angela Davis' (1981) *Women, Race & Class*.
4 For research on the American eugenics movement, consider Edwin Black's (2012) *War Against the Weak: Eugenics and America's campaign to create a master race.*
5 There is much homeopathic research on herbs such as Queen Anne's lace, also known as wild carrot, pennyroyal, cotton root bark, pulsatilla, and cohosh, among many others. See Loretta J. Ross, "African American Women and Abortion: 1800–1970," and John M. Riddle's (1997) text *Eve's Herbs: A History of Contraception and Abortion in the West* by Harvard University Press.
6 See Linda Gordon's 1973 work on the subject.
7 For a discussion on narrative control as birth control policy see Dorothy Roberts' "Killing the Black Body" (2017) on how "racism helped to create the view of birth control as a means of solving social problems" (p. 56).
8 Treb Allen's (2015), "The Promise of Freedom: Fertility decisions and the escape from slavery." Allen argues that the promise of freedom played a major role in the everyday lives of the enslaved and thus Black women's fertility ebbed and flowed with the promises of freedom.
9 Roberts, "Killing the Black Body."
10 For more information on the history of private prisons, see the September 23, 2020 article in the *Harvard International Review* "Capital and the Carceral State: Prison Privatization in the United States and United Kingdom." Found at: https://hir.harvard.edu/us-uk-prison-privatization/

References

Davis, A. Y. (1981). *Women, race & class*. Random House.
Harvey, L. (2020). *Lived experiences of young Black women who adopted Norplant between 1990–2000* (Publication No. 28029411) [Doctoral dissertation, Widener University]. ProQuest Dissertations & Theses Global.
Jackson, A. V., Karasek, D., Dehlendorf, C., & Foster, D. G. (2016). Racial and ethnic differences in women's preferences for features of contraceptive methods. *Contraception*, 93(5), 406–411. https://doi.org/10.1016/j.contraception.2015.12.010
Lawrence, S., & Travis, J. (2004). *The new landscape of imprisonment: Mapping America's prison expansion*. Urban Institute, Justice Policy Center.

NPR. (2016, November 11). Women rush to get long-acting birth control after Trump wins. *NPR.* https://www.npr.org/sections/health-shots/2016/11/11/501611813/women-rush-to-get-long-acting-birth-control-after-trump-wins

Pember, M. A. (2008). Diversifying pedagogy: Indigenous ways of knowing has been making its way out of tribal colleges into mainstream universities, but this method has its critics. *Diverse Issues in Higher Education, 25*(5), 18–20.

9 Sexual Health Is Mental Health

Shifting From Sex ~~Negative~~
Avoidant Society Into a Stigma-
Free One

Courtney Brame

Key Terms

- **Stigma:** a mark of disgrace within a particular circumstance, according to Google.

    Author's Note: I have come up with an interpretation of stigma that I believe is much deeper and serves as the concept to be used in this chapter therefore:

    > **Stigma** *is a universal stereotyping of invalidation of an individual's identity, causing themselves and others to be viewed as someone unethical, untrustworthy, unsafe, and as a person to avoid. Stigma, while seemingly harmless, is the core perpetuator of over a third of people with herpes having suicide ideation; the reason some people isolate themselves, why some may choose to withhold their positive status, and perpetually enable harm to be done to them out of feelings of guilt and shame that they ought to be punished for the act that they "committed" to get that which has caused them to be associated with their condition.*

- **Sex Avoidance:** is the aversion of individuals from verbal communication around sex beyond entertainment (mainstream media implications of sex) versus the reality of sex, which is inclusive to the broader aspects of sexuality rather than sex for intercourse and reproductive purposes, pregnancy, and STI prevention.
- **Intercourse Education:** a proposed term that speaks to how much of contemporary sex education is focused solely on how to engage in STI and/ or pregnancy-free sexual intercourse.

What?

We live in a sex-AVOIDANT society. It isn't that the general public is talking down to or negatively about sex. It's that there aren't any conversations happening about it at all. The most relevant spaces where conversations about sex

DOI: 10.4324/9781032615479-13

are introduced typically speak about INTERCOURSE and not sex itself. This hyper focus is on one aspect of sexuality, which is *related* to a much broader range of being human. Things like emotions, identity, self-relation, relation to others, and gender are completely disregarded from the general public as being part of sexuality, all because the focus on sex education is generally a belief that it is intercourse education. The mark has been missed so far particularly in STI prevention because it really only speaks to intercourse, when there are so many dimensions that comprehensive sex ed covers but get missed when we look at education that focuses on pregnancy prevention, abstinence, and STI prevention. These aspects of sexuality don't involve the outcome of pregnancy . . . which our early education aims to avoid, but that's not my chapter and I know it has been covered already. (Actually, I don't know if that's been covered already.)

My main reason for opening this way is because this sex avoidant society impacts my work directly. I run the 501c3 nonprofit organization, Something Positive for Positive People (SPFPP), which currently supports people navigating herpes stigma. *Stigma* is defined as a mark of disgrace associated with a particular circumstance, quality or person (Oxford Dictionary). SPFPP was born in 2017 after learning through our own research that roughly one third of people diagnosed with herpes struggled with suicidal thoughts because of their health status–what we originally thought was a direct result of stigma, or the fear of revealing a positive STI status to one's significant others. Throughout the last seven years, however, my team and I have interviewed and counseled countless people on the subject, only to consistently hear that people don't know how to talk about sex and that no one taught them. This was found to be the case even when people didn't feel the sense of disgrace marked by their diagnosis; moreover, their reported sex education experience was abstinence-only. Even their adult education from the *CDC Recommendations for STI Prevention* led to a belief that just wearing condoms was sufficient enough to avoid the outcomes of pregnancy and STIs. Thing is, nearly everyone we've spoken to who has received a diagnosis and finds SPFPP says they believed they did what they were supposed to do, but still ended up testing positive for an STI (genital herpes specifically).

Sex Education – Beyond Intercourse

What I've found is that the non-sexual components of sexuality education – such as boundaries, consent, relationship negotiation (including giving and receiving rejection), accountability, support resources, identifying abuse and/or green flags – is the core of what's missing in STI prevention. These non-intercourse aspects actually contain the necessary communication skills that translate directly into STI prevention. We believe that when the education system stops locking into a narrative of sex education as intercourse education, we can shift from a poorly communicative, sex avoidant society that doesn't know how to enter healthy relationships, into one that is more knowledgeably communicative and enters relationships more intentionally. That is the core of our work!

So What?

I mentioned that we live in a sex-avoidant, not necessarily a sex-negative society. For perspective, SPFPP's 2023–2024 HSV Survey Data showed that of 980 respondents living with herpes simplex virus (HSV), 34% of their health care providers NEVER initiated discussions about STIs, sexual health, and or safer sex practices. Of that same number, 36% responded that their provider RARELY (less than 10% of the time) initiated the conversation. So if 60% of patients and providers aren't talking about sexual health, with each other, where are these conversations being had?

Avoidance in Sexual Health Education

We know that K–12 sex education essentially teaches youth not to have sexual intercourse, which is typically defined as penetrative sexual contact between two "healthy" individuals, specifically the insertion of a man's erect penis into a woman's vagina, usually culminating in the ejaculation of semen (Oxford Dictionary). We don't need to unpack the lack of inclusivity here . . . actually we do.

When I say we live in a sex avoidant society and come across this definition of what sex is, we see the following:

Sex involves a man and woman

- This omits same sex relationships leading to risk of ignorance with safer sex practices

A penis must be present

- This implies there are only health risks when there is a penis there
- This also implies "[sex] doesn't count" unless there's a penis

Ejaculation (typically) happen

- Risks of STIs and pregnancy only happen when these outcomes occur
- Sex isn't sex without ejaculation
- Orgasm is either (in the case of youth) avoided entirely or (in the case of adults) presumed to be universal and automatic

A man has a penis and a woman has a vagina

- Intersex and trans people are excluded from this conversation and not quite given tools and language for discussing what sex is to them.

Sex is between two people

- This omits masturbation and that group sex exists. The framework of education as it exists only speaks to what is socially accepted as normal, not what actually happens

Healthy sex does not willfully happen with people who have sexually transmitted infections (STIs)

- People assume that coming into contact with someone with an STI means they'll definitely get one, which we know specifically with herpes is not always the case per www.spfpp.org/data (I don't know how to cite it, but our 2021 survey shows that people consent to sex with a person with herpes, and without barriers, AND of the 1,100+ people who took the survey in 2021, 72% reported they have NOT to their knowledge passed herpes on to a sexual partner).
- This point assumes that people with STIs do not have partners who still desire them sexually and are willing to learn (or capable of learning) how to engage in pleasurable, healthy sexual activities with them.

The CDC's prevention efforts do not speak to the "how" of STI prevention. We aren't offered the language and communication skills to negotiate the execution of the STI prevention skills such as testing practices and barrier use. The CDC says that the accurate, consistent use of the latex condom is effective at preventing STIs – which is great to know; what happens, however, when a partner goes against that? While the CDC is where many adults I work with may go to get up to speed on safe sex practices, it doesn't give us the communication skills necessary to negotiate safe sex between partners and providers. With that in mind, how can we expect health professionals to bear the burden of promoting the use of prevention methods outside of simply telling people what they are?

The overall point is that we do not know how to talk about sex, and this is more than a sexual health issue. It's unfortunate, but there seems to be much more receptivity when referring to these topics as a matter of "sex," when this isn't even really about sex at all, but about mental health. There is a *stigma* we have about SEX that is larger than STIs themselves; this is a perspective I've gained based on in-depth conversations and interviews my team and I have had with people living with STIs. Stigma on the surface is the belief system perceived to be directly associated with STIs, but we're learning that it really manifests as avoidance of sexual communication, because it is believed to be dirty, or not adhering to the "Ten Commandments of STI prevention." Defaulting to stigma is a really good way of deflecting people's attention away from examining the truth, which is that we just aren't given accurate information about the complexities of sex, which leads to the mental health outcome of suicide ideation, along with self-harming, self-destructive behavior and other mental health insecurities, particularly when someone has a positive STI status.

Avoidance and STI Disclosure

One of the common misconceptions of STI stigma is that people who have them "aren't telling people." Per our 2024 herpes survey, we see that people ARE in fact discussing their positive sexual health status. When we asked our survey sample about the moments when they chose not to disclose their STI status and the reasons behind that decision, we found that it wasn't actually about stigma at all, but that in many cases, people didn't know how to talk about their status, they weren't taught to, or they were afraid of being rejected. The fear of actually being seen through the negative light they believe others see them can be enough to perpetuate the no-disclosure cycle and, at its worst, suicide ideation among people with STIs; this fear emerges as a result of not being able to clearly communicate with others and negotiate relationships. To discuss these topics, people often have to go out into the world and hope to find their own supports; if they are lucky they find those educators like us, who work against the tide to get relevant and necessary information in the hands of people, despite general resistance.

Addressing STI Stigma by Addressing Sex Avoidance

Seeing that the shame involved is usually meant to keep people from experiencing adverse circumstances, one might argue that on some level yes, stigma is useful. In reality, however, using stigma to change behavior arguably has worse outcomes than those unaffected directly by it would think. Those who are affected by STIs experience the REAL impacts of stigma: isolation, suicide ideation, self-harm, risking others' health by not disclosing their status, depression, and abuse. What if we were to take these impacts seriously, letting them inform better ways of teaching about STIs and their significance?

What would a stigma-free approach to sexuality education look like? Is such a thing even possible? Could we "sneak in" the necessary sexuality education tools that bypass gatekeeper avoidance bias? I have good news: these nonsexual components of sex education can be taught. I bring to you, Sexless Sex Ed: Minimizing Stigma for Youth. . . . Working on the title.

Now What?

So by now I hope to have gotten the point across that our society is sex-avoidant rather than negative, and that the stigma of SEX is the real issue, keeping out critical communication skills that would help young adults navigate all their relationships, including sexual ones. Learning the value of these skills within non-sexual contexts allows them to be translated seamlessly to sexual ones, eventually serving to hopefully reduce stigma leading to rising STI rates.

Currently, I teach from the work of Dr. Evelin Molina-Dacker who created the STARS Talk Framework for communication in healthy relationships. STARS is an acronym that stands for the following:

S – Safety
T – Turn-ons
A – Avoids (or boundaries)
R – Relationship intention
S – Sexual health status

This framework encompasses all aspects of navigating a new relationship by giving someone a template to work with that covers all bases to the depth of their choosing. Below is a review of each letter; I go over what it is, then offer a way youth educators can take into their teaching settings.

S is for Safety. We identify safe people by learning them and getting to know them. We want to ask ourselves how our bodies feel around them. We also want to look at safety outside the normal lens of the physical and go deeper into our mental and emotional safety as well. In the classroom, I use the example of social awareness, referring to myself as someone in an interracial relationship. In this example, my white AFAB partner has to understand the social aspects of how others may interpret behaviors between them and myself (as a Black AMAB person) that we perceive as normal. Understanding that, for example, me raising my voice with her in public, is not something we can get away with in the same way that a same race couple might be able to, because of the socioemotional harm others who misinterpret my behavior may cause. Again, safety extends far beyond the physical (e.g., "would this person hit me?").

T is for Turn-ons, or as Dakota Ramppen (2024) stated in her presentation *Stigma Minimization for Youth Sexuality Educators,* "things you like." I don't think I need to explain turn-ons here; however, applying this concept to youth could get them to think about aspects of their relationships with peers that are compatible with themselves. For example, do we both like playing tag? Do we as a group enjoy painting? Are we all good at drawing? Understanding turn-ons as simply "things you like" is a critical component of compatibility that supports young people in identifying the intentions behind the relationships they build with each other. It's a practice of self-reflection to consider what you like and to identify others who like what you like, and it can save young people a lot of trouble in the dating world as adults to be taught how to do this when they are young.

A is for Avoids. Avoids are simply boundaries. Boundaries can be a new concept even still for adults; as of the time of this publication I am 35, and, I didn't even hear the word until age 32. Boundaries are how we protect ourselves from things and experiences we know we don't like or know we don't like. In adulthood, it could be a boundary to not have sex while alcohol is in your system. For youth, it could look like just not being friends with mean people. While we don't want to teach youth what not to like, we do want them to have the language and safety to respectfully say and be able to respectfully hear "no" and honor that. If they've had an experience they know they don't want again or already know that they don't want to go into an experience, they should have the power of choice taught to them and to be able to trust that those around them have been taught to respect their "no" or expect consequences.

On a personal note, I think the "A" should also stand for Accountability. We need to get it across that violating consent or not honoring one's "no" is unacceptable and that it has consequences. Simultaneously, I believe we should help people to understand that there is support for those who have not had their "no" respected in the past. I've seen this with people diagnosed with herpes who for YEARS have held in the fact that they were assaulted or that they didn't know where to go for support after their diagnosis. Of people we have surveyed, 91% did NOT receive a useful resource upon diagnosis and had to eventually stumble into something they learned was helpful to them at some later point in their diagnosis. This is unacceptable, because they should've had this offered to them upon diagnosis. With the right education they could've at least had the understanding of HOW to seek support or where to go for these resources so as not to drift into the impacts of stigma mentioned above.

R is for Relationship – intentions and expectations. This aspect of the acronym is about knowing what the nature of an existing relationship is with someone else – whether it be a friend, a partner, a relative, or even a rival. Understanding roles is a critical component of youth relationships, too. Respecting authority but also recognizing harmful/abusive behavior is a part of safety and support as it can prevent a lot of the sexual abuse minors face because they fear the consequences of telling someone. And when no abuse has occurred, we want to give youth the ability to assess their compatibility with others for where they are at the time. Big picture relationship intentions look like the "what are we?" conversation, eventually leading up to what they may want with others as life partners, business partners, etc. This is where lessons on negotiation can be brought into play, which again, so many adults have not been taught. For these early non-negotiable relationships youth have, however – such as family, school, work, and community involvement – helping young people recognize and communicate their intentions and expectations, while being able to set boundaries around who their significant others are and are not to them is a critical learning component.

Finally, the second *S is for STI Status* – though for youth, it could also represent Sexual Health overall. This is where sex education being solely focused on sexual avoidance becomes challenging, because sexual health is important outside of intercourse, a key part of understanding how body systems work. I remember a story of a young woman starting her period in elementary school and thinking that she was going to bleed to death because she did not have proper sexual health education. This is where an understanding of puberty and anatomy needs to be provided. Youth sexual health educators understand this at various levels; however, the challenge is the connection between these ideas and sex, connections that the gatekeepers responsible for providing funding and other access to this information just can't seem to get past. If we can integrate this one part of the acronym, then it gives youth a working foundational knowledge of their own bodies; then, when combined with the communication-based aspect of the other four letters, that provides the language and understanding of behavior in non-sexual relationships that minimizes the effects of stigma when sex begins later on in life for these populations.

I envision a world where stigma-free communication similar to the STARS frameworks is taught to adults AND youth who come into the doctors' office. When we can talk about sex as a normative part of life, we minimize the stigma of sex. And the minimization of stigma in sex minimizes the poor mental health outcomes we see as a result of adults being deprived of these critical communication skills as children. Whether playing tag on the playground as youth, planning a life together in a relationship, or even dating during the years in between, these communication skills are universal and can be applied to all stages of life.

I challenge you to reflect on ways you yourself may have internalized stigmas around sex. What do you believe about sexuality if you remove intercourse from it? How much of your beliefs are reflective of your mental health state? What communication skills were you taught in sex ed? Do you believe the trajectory of your own relationship to yourself and others would be different or the same if you had been given this communication resource? How can you use the information you gain from your answers to these questions to make different teaching choices in the future?

Reference

Ramppen, D. (2024, May). *Herpes stigma conference* [Stigma Minimizing Sex Ed]. Something Positive for Positive People (SPFPP), Virtual.

10 Childhood and Adolescent Sexualities

Alecia Rodriguez

Childhood and adolescent sexualities are intricate aspects of human development, demanding thorough examination with an intergenerational perspective. To grasp the continuum of sexual development from childhood to adolescence, one must acknowledge the interplay between personal experiences and societal norms. This approach sheds light on how societal values shape the sexual experiences of young individuals, enriching discussions about sexuality across generations. This chapter will explore cultural shifts and generational perspectives that shape attitudes towards sex education, consent, and the evolving discourse surrounding childhood and adolescent sexual identities, providing emerging educators with actionable recommendations for their practice.

Developmental Stages of Childhood and Adolescence

Educators should focus on teaching students about consent, boundaries, and respectful interactions to ensure they are well equipped to handle these natural explorations responsibly.

Early Adolescence (10–14 Years)

Ten- to fourteen-year-olds year olds experience physical changes from puberty, such as growth spurts and developing secondary sexual characteristics, often leading to body insecurities and self-consciousness. Sexual curiosity may emerge, and mood fluctuations are common as they explore their identity and navigate peer relationships. Adults can support them by discussing these changes openly, normalizing their experiences, and providing accurate information to reduce shame or confusion.

Concrete thinking at this age can intensify how adolescents interpret body changes, heightening self-awareness and insecurity. Open communication about puberty and reassurance that everyone develops differently can help ease their worries. Encouraging healthy habits like proper hygiene and promoting body positivity by celebrating diverse body types fosters a supportive atmosphere.

DOI: 10.4324/9781032615479-14

Teaching coping strategies like mindfulness, positive self-talk, and resilience helps adolescents manage insecurities and peer teasing. Providing a safe environment where they can express concerns and ask questions supports their emotional and physical well-being during this critical developmental stage.

Mid-Adolescence (15–17 Years)

Fifteen- to seventeen-year-olds experience continued physical changes and cognitive development, deepening their emotional quest for identity and independence. Friendships grow in importance, and they explore romantic relationships, often involving serial monogamy or brief relationships with multiple partners. While they begin to imagine the consequences of their actions, they may still engage in risky behaviors like substance use or unprotected sex.

To address these challenges, it's important to strengthen protective factors such as strong family connections, positive peer relationships, and involvement in extracurricular activities. Education on the consequences of risky behaviors and decision-making strategies can also help adolescents make informed choices.

Adolescents think more abstractly and critically as their cognitive abilities advance, allowing them to understand complex situations more deeply. Providing guidance, support, and a safe space for open communication during this transformative stage can foster healthier development.

Late Adolescence (18–21 Years)

Eighteen- to twenty-one-year-olds typically complete physical maturation, solidify their identity, and face the challenges of emerging adulthood. Socially, they focus on career and personal goals, with relationships becoming more serious and intimate. They also develop a mature understanding of their physical self, gender role, and sexual behaviors.

Despite increased maturity, they still need guidance on navigating higher education, career planning, mental health, financial management, and sexual health. Access to resources for relationship counseling and health care is also important.

Encouraging peer support networks and open communication fosters community and helps individuals recognize signs of distress or risky behavior, ensuring they receive the support needed during this transition.

Discourse on Sexual Identities

The binary notions of gender and the heteronormative standards that once dominated discussions about sexual identities are now being increasingly questioned and deconstructed. This transformation in discourse has significant implications for adolescents as they navigate their identities and experiences. Central to this evolving discourse is a growing awareness of the fluidity and complexity of human sexuality. Adolescents are learning that sexual identities are not fixed or predetermined but rather exist on a spectrum (Friedman et al., 2004). This recognition of the diversity of sexual identities highlights the importance of self-acceptance and representation.

Affirmation of diverse sexual identities fosters belonging and reduces suicidal ideation among queer youth. Research shows that up to 40% of LGBTQ+ youth have contemplated suicide, highlighting the need for supportive environments. Positive representation in media and culture validates queer identities, promoting self-acceptance, resilience, and healthier self-esteem.

Impact of Technology

Adolescents now access information about sexuality through various channels like peers, media, social media, and pornography, but the accuracy and reliability of this information can vary. Visual representations of sexual interactions online offer a platform for exploration and connection, allowing for anonymous exploration of desires and interests. However, these visuals also influence cultural norms and expectations around sexuality, potentially impacting real-life relationships and creating pressures, particularly among adolescents, related to sexual performance and communication in relationships.

Integrating comprehensive sexual education into digital literacy programs helps adolescents understand healthy sexual relationships amidst the complexities of online sexual expression. Educators can empower adolescents to discern accurate information from potentially harmful or misleading content by promoting critical thinking and media literacy skills. This approach fosters a proactive approach to digital sexual health, promoting positive messages about consent, pleasure, and diversity while mitigating the risks associated with unrealistic portrayals of sex in media.

Digital literacy education may include:

- Media Literacy: adolescents should learn to identify biased information, understand the impact of stereotypes and unrealistic portrayals of relationships, and differentiate between fact and fiction in online representations of sex. Therefore, they should be taught how to analyze and evaluate media content related to sexuality critically.
- Privacy and Security Awareness: by educating adolescents about the importance of privacy settings, secure communication methods, and the risks of sharing intimate content online, we provide them with a sense of security. They learn how to protect their personal information and maintain boundaries in digital interactions, reducing potential exploitation or harassment.
- Consent and Boundaries: adolescents should understand consent in digital contexts – such as messaging or sharing photos – and learn to communicate boundaries effectively to ensure respectful interactions.

- Digital Footprint and Reputation Management: adolescents should learn how to manage their digital footprint responsibly to avoid potential repercussions on their future personal and professional lives.

Social Media and Dating Apps

Social media and dating apps impact how adolescents form and maintain relationships, sometimes blurring boundaries. Social media platforms influence perceptions of body image, beauty standards, and sexual behavior. Adolescents may feel pressure to conform to idealized images of sexuality portrayed on social media, leading to issues related to self-esteem, body image, and sexual identity. Technology enables cyberbullying and sexting, which can have severe consequences for adolescent mental health and well-being. Adolescents may experience pressure to engage in sexting or may be victimized through cyberbullying, leading to feelings of shame, embarrassment, and isolation. Sexting and online interactions enhance sexual exploration but require careful attention to digital safety, consent, privacy, and the risks of hookup culture.

Pornography

Adolescents may be exposed to pornography at a young age, which can shape their attitudes, beliefs, and expectations about sex and relationships. Exploring sexual communication among adolescents in the digital era can enhance parents' and healthcare providers' comprehension of the obstacles adolescents encounter while navigating sexual communication and relationships, as suggested by (Richards et al., 2022).

Generational Perspectives on Consent

Younger generations are increasingly rejecting rigid gender norms and promoting a culture of consent, fostering healthier relationships and combating sexual violence. Adolescents now emphasize clear communication and verbal consent, challenging outdated silence or assumed consent norms. This shift encourages open discussions about boundaries, desires, and respect, empowering individuals to make informed choices and approach sexual encounters with autonomy and mutual respect.

This movement aligns with broader efforts to promote active consent and healthier dynamics in relationships, prioritizing enthusiastic participation and mutual respect. It highlights a cultural shift towards more equitable, consensual sexual interactions.

Deviating From Societal Norms

Problematic or non-normative childhood sexual behavior refers to actions that deviate from expected developmental norms, occur excessively, are socially unacceptable, or lead to harm to oneself or others. Societal norms like heter-onormativity, stigmatization, and biased media representation often lead to the repression of non-normative sexual identities, such as bisexuality, causing adolescents to feel shame and suppress their true desires. This repression can exacerbate mental health issues and increase vulnerability to engaging in socially unacceptable behaviors.

Conversely, a lack of repression allows adolescents to explore their sexual identities openly and without shame. This includes feeling empowered to express their desires and preferences authentically, seek support for their mental and emotional well-being, and engage in healthy discussions about sexual health and relationships. When diverse sexual identities are positively represented in media, education, and public discourse, adolescents are more likely to develop a healthy sense of self-esteem and acceptance of their sexuality. Comprehensive sex education programs can provide accurate information about sexual diversity, consent, and respectful relationships, thus equipping adolescents with the knowledge and skills needed to navigate their sexual journeys confidently and responsibly.

Entitlement in adolescents can appear in their attitudes towards sexuality, such as pressuring partners or disregarding boundaries. This may include expecting sexual favors without regard for consent, prioritizing their desires over their partners' comfort.

Allow Space for "Safe Behaviors"

Affirming sexual identities involves validating and respecting the diverse ways adolescents may express their sexuality, whether through orientation, gender identity, or personal preferences. Providing access to resources and support ensures that adolescents can seek information and assistance related to sexual health and relationships without fear of stigma or judgment. Cultivating non-judgmental and supportive environments involves fostering understanding and empathy among peers, educators, and communities, promoting acceptance and inclusivity. Empowering adolescents with comprehensive education and awareness about sexual diversity, consent, and healthy relationships equips them with the knowledge and skills to make informed decisions and navigate their sexual and emotional development confidently.

Adolescents are entitled to comprehensive sexuality education encompassing social, emotional, physical, and mental aspects of sexuality and sexual health that's accurate and gives explicit information about healthy relationships, communication, gender roles, and consent, as advocated by Speak About It (2020) and Santelli et al. (2018). Provide comprehensive education about sexual health, consent, and healthy relationships to equip adolescents with accurate information about their bodies and rights, empowering them to make informed decisions and navigate relationships safely.

Supportive resources, such as counselors, educators, or support groups, would be readily available to provide guidance, information, and support to adolescents navigating their sexual development empowering them to speak up about their needs and seek help.

Create judgment-free environments where adolescents can safely express themselves and explore their identities without fear of stigma or discrimination, supported by adults and peers who promote inclusivity. Access to comprehensive resources, including sexual health services, counseling, and education on consent and healthy relationships, is essential for their well-being.

Accepting Fluidity Without Sexualization

Adolescents experience stress related to sexual identification influenced by societal expectations favoring stable identities and pressure to conform to heterosexuality and cisnormativity. They navigate a period of self-discovery, questioning gender roles, experimenting with self-expression, and exploring sexuality. It is necessary to understand the complexity of their identities beyond just sexuality, recognizing that they may experience fluidity in gender or sexual orientation without necessarily being sexually active (Hall, 2019). For example, a teenage girl may feel conflicted about her attraction to both boys and girls, leading her to question her sexual orientation. She may feel pressure to conform to heterosexual norms but also feel drawn to exploring her attraction to individuals of the same gender. This internal conflict can cause stress and confusion as she tries to reconcile her feelings with societal expectations.

Similarly, a teenage boy may feel pressure to adhere to masculine stereotypes but finds himself drawn to activities or interests traditionally associated with femininity. He may want to experiment with different clothing styles, hairstyles, or hobbies as he explores his gender identity and seeks to express himself authentically but may be discouraged to do so because of conventional gender roles.

Adults must understand and respect this fluidity to create supportive environments where adolescents are safe exploring and expressing their identities without judgment or stigma. By acknowledging the complexity of adolescent identity and providing affirming support, we can help young people navigate this period of self-discovery with confidence and resilience.

Communication Between Adolescents and Their Parents/ Guardians

Adolescents frequently refrain from engaging in conversations about sexual health with parents or other trusted adults, leading them to depend on peers instead. This reliance leaves them inadequately equipped to navigate the intricacies, such as social, emotional, and romantic aspects, of sexually explicit content (Hall, 2019). Parents may hesitate to offer comprehensive sex education to their children due to various factors such as parental lack of education, the nature of the parent-child relationship, negative parental attitudes towards sexuality, concerns about their children's safety, and feelings of discomfort or awkwardness when discussing sex with their kids (Hegde et al., 2022).

Open communication between adolescents and their parents or guardians about sexuality fosters trust, allowing adolescents to seek guidance and accurate information from reliable sources. This trust provides a foundation for understanding healthy relationships, consent, and responsible sexual behavior. When adolescents feel supported and respected in discussing these topics with their parents or guardians, they are more likely to develop a clear understanding of boundaries, respect for themselves and others, and the importance of mutual consent in any relationship. This communication also facilitates discussions about personal values, beliefs, and expectations regarding sexuality, helping adolescents navigate peer pressure and societal influences with confidence.

It helps dispel myths, reduces the likelihood of risky behaviors, and supports emotional well-being by addressing concerns and promoting a positive attitude towards sexuality.

Open dialogue between adolescents and trusted adults creates a supportive environment where adolescents can navigate this critical development aspect. By fostering open dialogue, adolescents feel empowered to discuss their thoughts, feelings, and questions about sexuality without fear of judgment or misunderstanding. This dialogue enables them to explore and clarify their own beliefs and values regarding relationships, sexual health, and personal boundaries. It also provides opportunities for adults to offer guidance, share knowledge, and provide accurate information tailored to the adolescent's developmental stage and readiness. Through these conversations, adolescents not only gain a deeper understanding of sexuality but also develop crucial skills in communication, decision-making, and respectful behavior. Open dialogue nurtures trust, strengthens relationships, and equips adolescents with the confidence and knowledge needed to make informed choices that support their overall well-being and healthy development.

Therapeutic Approaches for Working With Adolescents on Sexual Issues

Counseling approaches for adolescents on sexual issues are designed to meet their unique developmental needs, promote open communication, and empower them to make informed decisions about sexuality. Therapists create a safe, non-judgmental space where adolescents can express concerns without fear, fostering trust and addressing sensitive topics effectively.

Sexual education is traditionally focused on fundamental aspects of anatomy and physiology and preventing risky sexual behaviors (Navarro-Prado et al., 2023). Sex educators focus on providing comprehensive education about healthy relationships, consent, and communication skills. Unlike therapists, they emphasize education over intervention, creating supportive environments for adolescents to explore their sexual identities and build peer support through group discussions and activities.

Educators can involve parents in sexual education through workshops and open dialogue strengthens family engagement and promotes healthy attitudes towards sexuality. This collaborative approach ensures that parents are informed and involved in their children's sexual education journey, promoting healthy attitudes towards sexuality within the family unit. It is essential to comprehend the knowledge and perspectives of adolescents, along with the correlation between sexual behaviors and the resources utilized for sexual education. This understanding is vital for mitigating the repercussions of unsafe sexual practices and addressing gender disparities (Navarro-Prado et al., 2023).

As we embrace inclusivity, challenge outdated norms, and foster open communication, we create environments that support healthy sexual development and empower adolescents to navigate their sexualities with confidence and respect. By promoting affirmative consent and providing comprehensive education and support from various angles that support youth, we can cultivate environments that nurture positive sexual health outcomes and contribute to the well-being of individuals across generations.

Introspective Questions for Consideration

- How did societal expectations during your childhood shape your understanding of sexuality, and how do those experiences influence how you discuss sexuality with young people in your practice today?
- Based on developmental stages, how can you adapt your approach to meet adolescents' unique needs? What strategies ensure adolescents feel supported in exploring their sexual identities in a safe, non-judgmental space?
- How can you incorporate the complexity of adolescent identities, beyond sexuality, into your practice to affirm all orientations? What resources and support systems help adolescents navigate sexual development with confidence?
- How can you use technology to promote positive messages about consent, pleasure, and diversity in sexuality? What steps can educate adolescents about online risks while empowering them to make informed choices?
- How can you integrate consent discussions into your curriculum or therapeutic approach? What strategies can help adolescents assert boundaries and make informed decisions about sexual health and relationships?

References

Friedman, M. S., Silvestre, A. J., Gold, M. A., Markovic, N., Savin-Williams, R. C., Huggins, J., & Sell, R. L. (2004). Adolescents define sexual orientation and suggest ways to measure it. *Journal of Adolescence, 27*, 303–317.

Hall, W. J. (2019). Sexual orientation. In C. Franklin (Ed.), *Encyclopedia of social work*. Oxford University Press.

Hegde, A. V., Chandran, S., & Pattnaik, J. I. (2022). Understanding adolescent sexuality: A developmental perspective. *Journal of Psychosexual Health, 4,* 237–242.

Navarro-Prado, S., Tovar-Gálvez, M. I., Sánchez-Ojeda, M. A., Luque-Vara, T., Fernández-Gómez, E., Martín-Salvador, A., & Marín-Jiménez, A. E. (2023). Type of sex education in childhood and adolescence: Influence on young people's sexual experimentation, risk and satisfaction: The necessity of establishing school nursing as pillar. *Healthcare (Basel, Switzerland), 11*(12), 1668.

Richards, M. J., Bogart, A., & Sheeder, J. (2022). Communication and interpretation of sexual consent and refusal in adolescents and young adults. *The Journal of Adolescent Health: Official Publication of the Society for Adolescent Medicine, 70*(6), 915–921. https://doi.org/10.1016/j.jadohealth.2021.12.013

Santelli, J. S., Grilo, S. A., Choo, T. H., Diaz, G., Walsh, K., Wall, M., Hirsch, J. S., Wilson, P. A., Gilbert, L., Khan, S., & Mellins, C. A. (2018). Does sex education before college protect students from sexual assault in college? *PLoS One, 13*(11), e0205951. https://doi.org/10.1371/journal.pone.0205951

Speak About It. (2020). *Consent, boundaries, and healthy relationships taught with humor and humanity.* Retrieved September 26, 2024, from https://wespeakaboutit.org/

11 [Inter]Sex Ed

Delia Sosa

Content warning: the following chapter contains discussion of sexual assault and non-consensual medical interventions.

Key Terms

- **Intersex:** literally "between the sexes." Adjective used to describe a person whose combination of primary and secondary sex characteristics are different from those of an average 46,XX female or 46,XY male.
- **Endosex:** adjective used to describe a person whose combination of primary and secondary sex characteristics are those expected in an average 46,XX female or 46,XY male.
- **Intersex Variation/Trait:** the specific combination of internal reproductive anatomy, external reproductive anatomy, genes, chromosomes, gene expression, and hormone levels a person has that falls outside of the expected combination for a 46,XX female or 46,XY male.
- **Primary Sex Characteristics:** those anatomic and/or physiologic traits related to sex and sexual development that a person is born with. These include internal reproductive anatomy, external reproductive anatomy, chromosomes, and gene expression.
- **Secondary Sex Characteristics:** those anatomic and/or physiologic traits related to sex and sexual development that a person develops over time, often during puberty. These include public and axillary hair development; breast development; growth of genitalia; increases in levels of testosterone, estrogen, and progesterone; and changes in gene expression (Emmanuel & Bokor, 2022).

Have you heard the word "intersex" before? Do you remember learning about intersex people in school? If your answer to either of these questions is "no," you've turned the page to the right chapter.

Intersex people have historically been excluded from public discourse and society at large. We exist in a society and culture where only the two binary

DOI: 10.4324/9781032615479-15

sexes, male and female, are common knowledge, taught in school and openly discussed. As medicine and the social sciences have evolved, we have learned more about the commonality of intersex existence in society and the variety of over 40 known intersex variations.

But where did this norm of the sex binary come from? In the 1960s, a prominent psychological researcher by the name of John Money began to experiment with gender identity on David Reimer, a child who had been designated male at birth but whose penis was accidentally damaged during a circumcision. Rather than receiving the truth about what happened to his body and being raised as a boy, David, an identical twin, was raised socially as a girl per the instruction of John Money, despite David's persistent discomfort and disapproval. John Money published research claiming that David's upbringing as a girl was successful, but David publicly spoke out against his upbringing, sharing that he was never happy as a girl. He later died by suicide (Intersex Society of North America, 2008a). John Money's works were later redacted, but the foundation laid by his work continues to erase intersex individuals from social narratives. What might have happened if David had been raised as a boy but knew the truth about his body?

Although David Reimer himself was not intersex, the research conducted on him established a societal standard of erasing intersex people from dialogue. His story set an example that bodies outside the male/female binary are somehow shameful, to be hidden from others and made out to fit into the binary. This erasure occurs in every sphere – social, political, medical, educational, and yes, in sex education, too. We learn about basic male anatomy and basic female anatomy, but what about differences in anatomy? What about discordance between internal and external anatomy? What about differences in hormone levels that can affect libido? What about the difference between sex and gender identity, which can impact the way intersex individuals date and choose sexual partners?

This chapter breaks down the sex binary and begins to help you understand it. It discusses how social responses to intersex variations impact intersex people's ability to fully participate in society. We will take a closer look at several examples of common intersex variations and how a person's intersex variation may impact their understanding of their own body, pleasure, and safety in sexual experiences. Finally, we will look at ways we can better incorporate and advocate for intersex integration into sex education, sexual health research, and public policy.

Sex as a Spectrum

When we hear the word "spectrum," many of us think of the color spectrum; the same, however, can be used when referring to human reproductive anatomy. On one end of the spectrum, we have endosex females, who have XX chromosomes, uterus, ovaries, vulva, typical gene expression, and high estrogen/low testosterone. On the other end of the spectrum, we have endosex males, who have XY chromosomes, testes, penis, typical gene expression, and low estrogen/high testosterone. In between we have intersex folks, who have a variety of combinations of chromosomes, genes, gene expression, internal anatomy, external anatomy, and hormone levels.

There are over 40 known intersex variations, each with distinct combinations of primary and secondary sex characteristics. Not everyone with these intersex variations will use the term "intersex" to describe themselves, so it's important to mirror each person's language. Here are a few common examples of intersex variations an individual might have:

Complete Androgen Insensitivity Syndrome (CAIS)

Chromosomes: 46,XY
Internal Anatomy: testes
External Anatomy: vagina, vulva
Hormone Profile: no testosterone (T) receptor, T converted to estradiol

Congenital Adrenal Hyperplasia (CAH)

Chromosomes: 46,XX
Internal Anatomy: uterus, ovaries
External Anatomy: may be a vagina and vulva, or may be ambiguous
Hormone Profile: increased testosterone (T)

Klinefelter Syndrome (Intersex Society of North America, 2008b)

Chromosomes: 46,XXY
Internal Anatomy: testes (small)
External Anatomy: penis
Hormone Profile: decreased testosterone, may develop breasts

It is estimated that approximately 2% of the world's population (or about 150 million people) is intersex (United Nations Human Rights Office of the High Commissioner, 2024). This number may be greater than we realize due to under-recognition and reporting of intersex variations. Someone you know or even love may have an intersex variation, even if you personally don't know about it.

Difference Between Sex and Gender

It is necessary to differentiate between sex and gender in order to understand the difference between intersex and transgender. Although intersex and transgender individuals face similar stigma, discrimination, and have some shared lived experiences, there are also significant differences between the two.

Sex is the genotypic and phenotypic combination of a person's primary and secondary sex characteristics, while gender identity is a person's internal understanding of self. There is simultaneously a difference between gender identity and gender expression. Unlike gender identity, gender expression is a person's external manifestation of their understanding of gender. This may manifest through clothing, hair, body modifications, etc.

Let's use what we'll call the cake analogy to illustrate the differences between gender, expression, and sex. Imagine we're baking a cake. Each of the ingredients in the cake can be used to refer to the different primary and secondary sex characteristics that make up the cake, similar to how they would be in the body. Once our cake is baked and assembled, the layers of cake, icing, and filling inside would represent gender – how all those ingredients make us uniquely ourselves. Finally, the colorful sprinkles, icing, glitter, and decorations on the outside of the cake represent gender expression, the way in which we present ourselves to others on the outside.

Now let's apply this analogy to the experience of being transgender and intersex. People who are intersex may have different combinations of cake ingredients (primary and secondary sex characteristics) than people who are made from a different cake recipe (endosex). They still turn out to be a wonderful cake, just made with slightly different ingredients and proportions. On the other hand, people who are transgender typically have similar ingredients and proportions as their endosex cake counterparts; however, theirs make likely be a cake of a different flavor, such as chocolate or strawberry, or even confetti. In this way, although intersex and transgender people possess characteristics that separate them from endosex people, both groups possess characteristics that make them equally distinct from each other as well.

Intersex people can be transgender, too, if they have a different combination of primary and secondary sex characteristics AND their gender identity is different from what was designated at birth and/or socialized as. In our cake analogy, an example of this might be a cake made with more baking powder than a traditional recipe, with cocoa powder also added into the cake mix itself. In this cake, the ingredients to make the cake's core components would be different, and would shift the cake from being a general cake with variations, to a chocolate cake with variations. The recipe would be different than traditional recipe cake with less baking powder but would still be a chocolate cake.

Effective Intersex-Centered Sex Ed Instruction

The next three sections will cover three necessary threads of discussion in education regarding intersex-centered sex ed. These are not intended to be discrete, one-lesson topics but rather themes to be incorporated into each lesson.

Consent and Trauma

Perhaps one of the most important aspects of intersex sexual health, as well as intersex health more broadly, is an understanding of trauma and consent. The intersex community has faced significant trauma from the medical system, from invasive non-consensual procedures, hidden information about their own medical histories, to unwanted medical judgment (Khanna, 2021; Grimstad et al., 2021). Intersex bodies are often manipulated, scarred, and disfigured without their owners' knowledge or consent (Carpenter, 2018). Some intersex people have even experienced trauma so significant that they have a difficult time seeking general medical care due to the mistrust these systems have caused. As one might imagine, these experiences have had the power to cause lasting harm and a lifelong psychological impact.

When teaching about intersex sexual health, it is necessary to engage in a complete and meaningful discussion of consent. An example of this would be having students answer the question of "How might you feel if a partner touched you in a way you didn't want them to without asking you first?" This could be followed by a discussion of how intersex people may have differences in their physical bodies that students might not be familiar with, but that does not automatically give others permission to touch or explore without the intersex person's consent. Many intersex people have had their bodies touched in ways they never asked for, and their autonomy taken from them before they even knew it existed. Creating space for discussions of consent gives some of this power back to intersex students who may be in the room and helps endosex students learn how to practice more care with both themselves and fellow intersex learners they may be or become involved with in the future.

Other teaching strategies involving consent and intersex experiences could look like Q&A conversations with intersex educators, or scenario-based learning in which students are interacting with an intersex partner for the first time. In creating safe, consensual spaces, the burden should not be placed on intersex individuals to educate others about their trauma and how consent plays a role in that. Forcing them to do so takes power away from intersex learners and defies the purpose of the consent discussion entirely. Instead, the onus of education should be placed on educators to explain the importance of consent and how intersex bodies fit into this discussion. Here are some reflection questions to consider in how to best incorporate intersex lived experiences into discussions about consent:

1. Do my lessons about consent include binary discussions of sex?
2. Have I myself learned about the history of intersex medical trauma?
3. When discussing sexual assault, do my statistics include intersex folks?
4. Are my lessons discussing other forms of physical trauma besides sexual?

Education around consent should also include a discussion of what it means to respect boundaries and respect partners' bodies. No one is entitled to information about another person's body, and it is up to each individual person to decide how much they share and when they share it. Just as consent is required for physical contact, it should also be required for private information about our bodies.

Getting to Know Intersex Bodies

Because every body is a bit different, whether intersex or endosex, it may take time for each individual to get to know their own bodies. For intersex people, especially those with less common intersex variations, resources to help people get to know their bodies better may not be as inclusive or comprehensive as we may need. It can help to encourage endosex folks to learn about bodies different from their own, for example, teaching every student about variations in anatomy to encourage learning beyond their own lived experiences. It can also be beneficial to encourage intersex folks to get to know their individual anatomy, both internal and external, as well as what makes them feel safe and what brings them pleasure (De Brouwer et al., 2022). This will look different for every student and should be personally and privately guided by their own self-interests. Below are some guiding questions to help all students consider their bodies and what makes them feel good:

1. What body parts do I have?
2. Which of those body parts makes me feel good?
3. What actions or sensations allow me to experience pleasure? What actions or sensations cause pain or discomfort?
4. What helps me create a space where my body and I feel safe?
5. What information about my body (or these questions) do I want to share with a partner?

Endosex partners, as well as partners with different intersex variations, play an important role in creating safe sexual environments for intersex folks. Asking what their partners enjoy, what makes them feel safe, and what they feel comfortable sharing or doing can take some of the burden off of intersex folks to create a safe and enjoyable sexual experience.

Pregnancy and Prevention

Yes, some intersex people can conceive a pregnancy or participate in pregnancy. What exactly this means for each person depends on their specific intersex variation, as well as whether they were subjected to non-consensual surgeries that affected their reproductive potential. That said, intersex people can have testes, ovaries, both, a combination of the two (called "ovotestes"), or an early-stage variation of ovaries, called "streak gonads." Some intersex people can become pregnant through sexual acts, but other intersex people may need to utilize assistive reproductive technology such as sperm donation, surrogates, intrauterine insemination (IUI), or in-vitro fertilization (IVF).

Learning about intersex bodies is important not just for establishing pleasure and safety, but to also help intersex learners determine whether they may want or need pregnancy prevention. If an intersex person has a uterus and ovaries and does not desire a pregnancy, they may benefit from an intrauterine device (IUD) or another form of hormonal birth control. If they do not have that specific combination of internal and external anatomy, they may want hormonal birth control for other reasons unrelated to pregnancy prevention, including hormone replacement therapy. If an intersex person has a penis and testes, they may need to be reminded of their capacity to cause a pregnancy as well, and to be given correct information about how to prevent it if they choose. Even if an intersex person cannot participate in pregnancy through sexual activity, it is important for them to receive information about the options that are available to them if they do want to participate in pregnancy and/or parenting at some point, as well as the importance of barrier protection for preventing STIs regardless of reproductive capacity.

Other Thoughts to Consider

Although intersex people are gradually becoming more visible in the public eye, there is still so much progress to be made with regard to normalizing intersex variations and including intersex people in sex education and research. Centering intersex lived experiences and uplifting intersex voices in sex ed ensures that they are directing conversations about their own experiences, rather than listening to others direct them (Callens et al., 2021).

1. Community-Oriented Research

There is a profound lack of research on intersex communities in general and especially around intersex bodies. The general consensus throughout the literature is that more attention should be given to the lived experiences of intersex individuals, including with respect to consent, sex, pleasure, and trauma (Liedmeier et al., 2021; Grimstad et al., 2021; Berry & Monro, 2022). Research should focus on intersex patients and communities and center their lived experiences, rather than utilizing terminology, theory, and structures created by the systems that have harmed them.

2. Broader Education

Not every person understands the differences between sex and gender, transgender and intersex. Sex and gender are often conflated in society, which can make it difficult for the general public to learn about intersex variations and even more difficult for intersex people to be safely visible. Broader education around the diversity of sex and intersex lived experiences would help create a more accessible, safer society for intersex individuals (Berry & Monro, 2022).

3. Shifting the Educational Burden

In everyday life and in educational settings, the burden of educating people about intersex variations and lived experiences often falls on intersex people ourselves. More work should be dedicated to educating students regarding intersex lived experiences based on stories that have already been shared publicly, educational resources, and existing literature. When the best possible option is to have an intersex educator, it is crucial to ensure they are compensated equitably for both their intellectual and emotional labor. And when curricular and instructional decisions are being made that affect the intersex community, intersex voices should be at the table and leading the conversation.

Normalizing intersex variations and the experiences of people living in intersex bodies pushes the boundaries of sex ed by normalizing all bodies and their natural variations. By including intersex narratives in sex ed, educators and researchers have the ability to empower learners to see beyond their own bodies and discover the breadth of variety nature has created.

References

Berry, A. W., & Monro, S. (2022). Ageing in obscurity: A critical literature review regarding older intersex people. *Sexual and Reproductive Health Matters, 30*(1), 1–12. https://doi.org/10.1080/26410397.2022.2136027

Callens, N., Kreukels, B. P. C., & Van de Grift, T. C. (2021). Young voices: Sexual health and transition care needs in adolescents with intersex/differences of sex development – a pilot study. *Journal of Pediatric and Adolescent Gynecology*, 176–189. https://doi.org/10.1016/j.jpag.2020.11.001

Carpenter, M. (2018). Intersex variations, human rights, and the international classification of diseases. *Health and Human Rights Journal, 20*(2), 205–214. https://www.ncbi.nlm.nih.gov/pmc/articles/PMC6293350/

De Brouwer, I. J., Suijkerbuijk, M., Van de Grift, T. C., & Kreukels, B. P. C. (2022). First adolescent romantic and sexual experiences in individuals with differences of sex development/intersex conditions. *Journal of Adolescent Health, 71*, 688–695. https://doi.org/10.1016/j.jadohealth.2022.07.012

Emmanuel, M., & Bokor, B. R. (2022). Tanner stages. In *StatPearls [Internet]*. StatPearls Publishing. https://www.ncbi.nlm.nih.gov/books/NBK470280/#article-29871.s1

Grimstad, F., Kremen, J., Streed, C. G., & Dalke, K. B. (2021). The health care of adults with differences in sex development or intersex traits is changing: Time to prepare clinicians and health systems. *LGBT Health, 8*(7). https://doi.org/10.1089/lgbt.2021.0018

Intersex Society of North America. (2008a). Who was David Reimer (also, sadly, known as John/Joan)? *ISNA*. https://isna.org/faq/reimer/

Intersex Society of North America. (2008b). Klinefelter syndrome. *ISNA*. https://isna.org/faq/conditions/klinefelter/

Khanna, N. (2021). Invisibility and trauma in the intersex community. In E. M. Lund, C. Burgess, & A. J. Johnson (Eds.), *Violence against LGBTQ+ persons*. Springer. https://doi.org/10.1007/978-3-030-52612-2_14

Liedmeier, A., Jendryczko, D., Rapp, M., Roehle, R., Thyen, U., Kreukels, B. P. C. & on behalf of the DSD-LIFE group (2021). The influence of psychosocial and sexual wellbeing on quality of life in women with differences of sexual development. *Comprehensive Psychoneuroendocrinology*, *8*(100087), 1–10. https://doi.org/10.1016/j.cpnec.2021.100087

United Nations Human Rights Office of the High Commissioner. (2024). *Intersex people*. United Nations. https://www.ohchr.org/en/sexual-orientation-and-gender-identity/intersex-people#:~:text=Experts%20estimate%20that%20up%20to,as%20heterosexual%20(sexual%20orientation)

12 Blurring the Boundaries of Orientation

Aubri Lancaster

"As I am sure any cat owner will be able to tell you, someone else putting you in a box is *entirely different* from getting into a box yourself."

– bisexualbaker (2015)

Key Terms

- **Hermeneutics:** a method or theory of interpretation.
- **Queer:** an umbrella term for those who don't fit dominant social constructs of gender or orientation.
- **Essentialism**: oversimplifying a complex concept into a reliance on a single determining factor or qualification that maintains or creates inherent power structures.

How Do You Teach About Sexual Orientation?

If I were to ask you your sexual orientation, you could probably give me an answer pretty quickly. Maybe you've spent years deciding on your terminology, or maybe you've always considered yourself heterosexual. But what if you had a student who asked you "What is sexual orientation?" Would you talk about gender? About love? How would you answer questions about orientation labels you've never heard of?

In this chapter we will look at how sexual orientation has traditionally been framed, what progress has been made through that framing, and why this framing can lead to various forms of essentialism. We will explore effective analogies and practical exercises designed to empower learners to lean in with curiosity and incorporate additional variables such as differentiated attractions, degree and circumstance of attraction, fluidity, gender diversity, and the respect for personal agency and autonomy in the labels people choose for themselves.

DOI: 10.4324/9781032615479-16

Ways of Knowing

Traditional framing of sexual orientation centers gender and interpersonal sexual and romantic behaviors as the defining variables in how orientations are understood. This framing relies on binary gender constructs and prioritizes observable behavior over internal experiences. This has been used to justify medical, psychological, and religious conversion therapies on the one hand, while on the other hand empowering social gatekeeping of queer spaces. Bisexual, Asexual, and Aromantic people often face litmus tests to be accepted as queer. "Excluding asexuals from queerness under the belief that we do not experience discrimination and trauma 'enough' only serves to reproduce the same harms as cisheteropatriarcy" (Brown, 2022).

Miranda Fricker names *testimonial injustice* and *hermeneutical injustice* as forms of epistemic injustices, injustices of knowledge and ways of knowing.

> Testimonial injustice occurs when prejudice causes a hearer to give a deflated level of credibility to a speaker's word; hermeneutical injustice occurs at a prior stage, when a gap in collective interpretive resources puts someone at an unfair disadvantage when it comes to making sense of their social experiences.
>
> (Fricker, 2007, pp. 60–61)

As educators, how might we begin to disrupt ingrained assumptions and recognize the impact of bias on our perceptions? The following is a self-reflection exercise that can serve as a foundation for learners to explore their own experiences of epistemic injustices.

Self-Reflection Exercise

Think about a time when you shared your experience, feelings, or perspective with someone. Did you feel heard and validated or did you feel doubted or dismissed? Have you ever had someone else say the same thing and it was received differently?

- Consider conversations with a doctor, family member, friend, customer/client, government official, law enforcement, teacher, classmate, colleague, supervisor, etc.
- Consider whether it was a public or private forum.
- Consider how any of the following aspects of your identity, or perceived identity, may have shaped their response: age, gender (assigned/identity/expression), ethnicity/race/culture/caste, orientation, ability/disability/neurodiversity, profession, family dynamics, geographic location, socioeconomic status, body size/shape/modifications/attire, education level, religion/spirituality, relationship status, language/accent/dialect.

Inclusivity vs Essentialism

Advocates of inclusivity have often brought in slogans that tap into socially acceptable narratives. For example, the slogan "Love is Love" appeals to amatonormative[1] ideals to diminish the problematizing of gender as a restrictive precursor to marriage. It has broad appeal but reinforces structures that marginalize other groups such as those who are non-monogamous, single at heart,[2] or those in long-term committed platonic relationships.

Another argument that has been used to gain acceptance is to claim that queer people are just "born that way." However, Dr Lisa Diamond proposes that

> the 'born this way' argument is also unjust because it implies that LGBT individuals who fit a certain cultural stereotype, the ones who have been exclusively gay for as long as they can possibly remember, are somehow more deserving of acceptance and equality than someone who came out at age 60, or whose attractions have been more fluid, or who is bisexual rather than exclusively gay.
>
> (Diamond, 2018)

These challenges will grow as we use the internet to map intrinsic experiences of gender, orientation, relationship structures, neurodiversity, spirituality, culture, and many more growing or yet to be identified spheres of human existence. With new language comes new forms of essentialism.

Reclaiming Agency of Identity Labels

One of the strongest ways to counter essentialism is through making space for people to define the labels they use for themselves and to recognize the fluidity and variance in lived experience that contribute to the hermeneutics of these labels.

Here are three different exercises to work with balancing one's own interpretation with the interpretation of others who use the same language:

Exercise 1: Labels Are Tools

Equipment:

- A Swiss Army Knife or other multi-function tool (or a picture)
- A Banana Slicer or other single use tool (or a picture)

Objective: this exercise helps learners recognize and evaluate the utility of identity terminology in both broad and specific applications.

Script for Facilitator:

If labels are tools, let's think about other kinds of tools. First let's think about the Swiss Army Knife. It has lots of different functions and some of them will likely be used more often than others.

<<Invite learners to name some of the different ways to use this tool.>>

This tool is a lot like the umbrella terms of Queer or LGBTQIA2+ that may be used to describe their connection to larger groups or used as placeholders for lesser known labels.

Now let's think about the Banana Slicer. At first glance one might roll their eyes and wonder why anyone would need that. Yet as soon as we ask that question, we start to think of answers.

<<Invite learners to name some of the reasons someone might want to use the Banana Slicer.>>

Ultimately, it may only do one thing, but if that's the one thing someone needs a tool for, then it serves its function.

Exercise 2: Labels Are Expansive

Equipment:

• A large pack of crayons, or a color wheel, or assorted paint swatches.

Objective: this exercise helps learners recognize and appreciate the continual development of identity terminology while encouraging acceptance and curiosity when confronted with new or unfamiliar language.

Script for Facilitator:

Crayola and the paint industry have exploded our language of colors over the last century. Each color name describes a specific position in the color spectrum or a range of colors that share a similar hue, tone, tint, or shade.

<<Ask learners to identify and name colors other than ROYGBV.[3] If two people name colors that are very similar, ask how they might distinguish the two or if that's even possible. Invite learners to name colors in other languages they may know.>>

It's impossible to memorize every single color name that has been created, especially with multiple brands and thousands of languages around the world. The language of identity labels are ever expanding as well. The more terms are developed, the more we can identify specific positions within the spectrum of experiences or range of experiences and fill hermeneutical gaps. Some labels may describe similar positions or overlap in their range and use. While we may not be able to memorize all of them, we can choose to lean in with curiosity and ask what the label means for the individual using it.

Exercise 3: Labels Are Optional

Equipment:

• Hats, buttons, or some other item that has a variety of styles and sizes.

Objective: this exercise helps learners reflect on personal and contextual reasons for using or not using identity labels while recognizing the fluidity and multiplicity of such terminology.

Script for Facilitator:

<<Distribute items>>

At one point in your life, you may put on a hat/button/etc. because that was the one you were given. Maybe that's the one everyone else was wearing and you were expected to wear it too. Or maybe you picked one out yourself and wore it for a while because it was comfortable and it fit. If down the line you find another one, you may decide to wear that one instead.

<<Invite learners to trade with each other or trade with extras you have available or keep the one they have.>>

Processing questions:

• "Why did you trade or not trade?"
• "Do you like the fit?"
• "Is it comfortable?"
• "Do you like the aesthetics?"

Whatever your reason, you get to decide what each hat/button/etc. means to you and whether or not to keep wearing ones that no longer suit you. And you don't have to wear one at all. You don't have to pick a label. You don't have to disclose your labels. Labels can change. You may need to try on different ones to see how they feel.

Agential Re-Framing of Sexual Orientation

Working off reclaiming language already developed and through adding new terms and language combinations, we can explore different ways to not only describe directional gendered sexual and romantic orientations, but we can begin to understand more types of attractions and degrees and circumstances that attractions manifest. Invite learners to consider the following:

1. Different types of attractions such as Aesthetic, Sensual, Platonic, Romantic, Sexual, Emotional, and Intellectual

    a. What forms of attraction do they prioritize, and which forms do they find either unimportant, non-existent, or too similar to distinguish?

    b. How do different attractions influence each other?

2. Degree or Circumstance of Attractions

    a. Are these attractions experienced all the time, none of the time, or do they wax and wane? Are they tied to other specific circumstances? Are they strong or mild?

    b. How do they feel about having these attractions reciprocated? Does that increase the attraction? Decrease it? Are they only experiencing these attractions to themselves or to fictional characters?

3. Gender Variance

    a. Are any of these attractions different for different genders? Does gender impact how they experience these attractions at all? In what ways?

4. Relationship Dynamics

    a. How do these attractions relate to the sorts of relationships that appeal to them? Do they thrive in Singlehood? Coupledom? Polyamory? Communal Living?

    b. Do they feel drawn to a hierarchical dynamic with a primary partner? Or no primary partners but varying degrees of closeness with people in their lives? In what other ways might they relate to intimacy, closeness, and connection with the people they care about?

In our work as educators we need to be flexible enough to make space for new hermeneutics as well as keep a connection to the history that brought us to this point. "We need to hold onto many stories, even when they might be in contradiction, rather than searching for one simple truth" (Barker, 2018). Again and again we must lean in and ask the question, "what does that mean for YOU?"

Self-Reflective Questions for Consideration

- In what ways has sex education relied on essentializing narratives of what does or does not qualify someone for a particular label?
- How can you adjust your work to make space for terminology that is lesser known, stigmatized, or as yet undeveloped?
- What challenges do you foresee in how this expansive language will be received and what counterpoints can you build into your work to address these arguments before they are made?

Notes

1 "This consists in the assumptions that a central, exclusive, amorous relationship is normal for humans, in that it is a universally shared goal, and that such a relationship is normative, in that it should be aimed at in preference to other relationship types" (Brake, 2012).

2 "Single at heart" is a term coined by Bella DePaulo to describe those who love being single and want to stay single (DePaulo, 2023).

3 Red, Orange, Yellow, Green, Blue, Violet/Purple.

References

Barker, M. J. (2018). *Rewriting the rules: An anti self-help guide to love, sex and relationships*. Taylor & Francis.

Bisexualbaker. (2015, January 5). *A note on labels*. [Tumblr post]. https://www.tumblr.com/bisexualbaker/107266896941/a-note-on-labels

Brake, E. (2012). *Minimizing marriage: Marriage, morality, and the law*. Oxford University Press.

Brown, S. J. (2022). *Refusing compulsory sexuality: A black asexual lens on our sex obsessed culture*. North Atlantic Books.

DePaulo, B. (2023). *Single at heart: The power, freedom, and heart-filled joy of single life*. Apollo Publishers.

Diamond, L. (2018, December 18). *Why the "born this way" argument doesn't advance LGBT equality*. TEDxSaltLakeCity.

Fricker, M. (2007). *Epistemic injustice: Power & the ethics of knowing*. Oxford University Press.

13 Decolonizing the History of the Gender Binary

Understanding What the Gender Binary Is, Where It Came From, How It Affects Us Today, and How It Destroyed My Chance of Being a Princess

Arc Telos Saint Amour (they/them)

Key Terms

- **Colonialism:** refers to imperialist practices that established an ongoing, long-term presence in acquired territories but does not necessarily equate to mass displacement and/or genocide of native communities.
- **Decolonization:** is the process of dismantling settler colonialism through abolitionist practices in order to return to a pre-colonized state of being with one another and the land.
- **The Gender Binary:** the classification of gender into two distinct, immutable categories, "Man" or "Woman."
- **Settler Colonialism:** refers to colonialism that seeks to replace existing native communities and cultures with Western European settlements through complete eradication and enslavement.
- **Western Imperialism:** refers to the historical and ongoing practice, of dominant white Western European and North American nations spreading their influence, power, and dominance ever beyond their own borders in the name of wealth, resource acquisition, and white supremacy.

When I was four years old, I wanted to be a ballerina. Although my love for dance would continue throughout my life, there was something specific about this desire when I was young, and that was the pink tutu. I wanted so badly to wear that pink dress with the frilly tutu. To be honest, I actually wanted to be a princess and even told people at my elementary school to call me "princess." It was a magical time, until of course it wasn't. Until I was ridiculed, laughed at, and bullied, both at home and at a school.

See, at the time my sex assigned at birth was male. So instead of my love for dance, pink dresses, and frilly tutus being celebrated and nurtured, I was instead

DOI: 10.4324/9781032615479-17

shoved into "boy's" clothes and forced into little league baseball. On the field I spent so much time picking flowers I was eventually relegated to playing catch with the coach's daughter in the parking lot. When a stray ball hit me in the face, it ended my sportsball career since I "couldn't even catch a ball from a 'girl' in a parking lot."

Largely, as a society in the United States, we agree that childhood should be an idyllic time where kids get to be kids. They should be able to have fun, play, be creative, and discover themselves without a care in the world. Perhaps the brightness, innovation, and hope that some would consider innocence and or even the naivety of childhood, could be a glimpse into the potential of what the world could be, free of judgment, hate, and an abundance of inclusive spaces where all are welcomed to be their true selves and be present and play. Is it so wrong to have appreciative inquiry where the only intention is to learn and grow, adapt and change, to be curious not righteous?

Certainly, there is a difference between what childhood should be and what it is. This is where largely, as a society, we begin to disagree. To some, the world is a harsh and cruel place, and the sooner kids know that the better. To some, all kids have an equal chance at happiness, the "you can be anything you want to be if you believe and work hard enough" mentality. And to some, and I would include myself in this area, there are forces beyond our control as children that prevent us from thriving.

The Human Rights Campaign and The Williams Institutes estimates there are over 22 million LGBTQ+ people in the United States alone, while simultaneously, the ACLU is tracking anti LGBTQ bills throughout the US, and as of June 28, 2024 there are 527. It's no wonder that a report by The Trevor Project from January 1, 2024 shows that "LGBTQ+ young people are more than four times as likely to attempt suicide than their peers (Johns et al., 2020)," with "at least one attempt . . . every 45 seconds."

No amount of believing in myself – or learning early that the world was cruel – prevents the harm of being a queer and trans kid – or adult – in America. This nation actively and intentionally, devalues, erases, and threatens the lives of queer trans people through hateful and violent legislation, rhetoric, misinformation, and gender norms that tell those little starry-eyed princesses that they shouldn't exist. For me, all my hopes and dreams were beaten, both literally and figuratively, out of me till I wanted to kill myself. That's how powerful binary gender norms can be and why it is absolutely vital we dismantle them.

Understanding the history of the gender binary is an invaluable tool in this fight to save lives. It helps us understand the present moment and how we got here. More importantly, it can help us know how to move forward in happier, healthier, and more affirming ways. Understanding history helps us change the now and learn how to not repeat these mistakes in the future, and learning how to tell our stories, how to own and be proud of our stories, is a critical part of that.

As educators, we can empower our students with their understanding of that history by guiding them to tell their own stories of how gender has impacted them.

Exercise – Turning Reflection Into Storytelling

Have students begin to reflect about their own gender history and journey, then craft that into their own gender origins story. For example, some leading questions might be:

- How did gender first show up in my life and why? How does gender show up in my life now and how does it affect me?
- What is my sex assigned at birth, gender identity, gender expression, and sexual orientation? How do I know this to be true?
- Is there anything I ever wanted to do, that I wasn't allowed to, or maybe I was made to feel ashamed of doing, simply because "boys" don't do that, or "girls" don't do that? Why?
- Have I ever repeated this cycle, gendered someone or something, or placed specific gender norms on to someone or something? Why?
- Why is it important for me to know, own, and tell my story? What implications does this all have for me – and others – today?

My assumption would be the majority would have gendered, and have been gendered, both in affirming ways and in harmful ways. Knowing and understanding our pasts helps us understand who we are and where we came from, and telling our stories can help others who may be struggling in today's climate.

A Brief Historical Context to the Gender Binary

Starting around the 12th century three major things were happening and beginning to intersect, **the Doctrine of Discovery**, which contributed to the eventual **Settler Colonization in North America** in the 14th century and the spread of **Agriculture** and white, Western European agricultural norms; all of these informed the gender norms of the past, which led to the gender binary as we know it today. The intersection of these three factors directly led to the invention of the gender binary as a racial tool of oppression starting with the Doctrine of Discovery, which led to the Age of Discovery era. The Doctrine of Discovery is Christian legal theory that stems from a reinterpretation of biblical texts. White male Western European Christian religious scholars essentially "discovered" that they were chosen by God as the rightful owners to the whole of the earth and everything upon its heavenly land. This then became a legal doctrine that functioned as public and international law. The spread of this doctrine is known as the Age of Discovery, a time of growth of western imperialism and the colonization of foreign lands. This rapid resource expansion, under the shield of the Doctrine of Discovery, excluded women and any non-Christian people from rightful ownership of land and bestowed special rights of sovereignty on Western European Christian men in the name of God.

This reinterpretation did several things. It justified horrific practices (e.g. enslaving people, sexual violence, etc.), authorized rightful ownership of all land and everything on it to be transferred by mere European identity while also introducing the idea of European men as the superior race and gender (which eventually became any other race and gender were not actually fully human). The doctrine also allowed room to charge dissenters with a crime, since they were speaking against the church. Countries such as Portugal, Spain, France, and England all adopted this doctrine, and it has been used to inform US law as recently as 2005.

Over the next centuries, the Doctrine of Discovery was used to distribute Great Britain's colonial practices to countries across the globe, beginning with the continent of Africa, followed by Central, South, the Caribbean Islands, and the settler colonization of North America and beyond. This intentional spread of colonization led to the enslavement and cross-continental trafficking of millions of African people and the genocide of over 90% of the Indigenous populations of the Americas. The genocide and eventual near erasure of Indigenous communities and cultures was intentional for the benefit of Christian European nations to grow their wealth, land, and resources, in accordance with their God and biblical texts.

As the Doctrine of Discovery was beginning to take hold in the 12th century, agriculture was growing alongside it as a direct result, which planted the seeds of the gender binary. Christian monasteries owned and operated most farms within Europe while also running the schools where others learned large-scale, for-profit farming. With colonialism running parallel, physical land began to be seen as the largest wealth generator through the practice of agriculture during the Age of Discovery era. As a result, anything that added value to the land, such as animals and people, were highly coveted. More and more animals were domesticated and owned as property to generate more wealth through farming. And although ownership of domesticated animals was of great labor value for farmland, people themselves held even more value. Thus, enslavement of Native Indigenous people became all the more important and valuable, and led even to European children – and cisgender women who could produce those children – being domesticated and viewed as something to be owned as property for the sole purpose of generating wealth for European men (as was law through the Doctrine of Discovery). For this reason, cisgender women's roles became one of solely giving birth to farm labor (boys were valued as future owners, girls were devalued as future caretakers to the owners) and tending to men who worked the land by cooking, cleaning, and maintaining the household.

Meanwhile pre-colonization, global Native Indigenous cultures viewed both gender and farming completely differently than their European counterparts. Almost universally the gender binary didn't exist amongst native communities, which largely viewed gender as a diverse spectrum and oftentimes didn't even have language for individual specific gender identities. Additionally, most native Indigenous tribal nations practiced hunter/gatherer/forager and small plot horticulture life styles, all of which was in direct contrast to Western European culture.

Eventually, as these white Christian cisgender men made their way to the shores of Turtle Island with their religion, the Doctrine of Discovery, and settler colonialism, they "discovered" the Native Indigenous populations. They named them "uncivilized heathens" and "barbarian savages" that were practicing what equated to them as gender diversity and socialism. This was all the more proof that they not only weren't human but animals, in need of domestication and ownership or complete eradication. The manufactured gender binary as we know it today was then formally solidified as a racial tool of oppression to justify the horrific actions and genocide that came next, and that largely still continues today.

Recognizing history's imprint today gets us closer to decolonizing the gender binary. Making connections from the past to the present is the first step.

Exercise: Modern-Day Examples of Key Terms

- **Agriculture:** large scale crop farming involving non-Indigenous plants for the purpose of profit.
- **Gender Expression:** the outward expression of an individual's gender identity and societal gender norms that are forced upon us, in which we are socialized.
- **Gender Identity:** the gender that an individual self identifies as, knowing themselves better than literally anyone else within their mind, body, spirit, heart, soul, etc.
- **Horticulture:** small scale plot farming involving Indigenous plants for the purpose of feeding families and/or small local communities.
- **Sex Assigned at Birth:** the sex marker assigned at birth on legal documents such as an individual's birth certificate.
- **Turtle Island:** the native, pre-colonization term for the landmass of North America.

Connecting the 12th century to the current political climate of today can sometimes be difficult for students to see. Have your students review the key terms and provide modern day examples of each, and/or how the concepts still play out today, with a focus on the gender binary. We must be able to recognize our socialization to the gender binary, which happens all around us starting at birth, as a vital tool in dismantling it, and knowing its history is an important start. Critical thinking and being able to know and understand the past, in order to assess the present, then analyze them both together to recognize better paths forward is vital to our modern day liberation from the gender binary, the oppressive systems from the past we still live under, and toxic white culture norms.

Why Decolonization Is Necessary

So now what, what do we do? Well, one of the main things we can do to dismantle the gender binary is to begin to decolonialize. Although a lot has happened since settler colonialism came to the shores of Turtle Islan, being liberated from it was not one of them including all current systems of government, laws, policies, and all things that make the United States of America in 2025. So abolition work is critical to freeing us from this oppression. I know that may seem big and daunting at first, but starting small can still make a big impact. Center Indigenous knowledge around living beyond the gender binary. Follow and support Two-Spirit activists and join in direct action, etc. Anytime you are working around or outside of systems to find solutions to the issues you face, by community, for community, you are helping to destroy this harmful practice.

In the communities we teach critical thinking to, we want them to be activated and empowered to address these issues in their own lives. With the history we've taught them and drawing connections to how the oppression is still present today, they can begin to decolonize the gender binary themselves.

Exercise: Decolonize Your Classroom

Have your students assess your classroom for signs of colonization and the gender binary. Once they find something, have them generate innovative, creative, and inclusive ideas to replace it with something more affirming. As best as you can, decenter yourself as an educator – truly have the students build something for them and by them, to prove that they can work outside of established systems and order to truly create something that includes all of their whole selves.

The world has obviously changed since the 12th century. The world has even changed since my youth, in some ways for the better, and in some ways for the worst. Now as a queer and trans adult I still see the gender binary all around me, as clear and as enforced as ever. The true and accurate history of how the gender binary came to be matters as it shows that we are still killing people over something that never really existed. The gender binary doesn't exist in nature, in plant or animal life; neither did it exist within the human experience till some white men used it as an excuse to accrue wealth through mass enslavement, domestication, and genocide. This is why our gender journeys matter, why telling our stories matter. We are still here and the world needs to know it. So the next time you buy your wife the pink toolkit or berate your son for picking flowers and wanting to dance like a princess in a pink tutu, remember that this gender binary concept you cling to is an intentionally invented tool of oppression meant to cause harm. And I assure you, it causes immense harm; take it from this Two-Spirit trans person who just wanted to look beautiful and dance.

This was written by Arc Telos Saint Amour (they/them) who is Native Indigenous (Coahuiltecan) and Two-Spirit, with assistance from Dre Ceja and Eliza Davison (formerly of the Transgender Training Institute), Dr. Jessica Jennrich, and the lived and living experiences of Native Indigenous people and traditional ancestral teachings and stories passed down from generation to generation.

Reference

Johns, M. M., Lowry, R., Haderxhanaj, L. T., Rasberry, C. N., Robin, L., Scales, L., Stone, D., & Suarez, N. A. (2020). Trends in violence victimization and suicide risk by sexual identity among high school students. *Youth Risk Behavior Survey, United States*, 69(1), 19–27. http://dx.doi.org/10.15585/mmwr.su6901a3

14 Redefining Intimacy

Expanding Relationship Design Beyond Compulsory Heteronormativity and Monogamy

Sam Casanova

Key Terms

- **Relationship Structure and Style:** a phrase that refers to how a relationship or connection is built and/or designed based on the needs and wants of everyone involved. It also suggests that relationships (whether sexual, romantic, platonic, etc.) may have different boundaries, goals, and expectations.
- **Un(learning):** while learning is often described as the acquisition of knowledge through varying modes of study, unlearning often references the process of rejecting certain (sometimes social) values, beliefs, or outdated ideas, to allow for more informed, expansive, and accurate insights, reflections, and understandings.
- **Consensual Non-monogamy (CNM):** a term that generally describes relationships that are romantically and/or sexually open, with the consent of everyone involved. People in these types of relationships believe that "one person doesn't have to be all the things," says Liz Clark, clinical psychologist and director of counseling.
  Note: Ethical Non-Monogamy (ENM): some may use ENM and CNM interchangeably. For this chapter, we use CNM to center the importance of consent versus diving into the ethics of "right and wrong" within specific relationship structures and dynamics.
- **Compulsory Heteronormativity (comphet):**

  - Heteronormativity is the theory and concept that heterosexuality is the preferred, expected, and *normal* sexual orientation. It also centers the gender binary (i.e., the idea that there are exclusively two genders) and that sexual and marital relationships are most fitting between people of opposite and/or different sexes.
  - Heteronormativity creates and upholds a social hierarchy based on sexual orientation with the practice and belief that heterosexuality is deemed the societal norm.

DOI: 10.4324/9781032615479-18

- **Compulsory Monogamy (compmon):**
  - Compulsory monogamy culture assumes everyone strives to be married (or partnered) to/with one person and finds complete fulfillment in that romantic endeavor.

Combatting Compulsory Heteronormativity and Monogamy

... and ...
Sitting in a tree,
K-I-S-S-I-N-G.
First comes love,
then comes marriage,
Then comes a baby in a baby carriage.

As seen earlier, there are ample societal messages that suggest there are specific socially acceptable steps and progressions when it comes to measuring "success" within an intimate (sometimes described as romantic) relationship, often with a presumed end goal or expectation of monogamy and/or relationship exclusivity.

In *Stepping Off the Relationship Escalator: Uncommon love and life*, Amy Gahran (who uses the pseudonym Aggie Sez) discusses how assumptions are made regarding relationships and their expected progressions. Gahran/Sez describes the progressions, in both their book and blog series, as follows:

1. **Making contact:** connecting and getting to know one other (via talking, texting, dates, meetups, etc.) and can include intimate behaviors (such as kissing, affection, sex)
2. **Initiation and Courtship:** may involve feelings of infatuation and/or a limerence phase, which may include hanging out, dating, spending quality time together in order to increase emotional closeness, and often (but not always) includes sexual behaviors
3. **Claiming, Labeling, and Defining:** establishment of "couplehood" or "partnership," (becoming an "us"), adopting common relationship labels, and expressing romantic, sexual and/or social exclusivity
4. **Establishment:** creating habits and rituations to support both/all partners consistently. This includes forming habits for shared time (date nights, sex, sleeping over at each other's homes, etc.) and typically maintaining daily communication
5. **Commitment:** discussing, and/or planning for a long-term shared future as a [monogamous] couple or individuals with a shared commitment and agreement. This may include meeting each others' families, friends, and loved ones
6. **Merging:** cohabitation and sharing responsibilities and finances; in addition to planning to become engaged to be married or the equivalent (Note: this may happen before, during, or after the commitment.)

7. **Conclusion:** getting engaged, married, and/or having children, with an expectation to endure partnership. The marriage/arrangement is expected to remain intact until a partner passes

8. **Legacy:** building wealth and/or family-building legacy such as purchasing a home, property, and/or raising children. This is when someone reaches the top of the escalator and represents the culmination of the traditional relationship path (Gahran, 2017)

Note: the relationship escalator (described in the previous steps) can look many different ways, and the language provided by Gahran/Sez is meant to act as one example of anticipated hierarchical and linear progression. Some people may choose to engage in all, some, or none of the progressions, regardless of their relationship structures and styles.

As we can see, there is often an anticipated hierarchical and linear progression within the sequence of events related to the unfolding, development, and building of interpersonal relationships. There is an expected leveling up with clear goals and timelines, often rooted in monogamy and/or some form of relationship exclusivity. According to Gahran/Sez, "relationships that [become stagnant] and/or linger too long in an intermediate phase without 'progress,' are deemed 'dead ends (Sez, 2012, para. 11)." With the relationship escalator, some face challenges when asked to take a step back, adjust, and/or accommodate a new or different structure within the relationship.

These themes are also woven into the curricula of many sex ed classrooms and learning spaces. This escalator script *can* still be included in sex education curricula so long as (1) it's not at the expense of excluding other types of relationship structures and styles and (2) it is not the only script examined or discussed. Within sex education, there is often an (un)intentional omission of diverse relationship structures and styles that perpetuates the notion that only certain relationships are acceptable and valid while others are not.

In *Compulsory Heterosexuality and the Lesbian Existence*, Adrienne Rich deliberately examines how heterosexuality and heteronormativity are "imposed, managed, organized, propagandized, and maintained by force, [power, and violence] (Rich, 2003, pp. 26–27)."

How does comphet and compmon show up in our work as sex educators? How are we upholding and/or interrupting comphet and compmon within classrooms and learning spaces?

Our job as sex educators is to provide all of the information and options needed to support people in making the best decisions for themselves. When folks are told limited, pre-selected information–whether in regard to different relationship structures and styles or otherwise – it denies community members, including our young people, the opportunity to (re)explore, (re)imagine, and (re)discover the types of intimacy dynamics and relationship structures and styles they want or desire to experience.

Everyone deserves the space and opportunities to foster and consensually co-create the types of relationships they want to experience and explore. As sex educators, there is responsibility to teach beyond the confines and parameters of comphet and compmon, without judgment, bias, or stigma.

Relationships Exist on a Spectrum

Before colonization, there were more visible and revered examples of relationship structures and styles that expanded beyond traditional, heteronormative, monogamous relationships, as seen in many Indigenous cultures. According to TallBear, from the Critical Polyamorist (2014), an Indigenous thinker and writer, "colonial borders and institutions that included reservations/reserves, residential schools, and churches and missions [were] all designed to "save the man and kill the Indian" [which also] meant pursuing the righteous, monogamous, couple-centric, nuclear-family institution" (para. 5).Through ongoing colonization, compmon and comphet became dominant world views at the cost of erasing and denying people's identities, cultures, and experiences.

As named in Polysecure:Attachment, Trauma and Consensual Nonmonogamy, monogamy is often upheld as the standard and measure to strive for and continues to remain unquestioned (Fern, 2020). However, in reality, monogamy is one of many options when it comes to defining and creating the types of relationships people want to have and experience. Within sex ed settings, there needs to be conversations around relationship structures and styles such as: monogamish, polyfidelity, open relationships, swinging, throuples, asexual and polyamorous, poly-intimates, hierarchical polyamory, non-hierarchical polyamory, solo polyamory, relationship anarchy, and more.

Note: for this chapter, we will not be discussing every type of relationship style and structure. However, we do encourage folks to continue their learning by reviewing the resources at the end of this chapter.

It's important to ask oneself as a sex educator: what is the impact of (not) discussing some and/or all of these relationship styles structures?

The previously listed relationships structures and styles are not the only options; however, they offer insight into the many ways people might choose to engage and/or experience their intimate, romantic, and/or sexual relationships.

Unfortunately, some of the messages and/or stereotypes associated with those who engage in CNM include myths, judgments, and assumptions around sexual "deviance" navigating avoidant attachment, "sexual addiction," non-committal, etc. However, those who engage in CNM often believe in "transparency, consent, open and honest communication, personal autonomy, sex positivity, compassion, and freedom for themselves and others" while simultaneously embracing the following tenets (Fern, 2020, 3:09:00).

- Love is not possessive or a finite resource. It is instead abundant and plentiful
- It is common to be attracted to more than one person at a time
- There are ample ways to practice love and sexual, romantic and/or intimate relationships
- Jealousy is not a feeling to be evaded or feared; but instead, a feeling that can help people better understand and learn (Fern, 2020)

Instead of dating and/or seeking out one person who checks *all* the boxes for an "ideal" relationship, people who practice CNM may seek out considerations like sexual attraction, romance, parenting, finance, and lifestyle preferences among different partners. For example, a person might have one partner who they share finances with, another they raise kids with, another who helps them explore their sexual desires, and another who simply shares their interests in cooking and traveling.

Implementing CNM Expansive Activities and Conversations Within Sex Ed

When it comes to relationships, one of the common questions received from young people is whether or not it is OK to date multiple people simultaneously – often with a curiosity around what is considered "disloyal" or "cheating."

As sex educators, it is critical to uplift the message that relationships are not a one-size-fits-all. For some, dating multiple people simultaneously crosses a boundary while for others it might not. Our job is to offer insight around why some people, including our young people, might prefer to date or be in relationship with multiple people at the same time and why others might not, in age and developmentally appropriate/relevant ways.

These next few activities and suggested conversations not only support your professional learning as an expansive sex educator but also can be used with your students to discuss and explore values around diverse relationship styles and structures.

Activity 1: Values-Based Assessment

Below is a values-based assessment. There are 15 statements. Your job is to read and decide if you agree, disagree, or are uncertain/undecided. There is no right or wrong answer. This activity is intended to allow room for critical thinking and reflection.

This tool is meant to support folks in unpacking their current perspectives, biases, and opinions, both within and outside classrooms and learning spaces.

1. Sexual, romantic and intimate relationships should be between two people
2. It is common to be attracted or have feelings for more than one person
3. Elementary schoolers are able to understand consensually nonmonogamous relationships
4. People should be friends first before dating or having sex
5. It is okay for sexual intimacy to be shared between friends
6. Cheating and acts of infidelity can occur in CNM relationships
7. It is acceptable for a middle schooler to be dating more than one person at a time
8. Honesty, open communication and trust exist in both monogamous and CNM relationships
9. It is acceptable for platonic relationships to be prioritized over romantic/sexual relationships
10. It is possible for one person to meet all of the emotional, social, romantic, sexual and other needs of another person
11. It is acceptable for someone to have sex first and then decide if they're interested in a relationship
12. CNM is often practiced by those who are not seeking commitment
13. CNM people seek marriage and/or kids
14. It is acceptable to connect, interact, and/or engage with a previous partner
15. People should maintain clear boundaries between platonic and romantic/sexual relationships

Activity 2: Written Reflection

Think back to your experiences growing up and how you learned about relationship structures and styles. Take five minutes and respond to the following series of questions.

- What types of relationships did you most often witness growing up? What types of relationships did you not witness growing up? Were there examples of CNM relationships? How were they depicted?
- How have media sources impacted your understanding of these relationships? What other influences impacted your understanding of relationships?
- What messages did you receive about the types of relationships you were expected to explore?

Activity 3: Critical Conversations – *Supporting Students in Thinking Critically About Relationship Structures and Styles*

Lead an open discussion with students about why they think some folks may choose certain relationship structures and styles over others. This allows students to examine and think critically amongst themselves and is an opportunity to reflect upon their understandings.

For example, some reasons why someone might be interested in CNM are because of the following:

- More room for self-expression through the experiences that can come with multiple partners
- Interest in the growth and development that can come with non-monogamy
- Romantic and sexual diversity and curiosity
- Philosophical and personal values
- Authentic expression of self or maybe other reasons altogether

Similarly, someone might be interested in monogamy because of the following:

- More socially accepted and recognized
- Lack of availability and capacity for multiple partners
- [1]Personal belief or bias that suggests monogamy lowers chances of passing infections and/or creating unintended pregnancies based on the notion that fewer partners leads to lower risk
- Philosophical and personal values
- Authentic expression of self or maybe other reasons altogether.

Addressing Stigma Within Sex Ed Settings

In these conversations around relationship structures and styles, educators must ensure that we are interrupting stigmatizing language or behavior. As sex educators, we must remind folks that just because something is different, new, or unfamiliar [to us] does not mean it is inherently harmful, negative, or inferior.

When it comes to CNM, there are often concerns about "sexual promiscuity," a judgment that is often associated with someone who has or has had multiple partners. We see this begin at a young age. If and when students date multiple people, there are negative judgments and assumptions around one's behaviors and inability to commit – when sometimes, dating multiple people gives people, including our young people, the opportunity to learn what qualities, interactions, and experiences they like and don't like.

Similarly, there is often a stigma associated with friends with benefits (FwBs), a term used to describe relationships where casual sexual behaviors may happen between non-exclusive partners or friends who generally have little to no romantic connection – when FwBs can be an opportunity for someone to experience sexual and/or physical fulfillment and exploration without feeling pressured or expected to pursue a romantic and/or emotional connection.

These relationship structures and styles may appeal to some and not others and that is okay. Our job is to offer the space to discuss these options to support folks in defining their relationships for themselves. We also have to uplift that all relationships, regardless of the structure and style, are encouraged to have a foundation rooted in safety, respect, communication, honesty, trust, and equality.

Within sex ed settings, students benefit when we present a diverse representation of safe and fulfilling relationship structures and styles. This may sound like providing additional examples such as:

- Some people are asexual and have multiple exclusive romantic partners
- Some people are married and choose to have consensual sex outside of their marriage
- Some people simultaneously date more than one person with the consent of everyone involved
- Some people can choose to live and co-parent with one partner and have sex with a different partner

We do not need to give an example of every relationship possibility but, instead, want to offer room for questions and dialogue that expand beyond comphet and compmon. Ariana Brown, a queer Black Mexican writer, shared the following writing prompt:

- Write a poem with instructions on how to love you properly. What would someone need to know about you to love you right? What advice would you give to them?

Consider using this prompt as a starting point in supporting yourself and those you support in envisioning the types of relationships they want to experience.

Additional Factors for Approach and Consideration

Audre Lorde, self-described as a "Black, lesbian, mother, warrior, poet" reminds us, "If [we] didn't define [ourselves] for [ourselves], [we] would be crunched into other people's fantasies for [us] and eaten alive (Lorde, 1982, para. 13)."

Every relationship deserves the opportunity to grow into whatever it wants and chooses to be–without the pressures, influences and/or messaging from external and internal influences.

Sex educators can support this by deepening their own understanding of diverse relationship styles in order to (1) offer accurate information and available options beyond the confines and parameters of compulsory heteronormativity and monogamy, (2) combat the stigma and negative stereotypes often associated with CNM, and (3) foster opportunities for people to determine and design the types of relationships (and values) they desire and want to experience. Community members, including our young people, should be able to safely embrace, explore, and discover their sexuality and their diverse desires and expressions without judgment, stigma, or shame. Many of us have different sexual and romantic needs and desires, and that is beautiful.

Note: though this chapter focused predominantly on romantic and sexual relationships, that is not intended to diminish the intimacy that exists within platonic relationships. Some might want to create romantic and/or sexual relationships that overlap with friendships, while others might want these relationships to be mutually exclusive. Some might want platonic relationships that are equally or similarly intimate to their romantic relationships, while others might want one relationship to have be of a priority than the other. Everyone has different relationship structure and style preferences and that is to be celebrated. Ultimately, people can decide for themselves how they want to be loved, held, and cared for; and our many relationships – however designed, however described – support us in experiencing and accessing that.

Introspective Questions for Consideration

• Why do you think there is an emphasis on comphet and compmon in sex education?
• What are the impacts of (not) teaching beyond comphet and compmon?
• Given social markers (like race, gender, orientation, etc.), how might that impact or influence one's ability to define and design the relationships they want to experience?
• How can sex educators incorporate dialogue around CNM into their curriculum?
• How can sex educators interrupt stigma and harmful comments regarding those who engage in CNM?

Note

1 Note: there are multiple studies that examine whether monogamy is proven to statistically reduce the chances of passing STIs and/or creating unintended pregnancies. The results vary.

References

Fern, J. (2020). *Polysecure: Attachment, trauma, and consensual nonmonogamy* (read by Jessica Fern, Eve Rickert, Nora Samaran, Audible audio ed., 7 hr., 52 mins). Thornapple Press.
Gahran, A. (2017). *Stepping off the Relationship Escalator: Uncommon love and life*. Off the Escalator Enterprises, LLC.
Lorde, A. (2012, August 12). *"Learning from the 60s" (1982) Audre Lorde*. https://www.blackpast.org/african-american-history/1982-audre-lorde-learning-60s/
Rich, A. C. (2003). Compulsory heterosexuality and lesbian existence (1980). *Journal of Women's History, 15*(3), 11–48. https://dx.doi.org/10.1353/jowh.2003.0079.
Sez, A. (2012, November 29). *Riding the relationship escalator (or not)*. Solo Poly. https://solopoly.net/2012/11/29/riding-the-relationship-escalator-or-not/
TallBear, K. (2014). Couple-centricity, polyamory and colonialism. *The Critical Polyamorist*. http://www.criticalpolyamorist.com/homeblog/couple-centricity-polyamory-and-colonialism

15 Breaking Barriers

Sex Education Promoting Quality of Life for People with Physical Disability

Kim Andreassen, Alysha Oorjitham, and Hannah Smith

Key Terms

- **Dignity of Risk:** this term promotes the idea that each person has the autonomy and self-determination to make their own choices, including the choice to take risks in life. The person can make choices, take risks, make mistakes, and learn through this process.
- **Human Rights Model of Disability:** this model builds on the social model and sees disability as a natural variation. It affirms that people with disability should be respected, supported, and have the same human rights as people without disability.
- **Medical Model of Disability:** this archaic model of disability sees disability as impairments that need to be "cured" and often views people with disability as less than people without disability. For many with a physical disability, sadly, this is the lens of disability most used.
- **Physical Disability:** physical disability encompasses a wide range of differences in someone's physical body, including mobility differences, limb differences, sensory differences (Blind, low vision, Deaf, hard of hearing), facial differences, and chronic illness. The disability may be temporary or permanent and may have existed from birth or be acquired. Using the human rights model of disability, depending on the physical and sensory accommodations of an environment, a person may be more or less disabled. For example, someone with low mobility may not be disabled if sufficient accommodations ensure they can do all they want and need with no barriers to participation.
- **Educator:** when used in this chapter, we affirm that in addition to people who have studied and work as a sex educator, all people who are in the lives of or support people with physical disability are sex educators. That is, they can and do provide relationship and sexuality education to people with disability through modeling behaviors and discussions. It is essential to recognize this fact as many people with a physical disability may have been excluded from sex education elsewhere.

DOI: 10.4324/9781032615479-19

- **Social Model of Disability:** this model of disability notes that the way society is organized and structured is responsible for the barriers and problems that people with disability face. For example, if someone cannot access a building, it is not because they have mobility issues, use a wheelchair and need to be cured (medical model). Rather, the building is inaccessible and needs to be made wheelchair accessible.

Under a human rights model or social model of disability, physical disability arises from the interaction of an individual's personal factors (e.g., a health condition) and their environment, such as the physical infrastructure where they live or the attitudes of others in their community (Burchardt, 2004). Unfortunately, physical disability continues to be viewed through the medical model of disability and that of "functional impairments," although a standardized definition does not exist. Therefore, the data on prevalence is often reductive (Loeb, 2013). For example, the data may not include those who are Hard of Hearing or Deaf, have low vision or are Blind, but will include those with missing limbs and mobility challenges. Further, chronic illness, whilst known to be disabling, is often unreported. Experts do agree that physical disability and age are strongly interrelated and that most elderly have some form of physical disability (Reynolds, 2018). It is, therefore, valid to assume that physical disability is an eventual outcome of living life and getting older.

Further complexities in understanding physical disability arise because of the differences between a physical disability a person was born with (for example, born without legs) or one acquired due to an accident (for example, acquired brain injury), which may also be temporary (for example, a broken leg). The impact of – and the disability – may, therefore, change over time, affecting a person's sexual health and thus sexuality differently over their lifespan. It may also impact someone's ability to engage in meaningful activities and relationships or have a positive self-image. This is particularly relevant in the case of people who have intersectional identities such as folks who are Two-Spirit, lesbian, gay, bisexual, transgender, queer/questioning, intersex, and/or asexual (2SLGBTQIA+) or are not white, are from lower socio-economic background, or other such historically underrepresented groups who experience oppression across multiple characteristics of their identity.

As physical disability could happen to all people, the design of comprehensive sex education should be one of inclusion, safety, and support for all identities a person may have. However, current research shows that people with physical disability are less likely to have access to comprehensive, 2SLGBTQIA+ inclusive sex education (Esmail et al., 2010). Societal values, beliefs, and attitudes reinforce a lack of sexual health training on disability-specific issues and disproportionately focus on risk mitigation, thereby preventing people with physical disability from receiving equitable sex education (Esmail et al., 2010).

Therefore, the questions that drive this chapter are: what are common limiting assumptions about physical disability and sexuality, where do they come from, and what can we do about that as sex educators?

People With Physical Disability as Sexual Beings Deserving of Comprehensive Sex Education

A common, but harmful societal view is that people with physical disability are asexual. It is assumed they do not or should not experience sexual desire or sexual activities (Esmail et al., 2010). A systematic review conducted by Giles et al. (2023) revealed that youth with physical disability reported others did not perceive them as sexually desirable or capable. This perception is backed up by research completed by Ip et al. (2022), which found more than 80% of participants identified the presence of disability as an important factor when selecting a partner. The participants indicated they would either prefer not to date someone with disability or would only consider dating a person with disability if their disability caused minimal "functional impact" (Ip et al., 2022).

An intersectional factor such as gender can also contribute to a complex experience of privilege or discrimination. For example, it has been demonstrated that having a physical disability decreases the degree to which others perceive a woman to be physically or sexually attractive (Pebdani & Tashjian, 2022). Factors such as gender and type of disability also interact and can compound stigmatization and bias. People with physical disability are considered less likely to date (Pebdani & Tashjian, 2022). However, whilst men with physical disability are perceived as likely to be dating someone who is also physically disabled, women with physical disability are perceived as unlikely to be dating anyone (Pebdani & Tashjian, 2022). Unfortunately, research on additional gender identities and disability is negligible, and, thus, the experiences of trans, gender diverse, or non-binary individuals are unknown. However, it is likely more restrictive for dating than experienced by those who still identify as the gender they were assigned at birth.

Being a trauma-informed sex educator requires that you acknowledge your biases (across all intersections: race, culture, ethnicity, disability, gender, sexuality, etc.) within your work so you can have a judgment-aware practice. Permitting the existence of judgments whilst evaluating how they influence you and how you interact with individuals personally and professionally is typically best practice. A trauma-informed approach understands and reacts appropriately to the knowledge that the stigmatization of people with physical disability engaging in sexual activities, relationships, or expressions of sexuality excludes them from opportunities to find sexual partners or engage in experiences that help them learn about or develop their sexuality (Giles et al., 2023). It is also understood that this is amplified for people whose sexuality deviates from the traditional norms, such as 2SLGBTIA+ folks. In turn, the internalization of this stigma contributes to adverse health outcomes, such as an increased risk of developing depression (Ju et al., 2023). Some people with physical disability have also reported accepting harmful treatment from sexual or romantic partners, due to their internalized belief that they are undesirable and will not be able to find a new sexual or romantic partner (Giles et al., 2023).

Furthermore, research that included women with physical disability found that they have additional factors influencing their sexual health, including societal beliefs that they are unable to do their traditional gender roles (for example, housework and birthing/rearing children) (Parsons et al., 2017). Narrow standards for beauty projected on women's bodies add to this and burden women with a requirement for a "normal" attractiveness that is impossible to meet (Mady et al., 2023) and certainly does not include physical disability. It is, therefore, unsurprising that Holmes et al. (2019), who had a 70% female participant ratio, found that participants were actively allowing their partners the opportunity to seek sexual satisfaction outside their relationship due to feelings of inadequacy and guilt. This may be a desired relationship structure for individuals who engage in ethical non-monogamy. However, for these participants, this relationship structure was chosen due to internalized stigma and shame rather than free exploration and choice. Again, research that includes trans, gender diverse, or non-binary people with disability integrating these issues has yet to be completed. However, anecdotal experience indicates similar experiences in these communities; therefore, suggesting any sex education should consider the impact of gender assigned at birth and gender expression on sexual understandings and scripts.

Sex educators who work with people with physical disability are also affected by the societal attitudes mentioned earlier. The impact includes excluding people with disability from comprehensive sex education, either on purpose or due to environmental barriers. Research also shows that for people with physical disability, health professionals' ability to provide comprehensive sex education was compromised by unconscious beliefs about asexuality or their discomfort with the topic (Engelen et al., 2020), also limiting the comprehensive sex education that people with physical disability receive.

Many people who could provide comprehensive sex education wait for topics to be raised by their students before supporting them (Low et al., 2022). Some believe that comprehensive sex education is beyond their role (Valvano et al., 2014). However, many people with physical disability also identified this approach as a barrier to accessing comprehensive sex education and prefer that people initiate this topic with them (Engelen et al., 2020). The safest approach is, therefore, one that uses a trauma-informed lens by gently questioning the wants and needs of the person with physical disability to determine the information and knowledge desired before providing sex education.

Social, Emotional, and Physical Pleasure and Fulfillment Are Essential for People With a Physical Disability

The authors understand that the training for educators (Collier-Harris & Goldman, 2017; Ezer et al., 2022) around comprehensive sex education is minimal, even sex education that caters for people without disability. Research has shown that when addressing health and well-being, sexual and romantic relationships are vital (Gómez-López et al., 2019); the ongoing training gaps are, therefore, devastating to people with physical disability.

Romantic relationships can be deeper connections than friends, contributing to positive self-regard and increased social integration (Gómez-López et al., 2019). Therefore, the ongoing "crisis intervention" manner of comprehensive sex education increases the risk of sexual assault (Goldfarb & Lieberman, 2021) and removes autonomy, dignity of risk, and capacity for consent (due to lack of education) from people with physical disability. Interestingly, one group of individuals are typically provided not just the comprehensive sex education required, but additional accessibility tools to have a functioning sexual life – people with a penis who have a spinal cord injury for whom it is seen as vital for their quality of life (Soler et al., 2018). In fact, in Japan, an agency that provides masturbation assistance exists, catering to people with penises only (Sakairi, 2020). This gender inequality further reduces the autonomy, dignity of risk, and capacity for consent (due to lack of education) of people with physical disability. Other considerations include varying attitudes towards people with disability and sexual orientation. For example, Pebdani and Tashjian (2022) found that lesbian sexual activity is more accepted in people without physical disability than people with a vulva who have a physical disability.

Additional Factors for Consideration and Approach

When you are aware of your biases and judgments and considering how to approach giving comprehensive sex education to people with physical disability, it is vital to tailor the approach to the individual, their strengths, and their physical disability. This means that having a conversation about accessibility and supports with the person is an essential first step. Table 15.1 provides a short list of suggestions and prompts for exploration and consideration, as well as some resources to help you get started on delivering comprehensive sex education to people with physical disability.

Reflective Questions for Consideration

- How do my own biases and assumptions about physical disability and sexuality influence the way I approach sex education?
- How can I actively seek out education, training, and resources to better understand the intersectionality of physical disability and sexuality and incorporate this knowledge into my practice?

Table 15.1 Suggestions and resources for sex educators

Physical disability type	Suggestions	Further resources
Chronic conditions (e.g. endometriosis, asthma, diabetes)	• Acknowledge harmful social norms that stigmatize the sexuality of people who use medical devices (e.g., colostomy bags, walking aids, insulin pumps) and validate associated feelings • Facilitate learners to explore any ways they may have connected with their sexuality previously • Explore typical heterosexual sexual scripts and how these can be adapted to make sexual activities accessible and enjoyable (e.g. challenging the concept that "real sex" must involve penetration) • Support learners to find communities in which their sexuality is acknowledged and celebrated (e.g. online support groups, Instagram influencers, Only Fans)	• Podcast: Doing it! With Hannah Witton • Podcast: Sex and Chronic Illness • YouTube: Hannah Witton • Instagram: @Queeringsex • Website: The Pleasure Project Trainer Toolkit
Sensory disability (e.g. Deaf, low vision, stroke)	• Provide education across multiple communication formats to promote accessibility (e.g. sign language, closed captions, text-to-voice) • Provide the option to learn through different sensory mediums (e.g. tactile exploration of an appropriate anatomical model ensuring 2SLGBTQIA+ inclusivity) • Provide education on erogenous zones and different ways to explore pleasure (e.g. light touch, hot and cold sensations)	• Product: SEX-ED+ Genitalia Models Website: Deaf2 Informational Videos • Website: AMAZE sex ed video library • Model: Cliterate – Thrive Rehab • Instagram: @insert_here. prosthetics • Website: Sex Love and OT • Website: OMGYes
Body differences and mobility challenges (e.g. amputees, cerebral palsy, spinal cord injury)	• Provide education on options to grade and adapt sexual positions (e.g. wedge cushions, sex swings, intimate rider) • Exploring the implications of altered sensations of different genitals and potential solutions (e.g. exploring options like oral medications, vacuum therapy, and penile injections)	• Products: Liberator Sex Furniture • Products: XES Products • Website: Sex Ed + • Podcast: Disability After Dark • Podcast: OT After Dark

- What can I do to prioritize the autonomy, dignity of risk, and sexual rights of individuals with physical disability in my approach to providing comprehensive and inclusive sex education?

References

Burchardt, T. (2004). Capabilities and disability: The capabilities framework and the social model of disability. *Disability and Society*, *19*(7), 735–751. https://doi.org/10.1080/0968759042000284213

Collier-Harris, C. A., & Goldman, J. D. G. (2017). Could Australia have its own teacher professional standards for teaching relationships and sexuality education? *Sex Education*, *17*(5), 512–528. https://doi.org/10.1080/14681811.2017.1313159

Engelen, M. M., Knoll, J. L., Rabsztyn, P. R. I., Maas-van Schaaijk, N. M., & van Gaal, B. G. I. (2020). Sexual health communication between healthcare professionals and adolescents with chronic conditions in western countries: An integrative review. *Sexuality and Disability*, (38), 191–216. https://doi.org/10.1007/s11195-019-09597-0

Esmail, S., Krupa, C., MacNeill, D., & Mackenzie, S. (2010). "Best-practice: Sexuality education for children and youth with physical disabilities – Developing a curriculum based on lived experiences." Canadian Council on Learning. http://en.copian.ca/library/research/ccl/best_practice/best_practice.pdf

Ezer, P., Fisher, C. M., Jones, T., & Power, J. (2022). Changes in sexuality education teacher training since the release of the Australian Curriculum. *Sexuality Research and Social Policy*, *19*(1), 12–21. https://doi.org/10.1007/s13178-020-00520-3

Giles, M. L., Juando-Prats, C., McPherson, A. C. et al. (2023). "But, you're in a wheelchair!": A systematic review exploring the sexuality of youth with physical disabilities. *Sexuality and Disability*, *41*, 141–171. https://doi.org/10.1007/s11195-022-09769-5

Goldfarb, E. S., & Lieberman, L. D. (2021). Three decades of research: The case for comprehensive sex education. *The Journal of Adolescent Health*, *68*(1), 13–27. https://doi.org/10.1016/j.jadohealth.2020.07.036

Gómez-López, M., Viejo, C., & Ortega-Ruiz, R. (2019). Well-being and romantic relationships: A systematic review in adolescence and emerging adulthood. *International Journal of Environmental Research and Public Health*, *16*(13), e2415. https://doi.org/10.3390/ijerph16132415

Holmes, L. J., Yorke, J. A., Dutton, C., Fowler, S. J., & Ryan, D. (2019). Sex and intimacy in people with severe asthma: A qualitative study. *BMJ Open Respiratory Research*, *6*, e000382. https://doi.org/10.1136/bmjresp-2018-000382

Ip, I. M. H., Honey, A., & McGrath, M. (2022). Attitudes toward dating people with disability amongst young people in Australia and Hong Kong. *Sexuality and Disability*, *40*, 233–244. https://doi.org/10.1007/s11195-022-09734-2

Ju, H.-J., Harley, D., & Miller-Rankin, J. (2023). Manifestations of public and self-stigma of physical disability: A scoping review in rehabilitation and disability research. *Journal of Applied Rehabilitation Counseling*, *54*(3), 178–199. https://doi.org/10.1891/JARC-2022-0016

Loeb, M. (2013). Disability statistics: An integral but missing (and misunderstood) component of development work. *Nordic Journal of Human Rights*, *31*(3), 306–324. https://www.ncbi.nlm.nih.gov/pmc/articles/PMC4766593/

Low, M. A., Power, E., & McGrath, M. (2022). Sexuality after stroke: Exploring knowledge, attitudes, comfort and behaviours of rehabilitation professionals. *Annals of Physical and Rehabilitation Medicine*, *65*(2), e101547. https://doi.org/10.1016/j.rehab.2021.101547

Mady, S., Biswas, D., Dadzie, C. A., Hill, R. P., & Paul, R. (2023). "A whiter shade of pale": Whiteness, female beauty standards, and ethical engagement across three cultures. *Journal of International Marketing, 31*(1), 69–89. https://doi.org/10.1177/1069 031X221112642

Parsons, A. L., Reichl, A. J., & Pedersen, C. L. (2017). Gendered ableism: Media representations and gender role beliefs' effect on perceptions of disability and sexuality. *Sexuality and Disability, 35*(2), 207–225. https://doi.org/10.1007/s11195-016-9464-6

Pebdani, R. N., & Tashjian, A. (2022). An analysis of the attitudes of the general public towards the sexuality of individuals with disabilities through a systematic literature review. *Sexuality and Disability, 40*, 21–55. https://doi.org/10.1007/ s11195-021-09700-4

Reynolds, J. M. (2018). The extended body: On aging, disability, and well-being. *Hastings Center Report, 48*, S31–S36. https://doi.org/10.1002/hast.910

Sakairi, E. (2020). Medicalized pleasure and silenced desire: Sexuality of people with physical disabilities. *Sex & Disability, 38*, 41–56. https://doi.org/10.1007/ s11195-020-09618-3

Soler, J. M., Navaux, M. A., & Previnaire, J. G. (2018). Positive sexuality in men with spinal cord injury. *Spinal Cord, 56*, 1199–1206. https://doi.org/10.1038/s41393-018-0177-9

Valvano, A. K., West, L. M., Wilson, C. K., Macapagal, K. R., Penwell-Waines, L. M., Waller, J. L., & Stepleman, L. M. (2014). Health professions students' perceptions of sexuality in patients with physical disability. *Sexuality and Disability, 32*, 413–427. https://doi.org/10.1007/s11195-014-9347-7

16 Sex Education for Neurodivergent Learners

Addressing Gaps, Misconceptions, and Needs

Dylan Kapit

Author's note: there are many forms of neurodivergence and infinite ways to be neurodivergent. Since the experiences of neurodivergent people vary widely, it would be impossible to write a chapter that encompasses the sex education needs of all neurodivergent people. While neurodivergent is not synonymous with autism, for this chapter, neurodivergent is used as a term that is meant to encompass autism and ADHD, because both populations might need similar supports and strategies in the classroom.

Key Terms

- **Autism:** is a disability that impacts the way that people experience the world around them. Every Autistic person has different ways of being Autistic, but some of the traits that most Autistic people have in common are thinking differently, processing senses differently, moving differently, communicating differently, and socializing differently. There is no one way to be Autistic.
- **Autism Is a Lifelong Disability:** Autistic people are born Autistic and will be Autistic their whole lives. Autism is frequently diagnosed by a doctor, but myths about autism mean that it is more challenging for specific populations, such as Autistic adults, Autistic people who were assigned female at birth, and BIPOC Autistic people, to receive a formal diagnosis. Sometimes, this leads to Autistic people diagnosing themselves, and self-diagnosis is a valid and recognized form of diagnosis within the Autistic community. Autistic people exist at every intersection of identities and in all communities. (Autistic Self Advocacy Network, n.d.)
- **Neurodivergence:** neurodivergent (ND) means having a mind that functions in ways that diverge significantly from the dominant societal standards of "normal." Neurodivergence, the state of being neurodivergent, can be genetic and innate, caused by a brain-altering experience or some combination of the two. A person whose neurocognitive functioning diverges from dominant societal norms in multiple ways can be described as multiply neurodivergent. (adapted from a definition by Nick Walker, PhD from his website Neuroqueer)

DOI: 10.4324/9781032615479-20

Intro to Neurodivergent Inclusive Sex Education

Neurodivergent people have sex. For many, that information is surprising. A trend in older research incorrectly argues that neurodivergent people are asexual and generally not interested in having sex. (Sullivan & Caterino, 2008). There is also a pervasive myth that disabled "young people lack the desire or maturity for sexual or romantic connection, will not attract sexual or romantic partners, [and] are not subject to sexual abuse" (Holmes & SIECUS, 2021, p. 9). The myths mentioned earlier for why neurodivergent and disabled young people are not interested in having sex are frequently used to justify excluding students from sex education, or when neurodivergent students are receiving sex education, it is not education adapted to their needs. Based on newer research, my argument is that this population requires comprehensive, inclusive, relevant, and accessible sex education.

Risk of Abuse and Legal Risks

Neurodivergent students have a right to information about their own bodies, and there can be serious risks if these students are not getting this critical information (MacKenzie, 2018). Forty to seventy percent of disabled girls and 30% of disabled boys will experience sexual abuse before the age of 18. These are staggering and horrifying statistics (Holmes & SIECUS, 2021; Sullivan & Caterino, 2008). Researchers suggest that this happens because abusers target vulnerable disabled youth who "do not know they have a right to bodily autonomy, may not recognize abuse, and may not know how to make a report or tell someone when they have been abused" (Holmes & SIECUS, 2021, p. 26). However, a comprehensive, inclusive, and accessible sex education curriculum can teach neurodivergent and otherwise disabled students information that reduces the risk of abuse and boundary-violation incidents (Solomon et al., 2019). In addition to these risks, neurodivergent young people are significantly more likely to run into legal trouble than their neurotypical peers because of behaviors such as public masturbation, undressing or exposing genitals in public, sexual fixation on people or objects, and stalking or following (Sullivan & Caterino, 2008).

What Is Getting in the Way

Why isn't sex ed for neurodivergent individuals already happening everywhere? In my conversations with educators over the last few years, they frequently share that they don't teach sex education to their neurodivergent students for a variety of reasons, including that they hold unconscious beliefs about what their ND students can understand, and they do not believe that sex ed is relevant to their students. If teachers hold limiting beliefs about their students, an imperative solution is to spend some time unlearning and challenging their ableist beliefs.

Many educators are not aware that most neurodivergent young people develop at the same rate as their neurotypical peers, emphasizing the need for teaching neurodivergent people the same information as their neurotypical peers (Curtiss & Ebata, 2016).

It is critical that providing neurodivergent young people with comprehensive, inclusive, relevant, and accessible sex education is the responsibility of everyone who works with the community. To do so, people need to understand what to teach and how to teach it, which is the focus of the rest of this chapter. Please note that the author of this chapter is Autistic and neurodivergent and is writing from both professional and lived experience.

Central Topics and Strategies to Approach Neurodivergent-Inclusive Sex Ed

To get a sense of the important topics and strategies that should be included and used in a sex education curriculum for neurodivergent learners, I conducted a mixed methods survey on the sex education experience of LGBTQ+ Autistic adults. I chose to only survey LGBTQ+ Autistic adults because queer and trans people make up a significant portion of the Autistic community. (MacKenzie, 2018). In addition to several demographic questions about race, ethnicity, gender identity, sexuality, type of school attended, and location, the survey asked multiple questions about the sex education experiences of respondents and for explanations of ways that their sex education experiences were or were not accessible to them as Autistic learners. The survey responses will be used to build an LGBTQ+ inclusive sex education curriculum for Autistic learners, built by the community for the community.

The majority of respondents shared that the two main concepts they were taught in their sex education classrooms were pregnancy prevention and information about sexually transmitted infections (STIs). For the respondents, this was not nearly enough information, and even the methodology used when it was taught was not accessible to them as neurodivergent individuals.

There are an infinite number of topics that should be included in sex education for neurodivergent learners. Some of the most noted topics that respondents shared on the survey were: consent and boundaries, masturbation, gender identity and sexuality, porn, internet safety, sexual violence and abuse prevention, contraception and protections, sensory experiences associated with sex, and strategies for dating and romantic relationships. Respondents also identified that pregnancy and pregnancy prevention and STI information should continue to be included in any sex-ed curriculum meant for this population but must be LGBTQ+ inclusive and affirming. Other topics that respondents identified as important include information on puberty and hygiene, LGBTQ+ affirming HIV prevention education, and a discussion of PrEP.

Teaching Strategies and Approaches

The research revealed important teaching strategies respondents identified as helpful and accessible in meeting their needs. Overwhelmingly, respondents shared that lecturing does not work and is not engaging, causing them to zone out or not pay attention during class. People shared that roleplay or talking through real-life scenarios, videos, and smaller discussion groups were much more effective ways of teaching neurodivergent students. They also emphasized the need for engaging and accurate visual aids, lots of space for questions, and more wait time and processing time in general.

A critical approach for sex educators working with the ND community is to be explicit and concrete. This approach means avoiding euphemisms, not using words or phrases that might require inferencing, and using medically accurate language and clear language for sex acts, including slang terms. Many young people who are not neurodivergent get their information on sex education topics from peer groups, but since neurodivergent students are frequently excluded from peer groups, they sometimes end up learning misinformation from the media and the internet (Kohn et al., 2023; Solomon et al., 2019).

Context also matters. In an early elementary classroom, it might be logical scaffolding to start with lessons about consent and boundaries with family and friends and to introduce the idea of LGBTQ+ people and families. A fifth-grade teacher might start with a discussion on puberty and hygiene. Middle school is a great time to dive deeper into LGBTQ+ identities and to start talking about dating and relationships. The majority of sex education topics are not covered until high school and yet students benefit greatly from learning age appropriate information about these topics throughout their entire K–12 education. Even kindergarteners should be able to name all the parts of their own body, be able to say no to things that they don't want, be able to ask before they touch people, as well as have information about all of the different types of people who they will meet throughout their lives.

For planning curriculum topic areas, I recommend approaching your sex education planning by thinking about what is age appropriate and not what is developmentally appropriate. This language distinction is essential because many people assume that neurodivergent students have a different developmental age than they do an actual age, which is infantilizing. A neurodivergent ten-year-old needs to be taught information that any ten-year-old would be taught because they are also ten years old and are exposed to ten-year-old peer interactions and media and have ten-year-old bodies. Content should be differentiated and scaffolded based on the teacher's knowledge about how each student learns and those ways may be different from student to student, but it is inappropriate to be giving students of the same age different information based on assumptions about what they can and cannot understand. That is a widespread mistake that teachers make, but it is based upon ableist beliefs about neurodivergent students.

Key Adaptations

There are several ways to offer inclusive adapted practice in a classroom:

1. Have students practice!
2. Use activities like roleplay and act out real-life examples and scenarios to talk through, act out together, then problem-solve. This allows students to build some necessary skills (Solomon et al., 2019; Sullivan & Caterino, 2008).
3. Ensure that you give students explicit feedback during these activities so that they know what they are doing well and what they might need to adapt or learn.
4. Give clear and kind feedback if/when they do something in class or roleplay that may be perceived as inappropriate or unsafe.
5. Celebrate, affirm, and validate when they work it out in a way that would lead to success in a dating or romantic situation.

Critical Topics

One of the key topics that research respondents noted as relevant and important was how to date and build romantic relationships. Dating and romance involve understanding social nuance and making social inferences, which is challenging for neurodivergent, especially Autistic, individuals. (Hannah & Stagg, 2016; Kohn et al., 2023; MacKenzie, 2018; Solomon et al., 2019). Sex and dating both involve sets of skills that need practicing, and neurodivergent people might require more practice. While an effective sex ed curriculum discusses critical skills involved in sex, the majority of those skills cannot be practiced in a classroom setting. Many dating skills, however, can and should be practiced in a classroom setting in a neurodivergent affirming way.

Discussing sexual and romantic relationships and practicing the skills that accompany them is also a great time to reinforce content about consent and boundaries. It is important to think about consent and boundaries in terms of all relationships, which a comprehensive lesson on these topics can make clear. These consent lessons should happen as early in elementary school as possible. Even elementary school students need to learn about and understand consent and boundaries in the context of their relationships with friends and family. Consent and boundaries are highly relevant in all types of relationships, not just sexual and romantic ones.

Consent and boundaries should be a continuous discussion for all young people whether or not they are neurodivergent, and neurodivergent individuals must get explicit information on this topic. Someone might show that they are comfortable or uncomfortable during sex and might communicate that through body language or certain facial expressions. Deciphering facial expressions and body language can be trickier for neurodivergent people, and they might require explicit instruction on what the body language or facial expressions during both of these experiences might look like. Pictures, drawings, videos, and other visual aids can be a great teaching tool for helping to identify nonverbal cues related to consent and boundaries (Solomon et al., 2019).

Not only is it imperative to teach these populations of young people about boundaries and consent so that they can make reports if/when someone breaches their consent or crosses their boundaries, but it also helps prevent them from potentially breaching someone else's consent or crossing someone else's boundaries (Solomon et al., 2019). As mentioned earlier in the chapter, sexual violence and abuse are entirely too common for the disability community, and disabled young people need to be aware of what crosses the line and know how to advocate for themselves if/when that happens. It is also just overwhelmingly important for neurodivergent people, as well as everyone, to have knowledge about and feel empowered in making choices about their own bodies.

Conclusion

After reading this chapter, sex educators might wonder how to begin creating a neurodivergent-affirming sex education classroom. I wish I could tell you that the next step was to find a pre-existing Autistic sex education curriculum and implement it in your classroom, but unfortunately, I have not found a comprehensive sex education curriculum I would fully recommend, and I am still in the process of writing mine. However, several critical steps and adaptations can be done starting today.

First, make sure that content is taught through an intersectional lens. Yes, the focus of this chapter is on how to teach neurodivergent learners, but neurodivergence is just one part of a student's identity. Make sure that race, ethnicity, religion, age, family structure, citizenship and nationality, gender identity, sexuality, body size, ability and disability, socioeconomic background, and other intersections are all also considerations and an active part of all lessons. Individuals living at different intersections of marginalized identities need sex education instruction that is relevant and accessible to them as members of those communities, so do not forget to include information on ways that each sex education topic might impact marginalized communities in different ways. Next, make ongoing learning about effective inclusive sex ed part of your lens through which you develop your sex education skills, knowledge, and insights.

Introspective Questions for Consideration

• What do you already know about the neurodivergent students you are working with and their interests that you can use as a jumping off point to dive into sex education topics? (e.g. TV shows, special interests, etc.). How can you incorporate those interests into your lessons?

- What are some things that you learned about sexuality and relationships that worked for you or were especially helpful? And how might you adapt these key learnings for your own ND students?
- What do you wish had been done better for your sex education by your teachers or your parents? How can you bring this insight into your work with your students?
- Knowing that we live in an ableist society and were all raised with unconscious ableist bias, how are you going to work to actively unlearn that? What underlying ideas and assumptions do you need to challenge, both in yourself and in your classrooms?

References

Autistic Self Advocacy Network. (n.d.). About autism. In *Autistic self advocacy network*. Retrieved April 1, 2024, from https://Autisticadvocacy.org/about-asan/about-autism/

Curtiss, S. L., & Ebata, A. T. (2016). Building capacity to deliver sex education to individuals with autism. *Sexuality and Disability*, *34*, 27–47.

Holmes, L. G., & SIECUS: Sex Ed for Social Change. (2021). *A call to action: Youth with disabilities need inclusive sex education* [White paper]. SIECUS. Retrieved from https://siecus.org/wp-content/uploads/2021/03/SIECUS-2021-Youth-with-Disabilities-CTA-1.pdf

Hannah, L. A., & Stagg, S. D. (2016). Experiences of sex education and sexual awareness in young adults with autism spectrum disorder. *Journal of Autism and Developmental Disorders*, *46*, 3678–3687.

Kohn, B. H., Vidal, P., Chiao, R., Pantalone, D. W., & Faja, S. (2023). Sexual knowledge, experiences, and pragmatic language in adults with and without autism: Implications for sex education. *Journal of Autism and Developmental Disorders*, *53*(10), 3770–3786.

MacKenzie, A. (2018). Prejudicial stereotypes and testimonial injustice: Autism, sexuality and sex education. *International Journal of Educational Research*, *89*, 110–118.

Solomon, D., Pantalone, D. W., & Faja, S. (2019). Autism and adult sex education: A literature review using the information–motivation–behavioral skills framework. *Sexuality and Disability*, *37*, 339–351.

Sullivan, A., & Caterino, L. C. (2008). Addressing the sexuality and sex education of individuals with autism spectrum disorders. In J. K. Luiselli, D. C. Russo, W. P. Christian, & S. M. Wilczynski (Eds.), *Effective practices for children with autism: Educational and behavioral support interventions that work* (pp. 381–394). Oxford University Press.

Walker, N. (2022, July 19). Neurodiversity: Some basic terms & definitions. *Neuroqueer*. https://neuroqueer.com/neurodiversity-terms-and-definitions/

17 Sex Education for People with IDD

Concrete Strategies for Increasing Accessibility

Isabella Weber, Quinn Vermillion, and Sarah Dahlston

Note: the authors have chosen to use both person-first and pride-first language. Person-first language emphasizes the person before the disability, for example "person with IDD." Pride-first language emphasizes an identity first, for example "disabled person" or "Autistic person." Both options are equally appropriate depending on what a person prefers.

Key Terms

- **Intellectual and Developmental Disability (IDD):** IDD is a term that indicates the presence of an intellectual disability in addition to other developmental disabilities in a person. Developmental disabilities are differences that affect a person's physical, intellectual, and/or emotional development. Some of the most common developmental disabilities are Autism Spectrum Disorder, Cerebral Palsy, Down Syndrome, Fetal Alcohol Syndrome, and Spina Bifida, which may or may not be accompanied by an intellectual disability.
- **Social Model of Disability:** the concept of the social model of disability was developed in 1983 by Mike Oliver. This model identifies failures in the way society is organized as responsible for the problems that disabled people encounter (Oliver, 1990).
- **Disability Justice:** building on the disability rights movement, the performance project Sins Invalid coined the term Disability Justice in 2005. This term examines and recognizes the intersectionality of disability and other marginalized identities and aims to secure rights for disabled people.
- **Dignity of Risk:** this term describes the right of people to make their own life choices, even if it could have negative outcomes. The dignity of risk gives people the agency to take risks, make mistakes, and learn from them.

DOI: 10.4324/9781032615479-21

Barriers to Sex Education for People With IDD

All people, including disabled people, deserve access to sexual health information, as well as education about bodily autonomy, consent, healthy relationships, and self-advocacy. Access to comprehensive sex education increases appreciation of sexual diversity, expands understanding of gender and gender norms, reduces dating violence, increases positive bystander behaviors, and increases knowledge and skills for healthy relationships, personal safety, and touch (Goldfarb & Lieberman, 2020).

Despite the importance of comprehensive sex education, people with IDD are often excluded from sex education classrooms and conversations. They are less likely to learn about sexuality from their peers, parents, teachers, and health care providers than people without disabilities (Holmes, 2021). Numerous factors create barriers to sex education for people with IDD, such as:

Social and societal barriers:

- Disabled people are viewed as either asexual and/or infantile and not in need of sex education or as hypersexual, with their sexuality viewed as deviant and something to control (Treacy et al., 2018)
- People with IDD experience social isolation at higher rates than people without disabilities, leading to less opportunity to practice healthy relationship skills with peers (Lawsin, 2023)
- Parents are often anxious about teaching sex education to their children with disabilities and don't feel prepared to determine what content should be taught or in what manner (Treacy et al., 2018)
- Sex education for people with IDD is often reactive rather than proactive, occurring in reaction to an incident of inappropriate behavior (Treacy et al., 2018)

Education system barriers:

- Health educators often lack training in teaching students with disabilities, while educators with expertise in teaching students with disabilities lack training in health and sex education. Teachers may also be fearful of parental reactions to sex education being taught in school to their children with disabilities (Treacy et al., 2018)
- Educators with experience teaching sex education often lack the skills or confidence to teach information specifically relevant to LGBTQ+ students. People with IDD don't have access to experienced sex educators with the skills and knowledge needed to be inclusive of LGBTQ+ students (Treacy et al., 2018)
- People with IDD may be excluded from sex education classes intentionally or circumstantially in order to receive other services (physical therapy, occupational therapy, speech therapy, etc.)

Health care barriers:

- Disabled people's reproductive rights may be overlooked or denied through contraceptive coercion or coercive sterilization (Lawsin, 2023)
- Sexual dysfunction may be assumed to be a product of the disability, which leads to people with IDD not accessing care or providers not providing treatment for dysfunction (Lawsin, 2023)

Policy barriers:

- There are no federal – and few state – standards regarding sex education for people with IDD. With no standards, education systems aren't held accountable to provide this important information to people with IDD in a way that is accessible (Treacy et al., 2018)
- In tandem with a lack of standards, there is a lack of funding for sex education programs for people with IDD, which means very few schools or communities are able to provide this education (Treacy et al., 2018)

As a result of these barriers, a lack of sex education leaves people with IDD particularly vulnerable to experiencing sexual abuse or assault. If people with IDD are not taught bodily autonomy, they may not know that they are experiencing abuse or how to report abuse. In addition, without this knowledge, people with IDD may unintentionally become perpetrators of sexual violence (Shearer, 2019).

People with IDD experience some of the highest rates of psychological, physical, and sexual abuse. Adults with disabilities are seven times more likely to be sexually assaulted than their non-disabled peers (Lawsin, 2023). Children with disabilities are four times more likely to be sexually abused than their non-disabled peers (Treacy et al., 2018).

Therefore, it's crucial that educators break down these barriers through comprehensive sex education for people with IDD. In a systematic review of the literature, focusing on the voices of people with IDD on the issue of sex education, Brown and McCann (2018) found that people with IDD want sex education to focus on knowledge and skills for enhancing relationships and sexuality, not just on preventing the negative consequences of sex. People with IDD expressed a desire to have control over developing and maintaining relationships and wanted information about setting boundaries and making informed decisions. They also desired a person-centered approach where families and professionals supported them in exploring and expressing their sexuality.

This chapter will equip emerging and experienced sex educators with foundational skills for creating and adapting sex education lessons to be accessible to people with IDD.

Considerations and Strategies for Facilitating Sex Education for People With IDD

The Medical Model vs the Social Model of Disability

There are two main models of disability: the medical and social models. The medical model views disability as caused by a deficiency or abnormality within the person. In 1983, disabled academic Mike Oliver introduced the social model of disability, putting a name to concepts published in a 1976 pamphlet by the Union of the Physically Impaired Against Segregation. The concept that it is social inequities that disable people is in direct opposition to the narrative that a person's differences are what disable them (Oliver, 1990). According to the social model, the problems that disabled people face result from isolation, discrimination, and a lack of services, which create an inaccessible world. Therefore, changes to societal structures are the solution to enhancing the lives of disabled people.

The social model does not posit that with enough social change, there will be no more disability. Rather, disability is a "long-term social state" that is not in need of a cure (Oliver, 1990). However, the social *barriers* that people with disabilities face in our society can and should be removed.

Consider a person with Autism at the hairdresser: the medical model attributes their difficulty interacting with the hairdresser to their sensory sensitivities. The social model, however, points to the salon's rigid expectations (e.g., tolerating touch, small talk, sitting still) as the barrier. By offering accommodations like lower lighting, built-in breaks, forgoing small talk, and no music, salons can make haircuts accessible without compromising service. Similarly, sex education can be made accessible to more people by modifying teaching methods while preserving key content.

Educators Must Adopt the Social Model of Disability

Educators must lean into the social model of disability and adjust the learning design and environment to ensure it is accessible to people with IDD. Educators should meaningfully represent people with IDD in materials and activities. Inclusion approaches include offering parent/guardian education opportunities, increasing accessibility to materials by adapting them to meet the needs of the learner(s), ensuring access to competent health care providers, and providing culturally relevant and accessible sexual health resources.

In a classroom of students with IDD, students have varying strengths and need for support around verbal communication, reading, and writing skills. Educators who are uncomfortable teaching sex education often fall into the trap of using overly vague language, relying on euphemisms, or limited descriptions of the concepts. Conversely, educators' language may be overly technical, relying heavily on scientific terms and descriptions in order to mitigate their own discomfort with the topics. Below are some examples that illustrate different ways to teach concepts in sex education to meet the needs of students with IDD. Note that strategies and adaptations vary widely and are dependent on the audience. No one set of adaptations is effective for all audiences.

Lesson: Correct Condom Use

When demonstrating correct external condom usage, a sex educator often talks through the steps of using a condom while demonstrating on a penis model. Some learners may benefit from adaptations to help them learn the sequence of the steps:

- **Chaining:** print picture cards that illustrate the steps to condom use. Ask learners to put them in the correct order.
- **Multiple Choices:** help the learner build out the process of using a condom by showing two cards and asking, "which step comes next?"
- **Simplified Chaining:** have students place picture cards of condom use steps into categories of "before sex," "during sex," and "after sex."
- **Identifying the Errors:** demonstrate condom use with intentional errors. Instruct students to identify the incorrect steps.

Lesson: Understanding Consent

Consent lessons typically focus on the importance of getting consent for all sexual activities but assume that students are already skilled in expressing and interpreting thoughts and desires with words and/or body language. Students with disabilities may have more difficulty judging whether a given written statement signifies consent. Adaptations to this lesson might include instructors providing tangible examples that allow students to picture the whole scenario, see the body language, and recognize the intonations in someone's voice/signing.

- **Instructor Role Play:** with two instructors, act out low-stakes touch requests (e.g. high fives, fist bumps) and model asking for the touch and have a co-teacher give a variety of answers. Students decide if consent was present in each example
- **Role Play with Pictures:** show an image of two people who are standing close and looking at each other. Roleplay a consent conversation by shifting your position to show who is talking. Students decide if consent was present in each example
- **Props:** use puppets to act out touch requests and encourage students to pay attention to words and body language. A benefit of puppets is that they can do things colleagues cannot (e.g. kiss)

- **Identifying Emotions:** give students examples of different facial expressions and body language, either by demonstrating them or by showing images. Ask students to guess what is being communicated
- **Videos:** watch a (non-sexual) video where people ask each other for consent. Have students raise their hands when they see consent given or body language/words ignored

Lesson: Public vs Private

Recognizing the behaviors that are appropriate in public and private places requires social awareness and helps people understand what behaviors are safe and expected in certain places. It is important to present the material in a way that students can take away the main message without getting lost in the gray areas. Depending on how much nuance students can understand/perceive, educators might choose to teach public/private with adaptations such as these:

- **Concrete Categorization:** explain the difference between public and private by outlining that behaviors involving private parts *must* happen in a private place
- **Clarify Exceptions:** distinguish between public places, private places, and places like the locker room or doctor's office where certain private behaviors can happen (e.g. taking off clothes). Have students practice sorting place cards into these three categories
- **Use Familiar Images:** use images from students' lives to discuss what is appropriate in a given public or private place. Show the images and instruct students to determine if certain behaviors (e.g. pulling down pants, masturbating, using the toilet) are safe and expected in that place

In addition to leaning into the social model, educators, families, and disability-serving professionals can practice dignity of risk, which is the belief that people have the right to make their own life choices, make mistakes, and learn from them. Often, family members and support staff may feel that they know what is best for someone. They may prevent a person from making a choice for fear of negative consequences. Dignity of risk is equipping people with IDD with knowledge, skills, and confidence, while allowing informed choices, even if there could be negative outcomes. Educators, families, and support staff can lead with dignity. For example, a person with IDD may want to become a parent. Instead of categorically telling them why they cannot, take time to explain the nuances of having and raising a child and provide opportunities for the person to practice parenting skills. The goal is to ensure people can make informed decisions about their lives.

Additional Factors for Consideration and Approach

Evidence-based interventions (EBIs) are rigorously tested sex education programs that have proven positive outcomes for students who participate in them. Although these are the gold standard for sex education programming, EBIs often require significant adaptations in order to be accessible to people with IDD. Sometimes, these programs might require adaptation to the extent that the EBI can no longer be implemented with fidelity, i.e. maintaining the core components of the program. It may be more reasonable to use and adapt a program specifically designed for people with IDD, rather than attempt to adapt an EBI and claim that it can be implemented with fidelity.

Traditional program evaluation techniques may not translate well to sex education programs for people with IDD. Rather than focusing evaluation efforts on knowledge acquisition, evaluation of programs for people with IDD may focus on affective changes such as an increased comfort with the topic or knowledge application such as demonstrating a skill learned in class. This might involve asking students before class to raise their hand if they feel comfortable talking about private parts and then asking the same question at the end of class to assess the change. When writing proposals for funding, note how the program will be evaluated in a way that is accessible for people with IDD and what metrics will be used to measure affective changes and demonstration of new skills.

One of the essential tenets of the disability justice movement is "nothing about us, without us." It is important for educators creating sex education content for people with IDD to develop materials in partnership with people with IDD, their parents, and families (McCann et al., 2019). Involving people with IDD and their families in the creation of sex education content ensures that it is accessible and will directly apply to – or impact the lives of – people with IDD.

Introspective Questions for Consideration

- Where do I see the social model of disability showing up in my work? Where might I still be supporting a medical model of disability?
- Think about one sex education topic or lesson you feel confident teaching – what adaptations would you make to ensure it is more accessible to people with IDD?
- How can I meaningfully include people with IDD and their families in the planning, creation, recruitment, facilitation, and/or evaluation of my sex education lesson or program?
- What are the areas where I have existing knowledge on this topic, and what do I still need to learn? How can my mentors and colleagues help me explore my professional training needs?

References

Brown, M., & McCann, E. (2018). Sexuality issues and the voices of adults with intellectual disabilities: A systematic review of the literature. *Research in Developmental Disabilities, 74*, 124–138. https://doi.org/10.1016/j.ridd.2018.01.009

Goldfarb, E., & Lieberman, L. (2020). Three decades of research: The case for comprehensive sex education. *Journal of Adolescent Health, 68*(1), 13–27. https://doi.org/10.1016/j.jadohealth.2020.07.036

Holmes, L. G. (2021). Comprehensive sex education for youth with disabilities: A call to action. In *SIECUS: Sex ed for social change*. https://siecus.org/wp-content/uploads/2021/03/SIECUS-2021-Youth-with-Disabilities-CTA-1.pdf

Lawsin, C. (2023). Sex ed for people with disabilities is almost non-existent. Here's why that needs to change. *USA Today*. https://www.usatoday.com/story/life/health-wellness/2023/08/16/disabled-sex-education/70500471007/

McCann, E., Marsh, L., & Brown, M. (2019). People with intellectual disabilities, relationship and sex education programmes: A systematic review. *Health Education Journal, 78*(8), 885–900. https://doi.org/10.1177/0017896919856047

Oliver, M. (1990). *The individual and social models of disability*. Presented at the Joint Workshop of the Living Options Group and the Research Unit of the Royal College of Physicians. https://disability-studies.leeds.ac.uk/wp-content/uploads/sites/40/library/Oliver-in-soc-dis.pdf

Shearer, N. (2019). Sexual health education for individuals with disabilities: A call to action. *Nevada Today*. https://www.unr.edu/nevada-today/news/2019/sexual-health-for-individuals-with-disabilities

Treacy, A. C., Taylor, S. S., & Abernathy, T. V. (2018). Sexual health education for individuals with disabilities: A call to action. *American Journal of Sexuality Education, 13*(1), 65–93. https://doi.org/10.1080/15546128.2017.1399492

18 Integrating Porn Literacy Into Sex Education

N. Jasmine Johnson

Porn Literacy is an educational framework that helps people develop critical thinking skills to analyze and understand the content, messages, and impact of pornography. It aims to promote media literacy by raising awareness of how pornography influences ideas about sex, relationships, consent, body image, and gender roles. Additionally, Porn Literacy encourages discussions about sexual health, consent, and ethics, empowering individuals to make informed decisions about their sexual attitudes and behaviors while recognizing the difference between fantasy and real-life sexual experiences.

The purpose of this chapter is to provide sex educators with approaches for addressing pornography by integrating diverse teaching methods for both youth and adults. Given the widespread availability of pornography and how attitudes and behaviors are shaped through portrayals in media, it is essential to equip sex educators with the necessary skills to manage its complexities from a sex-positive perspective. This chapter aims to explore strategies for fostering safety and critical thinking when and if pornography is encountered. Sex educators can integrate these practical tools immediately, creating space for open conversations about sexuality, identities, and boundaries.

Porn "In Practice"

Porn in Practice is a strategy that empowers professionals and caregivers, especially educators, to address pornography through **Porn Literacy** and a sex-positive framework, avoiding shame or avoidance of the topic. This approach acknowledges the influence of pornography on attitudes and beliefs while encouraging critical thinking about its content whether visual, audio, or literary. Importantly, it does not involve bringing explicit content into the classroom but rather equips educators with tools to discuss the broader impact and influence of such material in an appropriate and thoughtful way.

In our society, pornography often sits at the crossroads of controversy and misunderstanding. Misunderstandings can pathologize normal sexual curiosity and exploration, stigmatize consumers and creators, oversimplify the complexity

DOI: 10.4324/9781032615479-22

of human sexual expression and agency, and overlook its potential to celebrate sexual liberation, expressions, and diversity. The purpose of this chapter is to offer sex educators approaches when preparing to discuss pornography and ways to integrate diverse teaching methods to youth and adults.

> The topic of pornography can produce intense emotional responses serving as a mirror reflecting our anxieties about sex and intimacy. Engaging with this topic requires confronting personal biases and societal taboos that shape our understanding of what is normative and acceptable. As you navigate through this section, consider how your background, experiences, and professional training influence your views on pornography. Reflect on how these perceptions might impact your ability to provide balanced, informed, and comprehensive care. Addressing these biases is crucial to fostering a healthy discourse for Porn Literacy.

Common Misconceptions About Pornography

Pornography is often surrounded by misconceptions that shape public perception and beliefs, leading to misunderstandings about oneself, relationships with others, sexual expectations, and relationships. Below are some common misconceptions about pornography, along with recommended corrections that offer a more nuanced view.

- *Misconception: pornography inevitably leads to addiction.*
  - Correction: pornography itself does not inherently cause addiction. Problematic consumption often reflects underlying personal or psychological issues rather than being the cause (Duffy et al., 2016).

- *Misconception: watching pornography negatively impacts all relationships.*
  - Correction: the impact of pornography on relationships varies widely. Constructive communication and mutual consent are vital to integrating pornography into a healthy sexual lifestyle. Literature highlights diverse outcomes based on individual and couple dynamics, including outcomes that the use of pornography together reports more open communication and greater relationship closeness (Kohut et al., 2018).

- *Misconception: pornography promotes unrealistic expectations about sex.*
  - Correction: while some genres may showcase exaggerated scenarios, an intentional consumer can find a range of body presentation and sexual dynamics. Distinguishing between fantasy and realistic presentations in entertainment is essential, with media literacy education playing an

important role. The inability to decipher performative sexual behavior from personal interaction is so necessary to why Porn Literacy must be included as an evolving objective in education.

- *Misconception:* all pornography promotes abusive dynamics in BDSM, objectifies performers through racial stereotypes, and enforces traditional gender power roles.

  - Correction: while much pornography misrepresents or presents these dynamics without proper context – such as BDSM, racial stereotypes, and unequal gender power roles – it's important to recognize that not all content does this. Porn Literacy helps individuals discern between harmful portrayals and content that aligns with more respectful and realistic representations.

These and other misconceptions demonize pornography as merely a vice, ignoring its potential to celebrate sexual liberation and diversity. This perspective harms those who produce and consume adult content and impedes educators, therapists, and caregivers – from providing comprehensive support due to shame. Dismantling these nuanced narratives allows a broader dialogue and plan forward about its role in society and how it can be used for inspiration and entertainment.

Activity: think about a myth or belief you had growing up about entertainment (movies, music, etc.). Did you believe it to be true, or did you just accept it without question? Once you learned the truth, how did it change your perspective?

Research and Theory

Addressing adolescent pornography consumption, from the perspective of sex-positive education, is critical given the high level of engagement. Despite an increase in efforts that aim to restrict access to pornography (Free Speech Coalition, 2023), research shows that about 68.4% of US adolescents have encountered online pornography, with 42% of youths aged 10 to 17 viewing such materials (Jhe et al., 2023). Additionally, studies show that around 60% of adults in the US have consumed pornography, with 87% of men and 31% of women reporting viewing pornography (Carroll et al., 2008). These demonstrate the need for accessible education that centers on sexual autonomy, consent, and sex/relationship positive communication and interactions.

Porn Literacy in Practice Across the Life Span

Like all aspects of human development, sexual attitudes and behaviors change over time. Recognizing that many adults have experienced the impact of pornography without Porn Literacy emphasizes the importance of offering retrospective education and a sense of urgency to course correct for future generations. Porn Literacy recognizes aspects of ageism, harmful gender roles, and unrealistic or stereotypical representations of sex on the continuum.

Tailoring Sexual Health Education: Age Appropriateness and Adult Readiness

Effective sexual education hinges on identifying and addressing the specific needs of different age groups, backgrounds, and abilities. By delivering education that centers on Porn Literacy, sex positivity, and safe online engagement, we ensure that individuals receive information appropriate to their readiness.

For Children: Emphasizing Age Appropriateness

- Developmentally sensitive approach: tailor discussions on body safety, boundaries, and consent to be comprehensible and non-overwhelming
- Empowering autonomy: teach children to assert their boundaries respectfully, such as the right to decline physical affection, emphasizing the importance of consent and personal space
- Interactive tools: show age appropriate character clips that either respect or violate boundaries. Discuss how they would feel in those situations, prompting discussion on recognizing when something doesn't feel right. Encourage them to develop language to describe feelings around boundaries and establish their own likes and dislikes

For Teens: Addressing Complex Social Dynamics

- Role-playing exercises: simulate real-life situations, such as peer pressure, to practice assertiveness and decision-making about personal boundaries. Create open ended discussions where teens share their scenarios as it relates to consent, communication, and realistic relationships
- Interactive tools: incorporate digital games that simulate social scenarios, highlighting the difference between realistic and unrealistic portrayals of relationships. Invite analysis to these portrayals, helping them identify what feels authentic and what distorts their understanding of relationships and consent, ultimately enhancing their Porn Literacy

For Adults: Enhancing Understanding and Communication

- Sessions on relationships: delve into interpersonal relationships, exploring consent and boundaries in various contexts
- Scenario-based learning: challenge adults to articulate needs and negotiate boundaries, enhancing their understanding of healthy relationship dynamics

- Interactive tools: show clips of popular media portrayals of intimacy and sex and reflect on how these portrayals can or have created unrealistic expectations. Further the conversation on how these types of portrayals show up in adult content

Adopting a structured approach that addresses developmental stages with specific objectives and strategies promotes comprehensive sexual health education. It ensures that learners of all ages not only receive appropriate instruction but also develop critical thinking skills to navigate media, including pornography, in a healthy and informed way.

Working With Parents and Caregivers on Porn Literacy

Parents and caregivers are influential teachers for young people about the exposure to all kinds of media including pornography. Modeling conversations about consent, boundaries, and healthy relationships while implementing technology safeguards provides a framework for developmentally appropriate sexual development. Clarifying the differences between an adult entertainment performance, biased casting, and real-life relationships helps demystify sexual content, therefore reducing its impact on attitudes and behaviors.

When working with parents and caregivers, sex educators are advised to first check in with them on their own values, attitudes, and beliefs as they relate to pornography. An example of a reflective question to encourage this self-examination can be, "How do your personal beliefs about pornography shape the way you talk to your child about consent, boundaries and relationships?" Supporting this self-assessment can frame their internal starting point towards conscious and effective communication with young people.

As parents and caregivers begin to feel more comfortable with their own understanding, they can simultaneously approach age appropriate discussions with their children. Here are some prompts to encourage critical thinking about sensitive media and how it relates to real-life interactions:

- "How did seeing that interaction make you feel?"
- "What was missing from that interaction?"
- "What types of interactions are appropriate for someone your age?"
- "Are there any stops we can take to avoid you having to see that type of content until you are old enough and want to see or learn about it?"

Using these prompt styles can help initiate meaningful conversations and affirm that children and parent's learning process can evolve together.

Sex educators have an opportunity to equip parents and caregivers with tools and knowledge about sex, porn, and online safety for their child. When they approach these conversations with confidence and care, they promote healthy attitudes towards sexuality and safe online behaviors. The following are focus areas for guiding parents and caregivers through this complex landscape.

1. *Promoting a Positive View of Sex:* by learning to highlight the healthy, comprehensive aspects of sexuality, parents and caregivers reduce shame and societal taboos
2. *Improving Online Safety:* teach privacy settings, safe browsing practices and tools, and responsible engagement with online content
3. *Teaching Body Autonomy and Consent:* equip parents with the skills to teach their children to respect their bodies and the boundaries of others, including emotional boundaries
4. *Sustaining Conversations:* support the planning of starting and maintaining age-appropriate discussions about sexual content at each stage of child development Encourage parents to maintain open communication and answer questions honestly, prioritizing safety, the child's emotional and mental development, age-appropriateness, and when appropriate, with the support of a professional, including a coach! This approach not only fosters a deeper understanding of sexual health and relationships but also builds trust, making it more likely that children will turn to their parents/trusted caregivers if they encounter inappropriate content or interactions.

Additional Considerations When Working With Parents and Caregivers

- Open Forums: create spaces where children feel safe discussing online content, ensuring they can approach their guardians without fear of judgment or punishment
- Educational Sessions for Adults: provide adults with sessions to explore their beliefs about sexuality to challenge misconceptions and discrepancies between media portrayals and real-life sexual experiences for a more open, informed perspective

Empowering Digital Awareness With Children and Youth

Clear labeling and responsible access controls for adult content while educating children and youth about the internet's potential challenges and benefits is crucial. Here are strategies empowering students with digital awareness:

1. While it's essential to set firm boundaries for underage individuals from inappropriate content, it's equally essential to oppose overly restrictive censorship laws that can harm sex workers and limit diverse expressions for consenting adults. This delicate balance requires informed advocacy to maintain rights and protections without stifling free expression of some of our most vulnerable and marginalized members of the workforce

2. Use age-appropriate role-playing exercises and lessons on privacy settings to teach indicators of risky online behavior or content. For example, an educator could simulate a scenario where a student encounters a "suspicious pop-up ad," guide the student in safely closing it and reporting it, and discuss why some content can be inappropriate, confusing, or curious. Additionally, provide resources, such as online safety guides or direct students to a trusted adult or counselor for additional support.

3. Encourage students to share experiences in a supportive, non-judgmental environment. For instance, a small group discussion could include students anonymously sharing experiences about encountering "inappropriate or uncomfortable" online content, followed by guidance on handling similar situations. This practice helps recognize the importance of seeking support without shame. When educators create and facilitate this space, they acknowledge students' likely exposure to sensitive media while teaching them how to disengage and seek trusted guidance. As promoted by the Family Online Safety Institute, open communication is a key strategy for fostering such an environment (Family Online Safety Institute, n.d.).

4. Discuss the nature of pornography and other adult content sensitively without any exposure:

   - Curiosity discussions: begin with broad discussions on internet safety, gradually introducing the concept of encountering inappropriate content. For example, "The internet has a lot of information, but not all is appropriate for your age. Let's talk about recognizing and avoiding content not meant for you. If you have questions or are curious about things you hear or see online, you can always come to me to talk about them without feeling embarrassed or worried."
   - Role-playing Scenarios: role-play a child accidentally clicking on a misleading link. Discuss the immediate steps to take, such as closing the window and informing a trusted adult, reinforcing that it's not their fault
   - Use of Age-Appropriate Analogies: simplify complex issues by using familiar comparisons, such as explaining inappropriate content as "similar to movies or games rated for adults," which helps children understand why certain online materials are unsuitable
   - Establishing Open Communication: regularly invite open-ended discussions about what children see online or discuss with others, ensuring they can discuss anything unusual or confusing without fear of shame or judgment

---

Understanding Ethical Practices in Media for Transferable Skills

In adult sex education, there is a growing emphasis on teaching how to inform consumers of ethically produced, sex-positive adult content by exploring legal production practices, fair labor standards, and authentic representation. This focus would not be appropriate to introduce to non-adult students; however, we can teach how to evaluate all media critically.

Combining myth debunking with empowerment techniques is essential. One approach to help students differentiate between accurate information and misleading portrayals is through interactive discussions. Encourage students to question the media they consume, exploring how it shapes their views on consent, representation, and power dynamics/roles. Incorporate critical viewing exercises that empower students to recognize stereotypes and negative or unrealistic portrayals, using prompts like. . .

- "Are any groups of people shown in a way that seems unfair or not true to real life?"
- "How could that change how we think about them?"
- "How might watching this commercial, show or movie change your thoughts about relationships or yourself?"

These discussions foster media literacy skills that help create a pathway for students to engage critically with media and challenge unhealthy ideas about self and relationships.

Empowering Adults: Using Pornography as a Coaching Tool

Pornography can serve as a medium to uncover desires, reframe narratives around sexuality, and facilitate neutral discussions that do not directly involve the sharing of personal experiences. This approach allows for a non-judgmental exploration of sexuality, helping adult students articulate their preferences and boundaries using what they know and feel about the third-party medium to facilitate a deeper dialogue. Here are some points to remember:

- Tools for Self-assessment: encourage adult students to use guided self-assessment tools, such as quizzes or reflective questionnaires, which are available through various sexual health resources and workshops. These tools can support the reflection of their feelings, behaviors, and motivations
- Guided Discussions: use pornography as a neutral topic to discuss personal feelings and thoughts about sexuality. This may sound like an open invitation, "If you'd like, we can talk openly about how porn fits into your sexual experiences"
- Education on Safe Exploration: teach adult students how to explore pornography, if they choose, in a responsible and ethical way. One tool to promote ethics is encouraging them to look into the sources of the content that interest them. You might follow up by saying, "So, when you have time, consider your style and source of porn, then ask yourself, 'Does this align with my values?' What other options are available that might better satisfy your need for entertainment or inspiration?"

Critical Viewing Practices

Encourage learners to critically analyze pornography to differentiate between harmful stereotypes and healthy expressions of sexuality. Porn Literacy will help them understand how content can influence their perspectives on sex and relationships, promoting healthier engagement with media. Identifying these common trends allows the viewer to reject the tropes and differentiate between entertainment that plays up to stereotypes and more accurate reflections of a humane sexual/intimate experience.

Expand accessibility and inclusivity by integrating discussions on gender identity, body inclusivity, race, and persons living with disabilities into educational and reference materials. To incorporate trauma informed care into sex-positive learning, facilitators should focus on creating an environment that prioritizes safety, trustworthiness, choice, collaboration, and empowerment (Fallot & Harris, 2009). Facilitators should aim to provide clear information, offer participants the choice to step away if needed, and use inclusive, person-first language. Start activities and discussion with content warnings, set non-judgmental ground rules, and have referrals to trauma-informed professionals available for extra support.

Including Porn Literacy helps add a nuanced understanding of sexuality and its diverse expressions, consent, and reality-based interpersonal relationships. Providing comprehensive, age-appropriate sex education from childhood through adulthood helps individuals navigate sexual content and relationships responsibly.

Reflective Questions for Consideration

- Develop Self-awareness: how do your methods for discussing online safety and pornography align with the comprehensive approach to sex education outlined in this chapter? Identify specific areas for improvement.
- Evaluate Policies: examine the policies affecting sex education in your setting. Are there any that need revision to support your students' diverse needs better? Propose actionable changes.
- Adapt to Diversity: how do you tailor sex education to accommodate all students' unique backgrounds, intersections, abilities, and needs? Provide examples of inclusive practices you can implement.
- Identify Gaps: assess any gaps in your current educational approach. What specific areas need enhancements to provide a more comprehensive and inclusive education?
- Address Sensitive Topics: consider your comfort and preparedness in addressing gender identity, body inclusivity, kinks, and or explicit feelings related to sex/intimacy. What resources and training do you need to improve your competency in these areas?

Acknowledgments

Gratitude to King Noire, Jessica Nater, Dr. Nicole Crawford, Anne Hodder-Shipp, The Gordans, Marcia Pinkett-Heller, Nanay, our DOPE children Mani, Star, Majesty, and Royal for their invaluable contributions to the Sex Positive Parenting initiative.

References

Carroll, J. S., Padilla-Walker, L. M., Nelson, L. J., Olson, C. D., McNamara Barry, C., & Madsen, S. D. (2008). Generation XXX: Pornography acceptance and use among emerging adults. *Journal of Adolescent Research, 23*(1), 6–30. https://doi.org/10.1177/0743558407306348

Duffy, A., Dawson, D. L., & das Nair, R. (2016). Pornography addiction in adults: A systematic review of definitions and reported impact. *The Journal of Sexual Medicine, 13*(5), 760–777. https://doi.org/10.1016/j.jsxm.2016.03.002

Fallot, R. D., & Harris, M. (2009). *Creating cultures of trauma-informed care (CCTIC): A self-assessment and planning protocol.* Community Connections.

Family Online Safety Institute. (n.d.). *Family Online Safety Institute.* Retrieved from https://www.fosi.org

Free Speech Coalition. (2023). *2023 annual report.* Free Speech Coalition. https://www.freespeechcoalition.com

Jhe, G. B., Addison, J., Lin, J., & Pluhar, E. (2023). Pornography use among adolescents and the role of primary care. *Family Medicine and Community Health, 11*(1). https://doi.org/10.1136/fmch-2022-001776

Kohut, T., Balzarini, R. N., Fisher, W. A., & Campbell, L. (2018). Pornography's associations with open sexual communication and relationship closeness vary as a function of dyadic patterns of pornography use within heterosexual relationships. *Journal of Social and Personal Relationships, 35*(4), 655–676. https://doi.org/10.1177/0265407517743096

19 Hoes Need Help, Too

Navigating Stigma and Violence as Societal Barriers to Sex Workers

Danielle Simpson-Baker

Key Terms

- **Sex Work:** the consensual exchange of sexual services for money or goods.
- **Whorephobia:** discrimination or prejudice against sex workers.
- **Bronfenbrenner's Ecological Model:** a theoretical framework illustrating the interconnected layers influencing an individual within a social context.
- **Decriminalization:** the removal of legal penalties and criminal sanctions associated with sex work.

In the field of sexology, sex work is both resilient and controversial, deserving special attention in sex education. It embodies bodily autonomy, a core principle in human sexuality education. This chapter defines sex work historically and presently, highlighting societal barriers like stigma and violence. It also offers guidance for sex educators on dismantling these barriers.

Sex work, often called "the world's oldest profession," has ancient roots dating back to at least 2400 BC, challenging the idea that it's a recent phenomenon. While Rudyard Kipling may have exaggerated by calling it the "world's oldest profession," this phrase reflects its enduring presence throughout history. Sex workers have made significant contributions to society, such as enriching the field of sexology and playing key roles in historic events like the Stonewall riots. Today, sex work is part of the "side hustle" culture, challenging traditional work perceptions. In the UK, many university students turn to sex work to quickly pay bills, prompting a reevaluation of the socioeconomic factors behind such decisions (Prostitution, 2020; Kipling, 1909; Walker, 2023).

While sex workers have shaped both academic discourse and contemporary cultures, they endure deep-seated societal biases, presenting a paradox between the stigmatization they face and the societal influence they've inspired. This paradox underscores the need for nuanced exploration, acknowledging both historical significance and the challenges faced by those involved. Despite societal contributions, sex workers have faced systemic stigma and violence for centuries. This chapter's thesis emphasizes dismantling this stigma and violence,

DOI: 10.4324/9781032615479-23

asserting the importance of this process for fostering inclusive and supportive spaces within sex education. Stigma and violence act as barriers to access of essential resources, leading sex workers to be more likely to have poor mental health outcomes and lower quality of life (Bloomquist & Sprankle, 2019; Martin-Romo et al., 2023). Thus, addressing the destigmatization of sex work becomes crucial when discussing topics like sexual liberation and even decolonization. This chapter provides a blueprint for sex educators wanting to engage in these conversations and examine their roles as either a perpetuator of stigma or a force for positive change in how we view sex work and treat sex workers.

What's in a Name?

Let's start with a clear definition. **Sex work** is the *consensual* exchange of sexual services, including but not limited to sexual acts or performances, in return for money, goods, or other benefits. The keyword, "consensual," is the main part of the definition that separates sex work from sex *trafficking*.

"Sex work" is an umbrella term, coined by Carol Leigh (1951–2022), used to describe different kinds of consensual exchanges, ranging from no contact with a client to hands-on contact. Some types of sex work include:

- Full service (i.e. prostitution, escorting)
- Sugaring (i.e., sugar baby)
- Cam modeling
- Only Fans
- Phone sex operators
- Adult film stars
- Dominatrixes
- Selling used underwear, etc.

Other forms of sex work not typically included in the nomenclature but worth mentioning include:

- Surrogate partners (formerly known sex surrogates)
- Sacred intimates
- Somatic sexuality educators

Remember that the work must be consensual to constitute sex work. Of course, there is no real consent to labor under capitalism – let's face it, no one really *wants* to work, we all just want to eat (and preferably under a roof). However, as a sex educator, it is imperative that you make the distinction between sex work and sex trafficking in all contexts. Sex work involves consensual transactions between adults, while *sex trafficking* implies force, exploitation, and coercion of individuals against their will. It's crucial to differentiate sex trafficking from consensual sex work due to the detrimental nature of trafficking.

Furthermore, we must watch our mouths when discussing sex work. Our choice of words influences our perceptions and behaviors towards a subject. Derogatory terms like "whore" and "prostitute" contribute to stigma and negative attitudes towards sex work, reinforcing harmful stereotypes. Using terms like "sex work" and "sex worker" helps to destigmatize and be respectful of those in the industry. If you hear disparaging language, especially from students, address it directly. Strategies for doing so will be provided later on in the chapter.

Stigma and Violence as Barriers

Let's define stigma and violence within the context of sex work. These forces create a formidable barrier for sex workers within our society. Here, *stigma* refers to the pervasive negative attitudes, beliefs, and stereotypes associated with individuals engaged in sex work. Stigmatization not only results in discrimination but also acts as a precursor to violence, meaning stigma perpetuates violence against sex workers. This intersectionality amplifies these challenges, pushing sex workers further to the margins of society (Schwartz et al., 2021; Singer et al., 2021; Potter et al., 2022).

Violence against sex workers includes physical harm, verbal abuse, and systemic oppression, often from those meant to protect them (e.g., police, doctors, therapists, educators). This reciprocal relationship between stigma and violence hinders their social integration, perpetuating marginalization and lack of resources. Figure 19.1 shows global data on this violence. As a sex educator, addressing these issues and your role in them is crucial for dismantling barriers and respecting sex workers' dignity and rights.

Whorephobia and the Whorearchy

Whorephobia refers to discrimination and prejudice against sex workers, involving irrational fear, hatred, or contempt. It perpetuates hostility, adding to the stigma and violence sex workers already face. *Internalized whorephobia* occurs when sex workers adopt harmful stereotypes to distance themselves from the negative connotations of their work and align with mainstream society. This internalized hatred supports the "whorearchy," which divides sex workers into hierarchical categories.

45–75%	More likely to experience sexual violence while working (Deering et al., 2014)
82%	Experience physical violence while working (Farley & Barkan, 1998)
68%	Report sexual assault while working (Farley & Barkan, 1998)
30%	Report violence or threat of violence from the police (Swift, 2022)

Figure 19.1 Violence Against Sex Workers by the Numbers

The *whorearchy* is an unofficial ranking of the different types of sex work (Figure 19.2), ranging in level of contact with the client; typically, the more contact a sex worker has with a client (bottom of the pyramid), the "dirtier" the work is considered to be and the closer to stigmatization the worker is. The problem with this is two-fold: first, there is strength in numbers. Sex workers have historically relied on their community via organizing and mutual aid for survival (Abel & Healy, 2021); thus, anything hindering solidarity is inherently harmful to sw's. Second, most people who are not sex workers tend to view us as a monolith, so the internal fighting really makes no sense from the outside looking in. While there are many reasons why some may choose not to identify as a sex worker, it is still true that this internal othering is not only harmful to all sex workers but also perpetuates the spirit of whorephobia.

Bronfenbrenner's Ecological Model (of Sex Work)

Bronfenbrenner's ecological model, developed by Urie Bronfenbrenner in 1979, offers a framework for understanding how stigma and violence against sex workers are perpetuated systemically (Härkönen, 2007). This model emphasizes considering an individual's societal environment to comprehend human development and societal attitudes. It consists of five interconnected layers: the microsystem, mesosystem, exosystem, macrosystem, and chronosystem. Each layer influences and is influenced by the others, illustrating their interdependence.

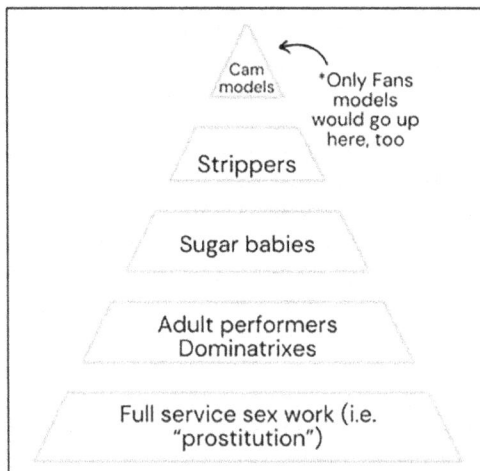

Adapted from The Sex Ed, 2022

Figure 19.2 The Whorearchy

Bronfenbrenner's Theory – What's Happening at Each Level
(Adapted From Harkonen, 2001)

1. Microsystem – Immediate environment (family, friends, peers, intimate relationships)
2. Mesosystem – Interactions between components of the microsystem
3. Exosystem – Broader social structures indirectly impacting life (local laws, community, resources, social services)
4. Macrosystem – Larger cultural and societal norms, values, ideologies (societal attitudes, religious beliefs, gender roles)
5. Chronosystem – Role of time and historical context (changes in norms, economy shifts, technological advancements)

Applying Bronfenbrenner's ecological model to sex work, we see how various systems shape perceptions and stigma. In the microsystem, individual biases, including those of sex educators, influence attitudes towards sex work, highlighting the need for self-reflection. The mesosystem examines how interactions between institutions, like schools and communities, perpetuate or challenge stigma. The exosystem includes legislative frameworks and societal norms that indirectly impact sex workers. At the macrosystem level, broader cultural ideologies influence the acceptance or marginalization of sex work. This model helps us understand systemic influences and develop strategies to combat stigma and violence in sex education.

So What? – Practical Applications

As a sex educator, you must do your part to challenge whorephobia as a way to dismantle stigma against sex workers and diminish the violence they face. You can do this by challenging the status quo on both a personal and societal level, as well as in educational spaces. This section will provide practical examples for how to do so.

A. On a Personal Level

Engage in self-reflection:

1. Remember, sex work is work! Challenge your biases by questioning assumptions and stereotypes
2. Consider the historical context and societal norms influencing perceptions of sex work in your profession
3. Evaluate and change any professional practices that may contribute to stigma to create a more inclusive and supportive environment

Educate yourself on how to be an advocate:

1. Research the decriminalization debate on sex work and understand the differences between decriminalization and legalization
2. Note that decriminalization, preferred by most sex workers, avoids restrictive regulations and has improved conditions and rights in places like New Zealand (*New Zealand: The ideal framework for decriminalized sex work*, 2023)
3. Link discussions on decriminalization to broader social justice movements
4. Study harmful legislation like FOSTA/SESTA (passed in 2018), and beneficial ones like the Prostitution Reform Act, (passed in 2003)
5. Advocate for policies prioritizing sex workers' rights and well-being, aligning with broader equity and justice movements

B. On a Societal Level . . . Leveraging Bronfenbrenner's Model

Leveraging Bronfenbrenner's ecological model, sex educators can analyze the various layers influencing stigma and violence. This enables you to develop educational practices that challenge societal norms, encourage empathy, and foster a more inclusive understanding of sex work. Chart 1 includes examples of how to take action at each societal level presented in Bronfenbrenner's theory:

C. A Note on Addressing Whorephobia in Educational Spaces

As a sex educator, you may encounter whorephobic attitudes from students or colleagues. Since sex workers come in many forms, someone may unknowingly express whorephobia in their presence. Address this by fostering an empathetic, reflective environment. Confront these attitudes directly, encouraging introspection and learning, even if it means deviating from the lesson plan. Here is a trauma-informed strategy for addressing microaggressions or whorephobia in academic settings:

1. Acknowledge the microaggression immediately, then address it privately to avoid embarrassment
2. Express empathy, emphasize the importance of addressing the issue, and use "I" statements (e.g., "I felt uncomfortable when you said X") to encourage dialogue
3. Provide specific examples to explain the impact and suggest alternative ways to convey their thoughts
4. Follow up if the microaggression occurred in your classroom

Level	What's Happening Here?	Possible Interventions
Microsystem	• Social isolation, fear to disclose • Negative labeling of sex work	• Educate family, peers • Providing safe spaces for peer support, counseling
Mesosystem	• Gossip, exclusion within social circles • Lack of communication btw law enforcement and support networks	• Creating community-based platforms for dialogue, collaboration • Developing protocols for info sharing btw support services and LE to enhance safety
Exosystem	• Discriminatory laws, criminalizing policies • Limited access to essential services	• Advocating for decriminalization, legal reform • Establishing services specifically for sex workers
Macrosystem	• Media portrayal of sex workers reinforcing negative stereotypes • Societal beliefs that devalue sex workers	• Conducting public awareness campaigns to challenge misconceptions • Encouraging people to PAY FOR THEIR PORN
Chronosystem	• Historical criminalization, moralistic attitudes • Tech advancements facilitating online harassment, exploitation	• Documenting, sharing the history of sex workers activism to raise awareness • Collaborating with tech companies to develop safer online platforms • Continuing to intervene at each level over time to create lasting change

Figure 19.3 Conceptual Model of Bronfenbrenner's Ecological Model of Sex Work

Finally, perhaps one of the most important things you can do to destigmatize sex workers is *talk to them*! Talk to sex workers about their experience (and pay them for their expertise)! If you want to know what sex work is really like, talk to those doing it. This will help to dismantle your own ideas of what sex work is and who sex workers are, further helping to destigmatize sex work altogether.

Additional Factors

In contemplating the multifaceted landscape of sex work, it is imperative to explore additional factors that extend beyond what we've discussed so far. Intersectionality and the pervasive influence of capitalism play nuanced roles in shaping the sex workers' experiences, particularly those at the intersections of race, gender identity, and socio-economic status.

Intersectionality in Sex Work

Sex work does not occur in a vacuum; rather, it intersects with various aspects of identity, amplifying the challenges faced by marginalized communities. Black and Brown sw's face heightened discrimination due to the compounding effects of racial biases and whorephobia. Trans sex workers, in particular, endure significant stigma and violence within the community, exacerbated by transphobia and whorephobia. Additionally, sex workers with disabilities may encounter their own forms of stigma. Recognizing these layers of intersectionality is vital for sex educators to comprehend the diverse obstacles encountered by individuals within the profession.

Sex Work and Capitalism

Understanding sex work within the framework of capitalism is also valuable. Economic disparities, fueled by capitalist structures, often drive individuals towards sex work as a means of survival. For Black, Brown, and trans sex workers specifically, sex work is a direct slap in the face to colonial capitalistic ideologies (but that's a conversation for another chapter). The commodification of sex under capitalism underscores the need to approach the subject with sensitivity and a critical lens. Sex educators must acknowledge the economic factors at play and advocate for systemic changes that address the root causes potentially leading individuals into the profession.

Whorephobia and Colonialism

Stigma and violence against sex workers contribute to internalized whorephobia, leading them to internalize negative beliefs about their worth and affecting their mental health. This internalized whorephobia can be viewed through a colonial lens, where historical legacies stigmatize sex outside traditional boundaries. Understanding this involves recognizing how colonial structures shape contemporary views on sex work. Therefore, analyzing sex work should include how it contrasts with colonial and capitalistic ideals, especially regarding internalized biases sex workers may experience.

Sex educators must adopt an intersectional lens and advocate for systemic changes that address the economic inequalities contributing to the existence of sex work. By acknowledging the specific challenges faced by Black and Brown sex workers, trans sex workers, and those influenced by socio-economic disparities, educators can work towards creating inclusive and empathetic educational spaces that strive for the dismantling of stigma and violence within the realm of sex work.

Introspective Questions for Consideration

- What assumptions do you still hold that contribute to the stigma against sex workers, and how might these biases affect your ability to educate inclusively about sex work?
- How can discussions on sexual liberation support the destigmatization of sex work?
- In what ways can you help dismantle stigma as a sexuality educator?
- How does the chapter's content influence your growth as a sexuality educator?

References

Abel, G., & Healy, C. (2021). Sex worker-led provision of services in New Zealand: Optimising health and safety in a decriminalised context. In S. M. Goldenberg, R. Morgan Thomas, A. Forbes, & S. Baral (Eds.), *Sex work, health, and human rights: Global inequities, challenges, and opportunities for action* (pp. 175–187). https://doi.org/10.1007/978-3-030-64171-9_10

Bloomquist, K., & Sprankle, E. (2019). Sex worker affirmative therapy: Conceptualization and case study. *Sexual and Relationship Therapy, 34*(3), 392–408. https://doi.org/10.1080/14681994.2019.1620930

Deering, K. N., Amin, A., Shoveller, J., Nesbitt, A., Garcia-Moreno, C., Duff, P., Argento, E., & Shannon, K. (2014). A systematic review of the correlates of violence against sex workers. *American Journal of Public Health, 104*(5), e42–e54. https://doi.org/10.2105/AJPH.2014.301909

Farley, M., & Barkan, H. (1998). Prostitution, violence, and posttraumatic stress disorder. *Women & Health, 27*(3), 37–49. https://doi.org/10.1300/J013v27n03_03

Härkönen, U. (2007). *The Bronfenbrenner ecological systems theory of human development.* University of Joensuu, Finland.

Kipling, R. (1909). *On the city wall.* University of California.

Martin-Romo, L., Sanmartin, F. J., & Velasco, J. (2023). Invisible and stigmatized: A systematic review of mental health and risk factors among sex workers. *Wiley Online Library.* https://onlinelibrary.wiley.com/doi/full/10.1111/acps.13559

New Zealand: The ideal framework for decriminalized sex work. (2023, September 5). *Decriminalize Sex Work.* https://decriminalizesex.work/why-decriminalization/briefing-papers/new-zealand-ideal-legal-framework/

Potter, L. C., Horwood, J., & Feder, G. (2022, February 11). Access to healthcare for Street Sex Workers in the UK: Perspectives and Best Practice Guidance from a national cross-sectional survey of Frontline Workers. *BMC Health Services Research.* https://bmchealthservres.biomedcentral.com/articles/10.1186/s12913-022-07581-7

Prostitution. (2020, March 19). *Historical timeline – prostitution – procon.org.* https://prostitution.procon.org/historical-timeline/#2400-bc-499

Schwartz, S., Viswasam, N., & Abdalla, P. (2021). Integrated interventions to address sex workers' needs and realities: Academic and community insights on incorporating structural, behavioural, and biomedical approaches. In S. M. Goldenberg, R. Morgan Thomas, A. Forbes, & S. Baral (Eds.), *Sex work, health, and human rights: Global inequities, challenges, and opportunities for action* (Chapter 13). Springer.

Singer, R. B., Johnson, A. K., Crooks, N., Bruce, D., Wesp, L., Karczmar, A., Mkandawire-Valhmu, L., & Sherman, S. (2021). "Feeling safe, feeling seen, feeling free": Combating stigma and creating culturally safe care for sex workers in Chicago. *PLoS ONE, 16*(6), e0253749. https://doi.org/10.1371/journal.pone.0253749

Swift, J. (2022, December 12). How to end violence against sex workers. *Gender Policy Report*. https://genderpolicyreport.umn.edu/how-to-end-violence-against-sex-workers/

Walker, K. (2023, October 20). More than 56,000 students now do sex work to make money at university. *ITV News*. https://www.itv.com/news/2023-10-20/more-than-56000-students-now-do-sex-work-to-make-money-at-university

20 Destigmatizing BDSM Through Education

Challenges, Mindset, and Strategies

Midori

Key Terms

- **Kink:** colloquial umbrella term encompassing BDSM and other erotic or sexual activities considered non-normative.
- **Stigma:** negative attitudes, beliefs, and discrimination.
- **BDSM:** activities leading to social exclusion and reduced opportunities.
- **Consent:** mutual agreement to participate in sexual or non-sexual BDSM activities.

This chapter equips educators with fundamental skills, practical tools, and strategies to introduce BDSM and kink into their curriculum. We will explore a discussion framework for BDSM, kink, and fetishes with various audiences, aiming to destigmatize while providing safe, accurate, and relevant information. We will cover compassionate educational facilitation practices and resources for educators and learners.

Kink, BDSM, and fetishes encompass a wide range of fantasies and activities. Media and academic literature usually describe these terms as bondage, discipline, dominance, submission, sadism, masochism (BDSM), and erotic arousal from non-reproductive body parts or objects (fetishism). Often, explanations do not extend beyond this expansion of initials.

Even this is rarely included in sex education and clinician training. In-depth discussions are rare despite studies showing prevalence of desires and activities throughout the general population. One study found BDSM-related fantasies are common (40–70%) in males and females, with about 20% reporting engagement (Brown et al., 2020), contradicting the assumption that these desires are anomalous.

BDSM and related activities have been historically stigmatized in Western cultures; stigma formalized in the first edition of the *Diagnostic and Statistical Manual of Mental Disorders* (DSM) in 1952, labeling them as pathological sexual deviance. Consensual BDSM remained classified as a disorder until DSM's fifth edition (American Psychological Association, 2013). Despite this, many in

DOI: 10.4324/9781032615479-24

the health/mental health fields continue to view consensual kinks and BDSM as dysfunction, exacerbating stigma (Gerson, 2015).

All forms of kink, BDSM, and fetishes share common stigmas and lack practical education for practitioners. Increasingly, comprehensive research, growing awareness, and society's gradual acceptance are driving change towards diverse expression of sexuality.

This chapter focuses on Western perspectives. "Western" refers to cultures influenced by Greco-Roman and European heritage. Attitudes towards sexuality, kink, behavior, language, and sex education are not universal and must be understood within their cultural context.

While discussions on human sexuality continue to be deemed sensitive, controversial topics, conversations about BDSM are more fraught with discomfort, judgment, and aversion. This often results in avoidance, exclusion from sex education curricula, mockery, and reliance on dubious sources including pop culture and social media. For people of color and other marginalized identities, additional minority stressors intensify challenges. Many BIPOC communities perceive BDSM as a "white thing," associated with privilege, ethnocentrism, able-bodiedness, and race-based exclusion. As a result, individuals may not receive support within their communities and may struggle finding acceptance or representation in BDSM social environments.

Discomfort and misinformation can affect educators, learners, families, health providers, and school administrators. Compassionate understanding of these attitudes is crucial for debunking myths and providing quality BDSM education.

Despite increased presence of BDSM imagery in popular culture, stigma persists, often portraying kink as deviant. This echoes past portrayals of other marginalized identities and sexual expressions, such as same-gender relationships, interracial sex, and non-binary identities. When kink is stigmatized, individuals may internalize shame, leading to adverse mental health and social outcomes (Hansen-Brown & Jefferson, 2023). Initially viewed as scandalous, these identities and expressions have become more normalized and affirmed within sexuality discourse, thanks to the collective and cumulative advocacy and social justice efforts.

Destigmatization can start by addressing common misconceptions, including that BDSM is:

- Caused by trauma or childhood abuse
- Inherently violent
- Consent to violence is invalid
- Coercive
- Non-consensual
- Mental illness
- Anti-feminist

- Linked to other problematic sexual behaviors
- Always sexual
- Engaged by few
- Cisgender white practice
- Indicates poor self-esteem
- Dominance equals bullying
- Men dominate, women submit

Considering destigmatization, it's helpful to address misconceptions through different activities such as anonymous Q&A or True/False exercises. These learning activities can help as a foundation for discussing BDSM.

Many BDSM practitioners face risks associated with disclosure, including harassment, job discrimination, child custody loss, and substandard health care. Awareness of these affects where and how they seek education.

Remember that BDSMers are in our learning environments, often enduring microaggressions. As educators, be prepared to encounter many challenging attitudes:

Joking: humor masking discomfort disrupts participation, reinforcing stigma. If appropriate, use levity to ease tension.

Oversharing: excessive contributions dominate discussions, discouraging others. Address this to maintain balance.

Avoidance: non-participation may indicate discomfort rather than disinterest. Low-pressure exercises can engage these learners.

Condescension: eye-rolling or dismissiveness negatively affects the learning environment. Address constructively.

Challenging qualifications: discomfort may manifest as questioning educator's expertise. Be open about your knowledge with willingness to research.

These behaviors often stem from BDSM stigmatization. Compassionate, accurate education can positively benefit stigma-affected learners, even if the impact emerges later.

Approaches Towards Destigmatization

How do we move beyond these stigmas, negative perceptions, and misconceptions? Efforts by researchers, clinicians, and mainstream influencers to undo stigma are gaining momentum.

By promoting comprehensive research and fostering accepting societal attitudes, we can create more inclusive understanding of human sexuality, including the subcultures within. Here are some effective approaches to help combat the stigma, starting with assessing our attitudes as educators.

Educator's Self-Inquiry

Acknowledging our biases, especially when experiencing ambivalence or uncertainty if BDSM is not a part of our lived experience, can influence how we facilitate discussions with learners. While Sexual Attitude Reassessment (SAR) programs include some components of assessing our attitudes and beliefs, SARs are often inaccessible or insufficiently thorough. To start, the following educator self-reflection questions can help identify biases and growth areas and deepen compassion and relatability with learners.

Describe:

- Can you clearly describe BDSM beyond the initials?
- Have you encountered different definitions of BDSM or kink?

Attitudes and feelings about BDSM:

- What were your past attitudes compared to today? What influenced any shifts?
- What are your past and current feelings about BDSM within your own sex life?

Impact:

- How do your attitudes support or detract from delivering BDSM education?
- Are negative biases evident in your language, humor, or expressions? How can you assess this?
- Do positive feelings cause you to minimize important risk information?
- What BDSM topics do you avoid and why?

Information sources:

- When did you first become aware of BDSM. What sources informed your attitudes about BDSM (e.g., comics, reality shows, movies, family, friends, dating sites, porn)?

Compassion/relatability:

- How can you show more compassion for learners' experiences and learning processes?
- Where can you find points of relatability and commonality with students?
- How prepared do you feel to handle student questions and reactions?

Reading the Room: Gauging Learners' Knowledge and Attitudes

Sharing your reflections can build relatability and trust, model sex positivity and pro-social behavior, while assessing baseline understanding of the audience's attitudes, feelings, and knowledge.

Adapting the self-inquiry prompts for learners through reflective writing exercises, surveys, or group discussions can be useful, encouraging reflection on views and biases, reducing anxiety, and fostering a compassionate atmosphere. Group discussions may lower stigma and create a safer space for open dialogue.

If considering large group discussions, gauge how to introduce these prompts in an inclusive and trauma-informed manner. Adjust the curriculum and goals based on students' language, assumptions, knowledge, experiences, and stigma.

Consider other variables affecting learner attitudes, ability, and capacity to engage with your lesson plan. This includes:

- In-person/virtual education
- Synchronous/asynchronous
- Age appropriateness
- Required/elective education
- Institutional/community settings (e.g., harm reduction programs, queer youth groups, religious organizations, sex-positive gatherings)
- Social norms of the area (sexually conservative vs. liberal communities, accessibility to sex education, cultural diversity)
- Cultural and linguistic background of the population and educator
- Degree of stigma or shame about BDSM and other sexual issues

Additional methods to help sex educators assess learner attitudes include:

- Passive listening to chatter
- Casual inquiry before class
- Pre-class anonymous surveys
- Level of engagement in large and small group activities
- Open discussions

When We, the Educator, Are Uncertain

BDSM/kink are relative to what is considered "normative" sexuality in a specific time and place. The idea of 'normal' sex shifts, and so do the concepts and terminologies of BDSM/kink. Trends in BDSM activities also change over time and across regions or communities.

For example, military uniforms and chaps with associated roleplay predominated gay male kink media in the 1980s. Today, events feature more diverse themes, such as superheroes and puppy play. In the late 20th century, leather and metal restraints were featured heavily in porn and BDSM media, but today more BDSM practices featured in sexual media, including an abundance of rope bondage classes and events accessible to wider audiences.

Given this evolving array, educators will encounter unfamiliar terms and practices. Use this opportunity to engage learners with discussions on the expansiveness of practices that may be both familiar and unfamiliar. Explaining the evolving nature of terms encourages curiosity and compassionate communication.

Here are some dialogue ideas on terms new to the educator:

- "That's new to me. Can you describe it to me?"
- "Where might this fall on the Appetite Grid?" (later discussed)
- "What challenges do you think people with these interests/labels/appetites face?"
- "I'll find out more information about ____. Would you want me to share my findings?"

Teaching Terminology and Incorporating Metaphors

The following are some common BDSM terms for educators to become familiar with. While these can be researched online, it's important to recognize assumptions, biases, and overt and covert stigmas associated with these. Prepare to address, explain, and discuss these appropriately for your audience. If uncertain, consult with resources from verified subject experts.

- Dominant
- Submissive
- Sadist
- Masochist
- Top
- Bottom
- Switch
- Fetishist
- Scene
- Negotiation
- Play
- Consent
- Safeword
- Safe signal
- Boundary
- Hard Limit
- Aftercare
- Check-ins
- Consent
- Consensual Non-consent

These terms originate from English-speaking cultures and can carry colonizing assumptions and, depending on the BDSM scene itself, can perpetuate stereotypes and discrimination as well as reinforce the exoticization of bodies, cultures, heritage, and race. In multilingual populations, discussing how these concepts translate – or do not – across languages can serve as a helpful exercise unveiling unconscious bias, helping to reduce harm, especially experienced by marginalized populations.

An example of discussing terminology is to reframe each as an "appetite." The term appetite for play can help bridge personal relatability and understanding.

Educators may begin by introducing audiences to consider these terms as recreation-seeking behavior, and much like satisfying hunger, it is aimed at creating a desired temporary state change. This shifts the focus away from unchanging attachments to personality, activity, or gendered roles (Malone et al., 2022).

Here are some examples of reframing into "appetites." I often use the catchphrase of "Verb, not Noun."

Identity statement		Appetite statement
"I'm a dominant."	→	"I'm feeling dominant."
"I'm a submissive."	→	"I want to submit to you tonight."
"I'm a switch."	→	"I enjoy switching."
"I top."	→	"I love topping you."
"I bottom."	→	"I enjoy bottoming."

Another helpful tool emphasizing Appetites for both educators and individuals is "Midori's BDSM Appetite Grid" (Midori, 2003, 2018).

This reframing approach helps expand learners' understanding and incorporate practical-use language. Many students successfully use this to clarify communication, enhance mutual satisfaction, reduce misunderstanding, and destigmatize consensual pleasure seeking. (Midori, 2018)

Incorporating good, relatable analogies helps one understand this charged subject. Following are some examples.

- *Masochism or masochistic appetites:* compare to people who enjoy spicy foods, roller coasters, or deep tissue massages. People enjoy these intense temporary experiences for fun, even if they don't look "happy" in the moment. Depending on their appetites, they may seek varying intensity, sometimes none
- *Dominance and submission:* lead and follow in paired dancing or grown-up versions of "Simon Says"
- *Consensual non-consent:* tag for grown-ups
- *Successful negotiation:* planning a meal together or deciding on movies to watch
- *Aftercare:* what a person needs to recover after a marathon or other sports

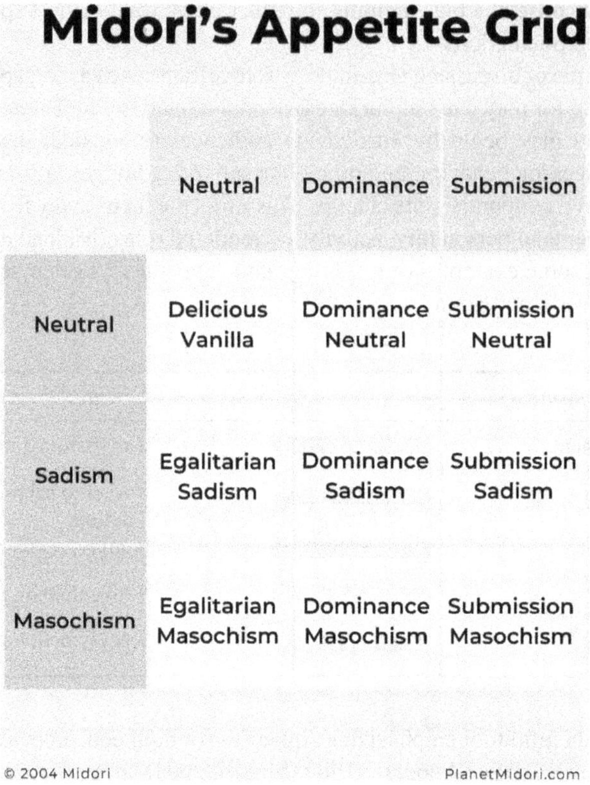

Midori's Appetite Grid

	Neutral	Dominance	Submission
Neutral	Delicious Vanilla	Dominance Neutral	Submission Neutral
Sadism	Egalitarian Sadism	Dominance Sadism	Submission Sadism
Masochism	Egalitarian Masochism	Dominance Masochism	Submission Masochism

© 2004 Midori   PlanetMidori.com

Figure 20.1 Chart 1: Midori's Appetite Grid

Now, create your analogies. Test these with others to see if they help clarify and demystify.

Media Awareness and Kink Destigmatization

For many, media (traditional, online, and social media) often serve as primary information sources. Unfortunately, these are rife with misinformation, prejudices, and reflect general cultural bias and stigma. Even sources for safer kink practices are not immune to biases.

Empower learners by broadening their awareness, identifying harmful biases with encouragement to seek more accurate information. Accomplish this through facilitating an intentional discussion on BDSM representation in mainstream and digital media. Here are examples of questions to incorporate in lesson plans:

1. Ask the class to name BDSM in pop culture, discuss and analyze embedded assumptions. Prepare by pre-selecting examples from various genres and platforms, such as movies, education sites, YouTube, advertising, TikTok, Reddit, etc.
2. Ask to identify commonly used terms in each example, critique and analyze assumptions underlying them. Consider modeling a conversation between two people on how different assumptions lead to misunderstandings, consent issues, and missed opportunities for growth in knowledge, agency, or intimacy
3. Ask how in this example, the cascade of misunderstanding and stigma could have been averted
4. Invite learners to reflect on how these ideas have evolved over time

On Consent and Negotiation

Discussing consent in the context of BDSM is essential in destigmatizing understandings of BDSM, highlighting the central role of mutual agreement, respect, and safety. Unlike misconceptions that BDSM is inherently abusive or coercive, focus on consent underscores the importance of clear communication and boundaries, ensuring all participants are fully aware and in control of their experiences. Emphasizing informed, enthusiastic consent helps dispel myths, portraying BDSM as consensual and legitimate form of sexual expression, prioritizing the well-being and autonomy of everyone involved.

Discover how learners understand consent. Often it's misunderstood as a one-time yes/no without nuanced considerations. Discuss the complex challenges impacting individuals' ability to consent fully enthusiastically.

Reframe consent as a collaborative agreement-making, leading to discussions on planning, also known as negotiation. Introduce resources and methods:

- Reflection: simple or more elaborate in-depth yes/no/maybe checklists
- Exploration: unidirectional or mutual question and answer
- Processing: co-writing or telling stories and fantasies
- Discussion: watching or reading kink material together and discussing plans based on ideas and inspiration

It's essential to debunk the myth that consent rules are different or not applicable in BDSM. Emphasize that healthy BDSM requires active, ongoing, fully, and freely given consent from all participants. The Planned Parenthood model "F.R.I.E.S." – Freely given, Reversible, Informed, and Enthusiastic – is a useful tool for remembering and recalling (Planned Parenthood, n.d.).

Helpful activity for those curious or experienced in BDSM is to (1) invite how they might design consent methods with different rules and structures, (2) explore questions and limitations of these consent methods, and (3) discuss where misunderstanding might occur and their consequences.

"Micro Cycles of Consent" describes the ongoing, circular nature of consent during play. This involves continuous verbal and non-verbal communication, similar to pair dancing (Midori, 2021):

Transmit: one sends a signal. (i.e. pressing a hand on a hip to indicate a step to the left.) Is the request clear and understandable?

Comprehend: the other interprets the request. Do they comprehend accurately?

Decide: they decide whether to act on the request. What's their decision?

Act: they act on their decision, either moving or not. Both are valid decisions.

In dancing and BDSM, continuous Micro Cycles of Consent create an pleasurable flow.

Imbalances in preexisting or perceived power dynamics, such as age, gender, race, experience, and social position differences, can influence consent. Have examples ready for discussion. For example:

- 30-year-old Black cis male negotiating potential scene with 30-year-old Black cis female. How is consent impacted when . . .

  - One is more experienced in kink?
  - Which one wants to top?

- 43-year-old white cis male approaches 25-year-old Asian cis female

  - When the male requests to dominate or submit?
  - When the female requests to dominate or submit?

- Experienced kinkster established in the local community negotiates with person new to kink and the local community. How is it different:

  - When the ages of the people are the same?
  - When the ages are different?
  - When one person is perceived to be wealthy, and the other is not?
  - When one person is trans and the other not?

Emphasize that agreeing to negotiate does not automatically lead to play. After negotiation, anyone can decline or suggest something different.

In conclusion, the destigmatization of BDSM through education is an essential multifaceted endeavor, demanding a compassionate, informed, and nuanced approach. By addressing deeply rooted misconceptions and societal biases, educators can create an inclusive and supportive learning environment. The integration of comprehensive research, reflective self-inquiry, and adaptive teaching strategies foster better understanding of BDSM and promote more accepting, respectful discourse around diverse sexual expressions. As educators, recognizing and mitigating our biases, utilizing practical communication tools, and employing culturally sensitive and critical pedagogies are foundational steps in dismantling stigma, empowering individuals to explore their identities safely and consensually. This chapter underscores the importance of continued advocacy and education in transforming societal attitudes, ensuring that everyone can embrace their sexuality free from judgment and discrimination.

Introspective Questions for Consideration

- How am I willing to make space for BDSM exploration by people who aren't of my culture, heritage, or linguistic groups?
- In what ways can I address colleagues or administration making prejudicial or stigma-enforcing comments about kink/BDSM?
- What are my plans or supports when I encounter consensual kink/BDSM interests that appall or disgust me personally?
- If I incorporate visual aids, what indicators do I look for that don't reinforce stereotypes and stigma?

References

American Psychiatric Association. (2013). *Diagnostic and statistical manual of mental disorders* (5th ed.). American Psychiatric Press.

Brown, A., Barker, E. D., & Rahman, Q. (2020). A systematic scoping review of the prevalence, etiological, psychological, and interpersonal factors associated with BDSM. *The Journal of Sex Research, 57*(6), 781–811. https://doi.org/10.1080/00224499.201 9.1665619

Gerson, M. N. (2015, January 13). BDSM versus the DSM: A history of the fight that got kink de-classified as mental illness. *The Atlantic.* https://www.theatlantic.com/health/archive/2015/01/bdsm-versus-the-dsm/384138/

Hansen-Brown, A. A., & Jefferson, S. E. (2023). Perceptions of and stigma toward BDSM practitioners. *Current Psychology, 42,* 19721–19729. https://doi.org/10.1007/s12144-022-03112-z

Malone, R. M., Stewart, M. R., Gary-Smith, M., & Wadley, J. C. (Eds.). (2022). *An intersectional approach to sex therapy: Centering the lives of Indigenous, racialized, and people of color.* Routledge.

Midori. (2003). *Best kink advice nobody told you.* ShibariCon.

Midori. (2018). *Moving toward pragmatic judgment-free language in discussion of BDSM desires* [Conference presentation]. AASECT Annual Conference.

Midori. (2021, April 23). *Best kink advice nobody told you* [Conference presentation]. International Kink for the Professionals, Sexual Health Alliance.

Planned Parenthood. (n.d.). *Sexual consent.* https://www.plannedparenthood.org/learn/relationships/sexual-consent#

Part IV

Skills and Considerations for Increasing Impact and Inclusivity

21 Making Mistakes and Practicing Accountability

Jennifer A. Hart and Hilary F. Towle
(Introduction written by Bianca I. Laureano)

Key Terms

- **Accountability:** the act of owning one's responsibility and justification of their words, actions, deeds, and lack thereof.
- **Calling On:** a public request for a person or entity to be accountable through action. Different from calling in or calling out, which are focused more on naming harm through discourse.
- **Interdependence:** reliance, engagement, collaboration of two or more entities to be present in centering accountability towards collective healing.
- **Reproductive Justice:** the human right to maintain personal bodily autonomy, have children, not have children, and parent the children we have in safe and sustainable communities (SisterSong, 2024).
- **White Supremacy:** the belief that white people constitute a superior race and should therefore dominate society, typically to the exclusion or detriment of other racial and ethnic groups (Dictionary.com, 2024).

Introduction

Accountability is an act of revolutionary love. The kind of love that shows up for the growing up, the growing into, and the calling on one another that can only arrive when we are practicing interdependence. To be held accountable is to be held in a way many of us may have never experienced before and so it may feel the opposite of what we think love is supposed to be: scary, frustrating, overwhelming, painful, uncomfortable, embarrassing. Feeling these emotions and having these experiences are ways to feel alive!

Because sexuality education in the US is fraught with the legacy and stains of white supremacy and settler colonialism, the accountability that is needed requires a lot of practice and work. We won't get it right the first, second, or even the third time. It is a lifelong practice of messing up, trying again, listening with our entire bodies, receiving feedback, thinking, exploring, implementing, redistributing, relearning, and messing up again. It is a cycle, a process and not a

DOI: 10.4324/9781032615479-26

destination. To think accountability has a beginning, middle, and end is to ignore the rehumanizing healing that is being offered.

When accountability emerges and is focused on the US sexuality field it is often those most impacted by oppression and -isms that lead this calling on for collective shared power and healing. Often when some think about accountability they imagine a binary of us vs them or of those with power and those without. Yet, accountability is not a binary, it is a circle. When we begin to listen with our whole bodies, to our elders, peers, youth, children, and those with different experiences and training than ourselves, we begin to fully move into the interdisciplinarity that sexuality education requires.

There is so much harm that exists in the US sexuality field, and it is being replicated, evaluated, endorsed, and then deemed "evidence-based" and thus continues to be funded. Those evaluations rarely ever consider the harm that always already exists. If we are to really believe "sex ed saves lives," then whose lives are we trying to save if we are allowing for the continued violence of erasure, silencing, exclusion, medical inaccuracies, and more? This chapter offers a glimpse into a correction, an attempt, a vulnerability that invites us all to rehumanize and rematriate to our bodymindsheartssouls.

Content

Writing a chapter on "Making Mistakes and Practicing Accountability," as current and former employees of a Planned Parenthood (PP) affiliate, and also as two white, straight, cis, able, neurotypical, Ivy League educated, city-dwelling women, is – to put it mildly – no small task. And, it *may* make the most sense that people like us write this chapter. Our identities overwhelmingly reflect the historical and contemporary realities of PP employees across the country. Our identities hold privilege in this country, and therefore power. And unfortunately, that power means that, even unintentionally, we have oppressed, marginalized, and otherwise caused harm to our Black, Indigenous, and People of Color (BIPOC); Lesbian, Gay, Bisexual, Transgender, Queer (LGBTQ)+, disabled, and neurodivergent colleagues, patients, community partners, and students. Coming to terms with the harm we've caused has been a matter of radical acceptance of the impact of our identities on the people and spaces with which we engage, and the life-long commitment to unlearn, relearn, and practice anti-oppressive approaches in our personal and professional lives.

We, Jennifer and Hilary, hope to offer you, the reader, this chapter as a small offering to get you thinking about how you have made mistakes, how it will feel to keep making them, what accountability could look like in your work, and what you are actively doing to continue to strive for equity. To those entering into the sexuality education space for the first time, or if you're reading this book and chapter after many years in the field, we encourage you to get comfortable with discomfort, leave your ego at the door, roll up your sleeves, and lean into the hard yet critical work to create more equitable learning environments in sex education.

Planned Parenthood

Planned Parenthood (PP), as a national entity and brand, is the largest provider of sex education in the country. Planned Parenthood Federation of America (PPFA) is the national office and serves as an umbrella for nearly 50 affiliates across the United States, each with their own affiliate names, CEOs, boards of directors, staff, budgets, strategic initiatives, and health and race equity approaches.

PP began more than 100 years ago, by its founder Margaret Sanger, who was involved from 1916–1959. Sanger was an avid advocate for birth control, and also had racist alliances and believed in eugenics.[1] One of the most notable examples of this was in her invitation to speak to the women's auxiliary of the Ku Klux Klan in 1926. In 1927, Sanger endorsed the US Supreme Court's decision in *Buck v. Bell*, allowing states to sterilize people deemed "unfit" without their consent and sometimes without their knowledge; the ruling in that case led to the sterilization of tens of thousands of people during the 20th century. Later on in her career, Sanger backed the first human trials of the birth control pill conducted in Puerto Rico, where as many as 1,500 women were exposed to an experimental version of the drug that contained 20 times more hormones than birth control pills on the market today and came with many dangerous potential side effects of which the women were not notified.

Since Sanger's leadership, PPFA has had to step up to the accountability plate after being called on by leaders in the reproductive justice movement on similar and related oversights. In 2014, Sister Song's CEO, Monica Simpson, wrote an open letter to PPFA and Cecile Richards, PPFA's president at the time, naming PPFA's "single-issue organizing strategies," not including Reproductive Justice (RJ) leaders in strategic decision-making, and history of taking credit for work of RJ organizations and leaders (Simpson, 2022). In April of 2021, PPFA's current President and CEO Alexis McGill Johnson addressed PPFA membership at its national conference, explicitly naming the racist and ableist history of PP, its founder, and the irreparable impact of that legacy. Following that conference, the *New York Times* released an opinion piece from Johnson, publicly stating the same. At a more local level, the PP of Greater New York (PPGNY) affiliate renamed its Manhattan Health Center, removing Margaret Sanger's name from the building in 2020, and in 2021, PPGNY and City Council "unnamed" Margaret Sanger Square at the intersection outside their office.

Working for a sexual and reproductive health (SRH) and education organization with such explicit ties to historical and contemporary racism can be overwhelming to reckon with. And, it is a bold and undeniable reminder of the responsibility we have to dismantle white supremacy in our own workplaces and also in the greater field. PPFA's present day values support the "fundamental freedom of all people to control their own bodies, their lives, and their futures . . . in full health, dignity, and self-determination." How do we do this work so that PP is truly and authentically trusted by Black, brown, and Indigenous people, people with disabilities, and people with marginalized gender and sexual identities? That PP and others are known not for the violence caused but rather for the reliable, trustworthy, and safe health care and inclusive, trauma-informed comprehensive sex education? We must strive towards that reality, always.

PPLM

While Planned Parenthood League of Massachusetts (PPLM) has established and accomplished several strategies for achieving more accountable external relationships and internal practices, we know that the impact of white supremacy workplace culture will always disproportionately impact the experiences of our BIPOC colleagues, patients, partners, and participants. What follows is a small piece of how we have attempted to pursue accountability as it relates to sex education, both in curriculum and practice.

Accountability in Sex Education at PPLM

PPLM is the author and developer of the evidence-based curriculum, *Get Real: Comprehensive Sex Education That Works. Get Real* was originally conceived of and written by a team of all white SRH educators, many also holding other privileged identities. *Get Real* is an evidence-based curriculum established as such by the United States Health and Human Services' Teen Pregnancy Prevention Evidence Review and the Office of Population Affairs, which means it has been vetted through randomized control trial research to be effective at impacting STI, pregnancy, and other sexual health outcomes with a variety of diverse populations. *Get Real* is used across the United States and in multiple countries with thousands of middle and high school students with a variety of racial and ethnic identities. That said, we should not be surprised that our curricula, while evaluated with diverse student populations, doesn't resonate with every student or educator in the country, particularly those whose identities and perspectives are vastly different from the developers.

Before moving on, it is important to acknowledge the inherent inequities imposed by much evidence-based research and curriculum development, which are often created through projects funded by research bodies that target "high-risk" populations (usually Black and brown) with quick, short-term resources. Once research is complete and the curriculum has been made, many organizations leave those communities behind, waiting for intervention sustainability that never arrives. Evidence-based programs are also usually elevated as best practice, often devaluing practice-based efforts that have been used with great success in community settings for years. Through its *Get Real &*

Professional Training Institute (the Institute), PPLM has strived to identify gaps and increase access within our curricula and associated training opportunities to more equitably meet the needs of underrepresented BIPOC educators and often marginalized, invisibilized, and/or tokenized BIPOC young people, LGBTQ+ young people, and young people with disabilities, without perpetuating further harm. Consider the examples that follow as some efforts at accountability in this regard:

Race Equity

Over the most recent years, the Institute has received feedback that pieces of *Get Real* do not resonate for either students and/or educators of color alike, and that some of the content poses a risk of perpetuating stigma, shame, and marginalization of students of color. In 2024, we engaged a consultant team from Fact Forward, a Woman of Color (WOC)-led sex education organization in South Carolina with expertise in practicing racial justice within sex education. The consultant team was able to conduct a racial equity and cultural competency review of the full curricula and associated training materials, using the practice paper, *Centering Racial Justice in Sex Education: Strategies for Engaging Professionals and Young People* and a grading scale of "Critical, Moderate, Low" as a guide. Within weeks of receiving their assessment, all items that were marked with a "Critical" score were updated; over the next four months, all "Moderate" scores were identified and updated with additional support from Onyx Empowerment Collective (OEC), a Black woman-owned Diversity, Equity, and Inclusion (DEI) consulting firm. With OEC's guidance, all "Low" scored items were scheduled for completion by Fall 2024. Curriculum updates were incorporated into the evaluation of *Get Real* High School and upon completion of the evaluation, we intend to publish a culturally responsive third edition of *Get Real*.

Disability Justice

To ensure PPLM's ongoing work is effective in meeting the needs of people with Intellectual and Developmental Disabilities (IDD), PPLM hosted a convening entitled *State of Affairs in Sex Education for People with IDD* ("the Convening") in October 2018. We hired Nechama Sammett Moring, a consultant from Rebel Girl Research Communications who has expertise in disability and reproductive justice and anti-ableism approaches, to guide our work. A pre-Convening Planning Committee of self-advocates with IDD, parents, service providers, and clinicians provided additional guidance about the format and content of the event itself. The Convening brought together stakeholders from across New England, including general and adapted educators, skills coaches, public health officials, mental and physical health care providers, rape crisis counselors, parents with IDD, peer self-advocates with IDD, and others. Accessibility and inclusion were also key considerations; various accommodations were provided to make the Convening space and content physically and cognitively accessible.

Self-advocates served as keynote speakers, workshop leaders, and panelists and were supported and paid for their time and expertise. Workshop topics included: trauma-informed sex education; consent, autonomy and rights; educator best practices in sex education; parents as educators and advocates; and LGBTQIA+ inclusive sex education. In response to what we learned, PPLM and IMPACT, a Boston-based organization specializing in IDD, co-created a training, *Sexuality Education Tools for the IDD Community,* which is now co-facilitated twice a year.

LGBTQ+ Inclusivity and Trauma Informed Approaches

In 2017, *Get Real* Educators reported that their LGBTQ+ students felt tokenized by the gender and sexuality lessons in the curriculum. We further understood that the activities we were using supported peer empathy building at the expense of LGBTQ+ students. In response, we consulted with Lisa Schergen of WOC-led training organization Cardea to review *Get Real* for inclusivity and trauma informed approaches. Changes were made throughout the curriculum, including the Teacher's Guide, to make language more intentional, inclusive, and trauma informed and activities more meaningful and accessible to the lived experiences of young LGBTQ+ people. New lessons and activities were piloted with LGBTQ+ high school students before the second edition of the curriculum was published in 2019.

Unfortunately, in our attempt to improve the lesson for LBGTQ+ students, we inadvertently made it unsafe for BIPOC students, by including an activity where all students were asked to imagine having to hide their race. In the feedback, we were appropriately reminded that suggesting that someone could hide their race in the same way that someone might hide their gender and sexual orientation invalidates the unavoidable racism many students of color experience in the real world. In 2023, we re-wrote the Gender and Sexual Identity lesson plan to address this marginalization. We also incorporated sections into training for *Get Real* Educators on creating inclusive environments for all students, addressing harmful comments in the classroom and checking their own biases before they teach students who hold a variety of identities. The iterations of this lesson plan over the years have further underscored the intersectional experience of race and sexual orientation for students of color, and highlighted the need to move towards the Racial Justice-related curriculum changes noted earlier.

Individual Educators Can Make a Difference

We share these experiences with you to contextualize what comes next, which are tools and practices we can each utilize as individuals in our sexuality education work. There is so much that sex educators can do to advance equity at an individual level, without having to embark on months-long projects that are dependent on funding availability or wait for their school administration or organization leadership to catch up and invest in equity work. Sometimes schools and organizations are lightyears away from where individuals are because individuals tend to move more quickly than the larger entities they are a part of; the wheels of bureaucracy are often slow to turn and require the uplifting of voices and input from many.

As Dr. Laureano highlights in the introduction to this chapter, practicing accountability is a cyclical, lifelong practice. There is an opportunity with every school/program year, in every classroom, with every student, to try, mess up, listen, receive feedback, and try again. PPFA, PPLM, us as individuals, and many of you within your own organizations and teaching practices have already made mistakes as players in this field. Rather than being cast aside and removed from the work (Dr. Laureano calls this disposability), we are called on to address the harm we have caused and do the work to be and do better. No matter the limitations of your school or organization, there are always ways that sex educators can work to be as inclusive as possible. When it comes to young people feeling valued, respected, seen, heard, and safe in their classrooms and communities, they *require* us as adults and educators to be actively and consistently thinking about and working on inclusivity and showing up for them. So even if you're not able to move your school or organization along more quickly, what can you do in your individual power to ensure students feel that inclusivity is a top priority for you and therefore feel included and seen?

At the interpersonal and classroom level, Group Rights and Responsibilities is a tool that educators can use to co-create to establish shared accountability practice for words and actions in the learning space. Calling this a list of rights *and* responsibilities is intentional since while many of the agreements are rights that all people have, other agreements require individuals to take responsibility for enacting them in the shared environment. Here are a few Group Rights and Responsibilities that come to mind when thinking both about how to establish more responsible learning spaces and to navigate the cycle of learning towards anti-racist sex education.

1. Mistakes Are Inevitable

Humans are imperfect; we are not born knowing everything. It is precisely because a person does not know something already that they make mistakes when trying something new for the first time. Mistakes are often made when we rush to do things just to have them done. Rushing in circumstances that are not life-threatening often reflects a sense of urgency, which is a characteristic of White Supremacy (Simpson, 2022). This sense of urgency can result in increased difficulty to be inclusive; instead, commit to making intentional, thoughtful decisions, and consider their long-term impact.

As part of the *Get Real* curriculum development team we have, at times, felt held back by a fear of messing up while doing the race equity work on our curriculum and training (another characteristic of White Supremacy). This is a common concern among sex educators, that saying or doing the wrong thing in their sex education spaces might unintentionally cause harm. How do we make it okay, or even acceptable, to make mistakes? One way is to create environments where we feel safe enough to mess up and that offer support when mistakes occur. What's in place before, during, and after mistakes are made in an environment like that? Since mistakes are inevitable, what do you do once one is made? These are some questions we have found important to answer.

2. Acknowledging Intent, Owning Impact

The group right of "Acknowledge Intent, and Own Impact" is about holding ourselves and each other accountable. While a person may be well intentioned, the result of one's words or actions may have a hurtful impact. As sex educators and facilitators, redirecting someone or pushing back on harmful comments is not about shaming, being argumentative, or punitive. Providing feedback that will help participants learn and grow, while naming the injustice, is a responsibility of sex educators to create and hold a safer container for learning, constructive discourse, and accountability. The authors of *Centering Racial Justice in Sex Education* offer "accountability circles" as a way to unpack harm that has occurred. This cycle facilitates a healthy and constructive learning environment for everyone, a hallmark of interdependence.

3. Work in the Growth Zone

So, you've made a mistake. You've acknowledged your intent and owned your impact. From there, strive to do the learning and reparative work from the growth zone. The growth zone is where you feel challenged (as the aforementioned practice paper states, getting comfortable with discomfort), and know that you are supported by everyone in the space to work through those challenges. Dr. Laureano introduced the concept of "calling on" our community, our interdependence to each other, in order for there to be shared power and healing. There are no expectations that by simply being a sex educator, we know how to do this work "right." We have so much opportunity to learn and grow from those around us – the young people we teach, the colleagues we collaborate with, and from those who came before.

Additional Factors

Dr. Laureano states that "learn[ing] how to genuinely apologize and decenter [ourselves] are amazing life skills" (Laureano, 2019). There is symmetry between what she sets up for us in her introduction to this chapter and how we as the authors think about comprehensive sex education. Sexuality education and accountability work are both lifelong practices. They each require a strong grasp of social and emotional learning competencies, such as having self-awareness, social-awareness, and relationship skills. They both ask a person to check their biases, understand their personal values, and identify their roots, for better or for worse. Each is most successful when they center marginalized students and communities. And, neither is done fully without making mistakes. If comprehensive sex education is truly inclusive and trauma-informed, it MUST also be racially equitable and culturally responsive because the harm done in sexuality education has disproportionately impacted those with marginalized identities – BIPOC, LGBTQ+ people, people with disabilities, and those with intersecting marginalized identities. Harm will be perpetuated without individual dedication to the lifelong practice of taking accountability.

That said, it's important to note that the cycle of accountability can occur and the repair of harm is not possible. Just as self-awareness is crucial in the cycle we've described, it is alsocritical in this instance. Putting all good intentions and ego aside, it is important and respectful to give grace to an offended person or community, and to support their decision to protect their boundaries and psychosocial safety. It's possible that you are not a safe person for them right now, or in the future. This does not mean you are a horrible person. It is also not an excuse to stop the hard work towards equity. Rather, use this experience as another opportunity to learn, forgive yourself, grow, and keep on fighting the good fight towards liberation.

Conclusion

When harm is caused, redirection is received openly, an apology is sincerely given and accepted, and action to do better is conducted, a stronger, more beautiful relationship can be nurtured. Think of the beautiful Japanese art of Kintsugi where broken pottery is repaired by putting the pieces back together with gold, silver, or platinum to create a perfectly imperfect vessel – one that is even stronger than it was when it was originally whole. When we give ourselves grace to make mistakes while we are earnestly trying to be better, and the commitment to learn and grow together, trust can be built, and strong, productive, interdependent relationships and community partnerships can flourish.

Effective sex educators know how to relate to and talk to humans, meeting them where they are in all their messiness. Our job as sex educators is to literally hold this cycle and discomfort of people figuring out some of the most stigmatized issues in our society, making mistakes, and taking accountability, every day. Because of this, sex educators should be organically more poised to be able to engage each other with empathy, and with inclusive, trauma-informed and more equitable approaches. It only makes sense that we acknowledge that sexuality education work is not mutually exclusive from the work of equity and liberation.

Education is POWER, and as sex educators, we not only give power to others to identity and honor their true selves and determine the most important decisions in their lives for their own health, well-being, and safety, we also support and celebrate the inherent power in each other to access the care they need to live their most authentic and empowered lives possible. See you out there.

Introspective Questions for Consideration

- After reading this chapter, how would you describe in your own words why normalizing mistakes is important in anti-oppression work, and what it means to practice accountability in sex education?
- How might it feel to own the harmful impact of your words or actions even if you didn't mean to cause harm? How do you need to prepare yourself in order to harness that energy into active listening, unlearning, and trying again?
- In addition to Group Rights and Responsibilities, what else should exist in a sex education learning environment that allows it to be a space that is trusted enough to make mistakes?
- How is making mistakes and taking accountability among adults similar or different to how it may look among young people? What about between young people and adults?
- What spheres of influence do you inhabit (work, school, family, community, etc.)? How can you use your own influence and power within those spheres to make impactful change towards a more equitable, inclusive, and trauma-informed outcome or experience?

Note

1 Eugenics is an "inherently racist and ableist ideology, labeling certain people unfit to procreate, on the basis of improving society via planned breeding for "desirable traits" like intelligence and industriousness" (https://www.plannedparenthood.org/about-us/who-we-are/our-history).

References

Dictionary.com. (2024, October 4). *Definition of "White supremacy."* https://www.dictionary.com/browse/white%20supremacy

Laureano, B. I. (2019, April 5). How do we hold each other accountable when we mess up? *Medium.* https://medium.com/@bianca.i.laureano/how-do-we-hold-each-other-accountable-when-we-mess-up-a75d4d036c11

McGill Johnson, A. (2021, April 17). I'm the head of planned parenthood. We're done making excuses for our founder. *The New York Times.* https://www.nytimes.com/2021/04/17/opinion/planned-parenthood-margaret-sanger.html

Okun, T. (2021, May). *White supremacy culture – still here.* https://drive.google.com/file/d/1XR_7M_9qa64zZ00_JyFVTAjmjVU-uSz8/view

Planned Parenthood Federation of America. (2024, October 4). *Definition of "Eugenics."* https://www.plannedparenthood.org/about-us/who-we-are/our-history

Sex Education Collaborative. (2022, May). *Centering racial justice in sex education.* https://sexeducationcollaborative.org/resources/centeringracialjustice

Simpson, M. (2022, April 11). To be pro-choice, you must have the privilege of having choices. *The New York Times.* https://www.nytimes.com/2022/04/11/opinion/abortion-black-brown-women.html

SisterSong. (2024, October 4). *Definition of "reproductive justice."* https://www.sistersong.net/about-x2

22 Liberation-Centered Learning Spaces

Valuing Joy, Relationships, and Power-Shifting

Yael R. Rosenstock Gonzalez

> any radical pedagogy must insist that everyone's presence is acknowledged. That insistence cannot be simply stated. It has to be demonstrated through pedagogical practices. To begin, the professor must genuinely value everyone's presence.
>
> – bell hooks (1994), *Teaching to Transgress: Education as the Practice of Freedom*

Key Terms

- **Equitably-inclusive:** the centering and uplifting of those with identities that have been historically marginalized.
- **Liberatory:** disrupting "supremacist cultures by centering (1) joy, community, connection, and accessibility, (2) shifting power in tangible ways, and (3) dismantling our internalized relationship with systems of oppression" (Gray & Rosenstock Gonzalez, 2023).
- **Dignity:** an immutable right for all but given historical racialized oppression, for Black and Indigenous people, it is "the actionable affirmation of a person's inviolable and sacred personhood" (Mariam Davis, 2021).
- **Belonging:** a feeling – one in which people see themselves as valued community members whose voices matter.

How to Move Through This Chapter

This chapter supports educators both in nurturing what we seek to create and in dismantling what we seek to leave behind through centering values and community experience in all aspects of course development. Use the following pages to help you develop syllabi and lesson plans, create materials, and choose activities and assessments. As you evaluate your own spaces and the tools you will employ, consider (1) how they do/do not reflect your values, (2) how these tools are responsive to the community,

---

DOI: 10.4324/9781032615479-27

(3) where your tools fall within the liberatory practice framework, and (4) which of the three prongs of liberatory practice (described later) might require additional attention.

When we focus solely on what we seek to eradicate, we miss out on specifying what we will create and nurture in its absence. Before you continue reading, write out some values and/or attributes that you would like to see present and alive within learning spaces as well as some that you will work to dismantle. Return to this activity after you finish this chapter and after you have gone through the book. Reflect on what has remained the same, what has changed, and what motivated these directions.

Nurture	*Dismantle*

As an educator, I strive to nurture equitably-inclusive and liberatory spaces that center dignity and promote belonging. This entails recognizing and dismantling cis-hetero white ableist supremacist culture within learning environments at every level. I actively complicate my own power as a facilitator and holder of privileged identities by working to equitably redistribute power through shared learning and shared facilitation, relationship building, and centering participant dignity. I utilize an interconnected and non-hierarchical three-pronged[1] framework of liberatory practices (cultural, systems/institutional, and intra/interpersonal). Aysa Gray, Brianna Harlan, and I developed this framework through teachings and coaching about liberatory practices from members of the Racial Equity and Liberation Group (RE&L), the People's Institute for Survival and Beyond (PISAB), and one another during our time as leaders of the CUNY DEI Incubator.[2]

Non-hierarchical Three-pronged Framework of Liberatory Practices

1. Liberatory practices at the **cultural level** prioritize joy, connection, and ease in shared spaces. Examples include incorporating music and dance, facilitating authentic connections among group members, providing comfortable seating and breaks for self-care, and offering tactile items (fidget toys, doodling supplies, etc.) to support focus and grounding.
2. At the **systems/institutional level**, liberatory practices focus on creating tangible shifts in access to well-being and power. This involves dismantling unequal power systems by providing resources such as daycare options, financial

support for dependent care, accessible infrastructure, multiple assignment options, equitable recognition and compensation for work, and embracing abolitionist and transformative justice values.
3. Liberatory practices at the **intra/interpersonal level** involve deep internal work to dismantle internalized oppression (both as enacted on others and self). This includes raising awareness of problematic power dynamics, privilege, and white supremacy culture, followed by supporting individuals in practicing alternative ways of being.

Developing a Liberatory Culture

Sex is a topic wrapped up in social scripts, taboos, myths, and cultural and religious significance, making it crucial for facilitators and educators to create a brave space for exploring uncomfortable or historically inaccessible topics. Ethically navigating such impactful subjects requires fostering agency, community, and conflict-resolution skills.

1. Shared/Multi-Directional Learning

Embracing shared or multi-directional learning challenges hierarchical norms by valuing everyone's expertise and contributions. Activities like counter-storytelling, rotating roles, and asset mapping encourage investment in and ownership of the learning space.

Counter-Storytelling

The experiences, stories, and knowledge of historically marginalized peoples have been silenced, warped, or devalued by those in power while overvaluing knowledge and narratives by dominant groups. Counter-storytelling amplifies the voices and experiences of historically marginalized groups, challenging dominant narratives (Delgado, 1989). Welcome participants, as their whole selves, to share their experiences and knowledge, thereby fostering community and critical dialogue.

- *Inviting the whole self*: Matika Wilbur from the 562 Project asks people to share their familial lineages as part of introductions and Racial Equity and Liberation Group (RE&L) poses a broader question of "who are your people?" to open a space. Both methods introduce the value of community for grounding and as a resource, which is counter to white supremacist values of individualism.
- *Valuing lived experience*: ask an open-ended question. For example, "What does sex mean for you and what informs your definition?" bypasses concern about being "right" and instead generates a conversation that includes

personal experiences, beliefs/values, and critical thinking that also invites participants into a space of curiosity and building off one another through difference and similarity.

Rotating Space Holder Roles

Sharing space-holding responsibilities by rotating roles based on capacity develops facilitation skills, fosters learning space investment, and reduces the burden on individuals (while pushing back against white supremacist characteristics of individualism and paternalism). My favorite space holder roles that Nikita Mitchell taught me are the "Minister of Fun," someone who leads a fun grounding or closing, and the "Conductor," who keeps the space accessible through actions such as writing out spontaneous questions in the chat or on a board as they arise.

Asset Mapping

Identifying participants' interests, skills, and networks promotes collaboration and informs group projects or actions while developing an important social justice organizing skill. First, ask participants to respond to any or all of the following three questions individually. Then, invite them to combine the responses they are willing to share to paint a picture of the group's shared assets. Make it clear that just because someone has a skill or network connection does not mean that they must use them in the space.

1. Which, if any, of the topics we plan to cover are of particular interest to you? Are there any topics about which you are knowledgeable? Would you be interested in sharing some of that knowledge in this space? *This is a great question for those seeking to encourage peer-education skill development.*
2. What talents and skills do you have? These do not need to be relevant to our current space.
3. Who are you in community with? This includes individuals, clubs, local businesses or organizations, religious communities, neighborhoods, etc.

2. Navigating Grace, Relations, and Conflict Through a Justice and Community Lens

Not every day is a great day and people don't always show up as their best selves. When nurturing a community, there must be a balance between creating space for human emotions and current capacity without excusing harmful behavior. Establishing a set of mutually agreed upon community agreements at the start of a space can support a group in navigating whatever arises along with a toolbox of options for support and addressing conflict.

Support Toolbox

Support is not the responsibility of any one person, and it is not sustainable for individuals to support others without boundaries. The following are tools that can help you identify capacity and containers for support without burnout.

- **Establishing capacity:** naming one's capacity at the beginning of a meeting is a tool I learned from Chris Novaton that can be used within learning spaces as well. For multi-session spaces, the community can develop a shared language that easily and quickly communicates capacities, limits, and needs, which allows the group to move forward from a non-stigmatizing and informed space
- **Building containers:** proactively establishing containers for different needs can prevent spontaneous concerns from turning into a complete detour. Example needs include (1) requiring solo time, (2) desiring support from a peer and/or the facilitator, and (3) desiring the whole group take a break, ground, or explore something together. Containers to address these needs can take various forms. For example, Dr. Lexx Brown-James uses a four-point system in her classroom where students can hold up a certain number of fingers to indicate what kind of support they are requesting. In their workshops, Novaton establishes a care room that can be accessed by participants at any time. If someone enters, either another facilitator (or participant volunteer) can check in with them, or if facilitating solo, it might be a good time for a break to check in with that person.
- **Identify values and expectations early:** not all opinions are created equal and not every thought deserves a space. This might sound counterintuitive but if you remember the value of equitable inclusivity, it begins to make sense. Within any given space, you, and those present must identify the values and intentions. Each community is different so sex education within a homophobic community will look different than within a QTPOC social justice-oriented community. However, most spaces benefit from values and expectation commitments. In the former, you may have common agreements around not engaging in hate speech or using homophobic slurs while hosting an honest conversation about anti-queer sentiment (but you must also prepare ways to hold and support both closeted and out queers in the space). In my university classrooms, shared space isn't a time to debate the validity of people's identities or the existence of oppressive structures. Those who need time to process or voice opinions that might be invalidating may use office hours where harm to others is minimized. It is helpful to name (and agree to) these expectations in the beginning to avoid participants feeling rejected or called out in moments when the agreements are enforced as an unexpected upholding of agreements might prevent participants from feeling comfortable to engage as you move forward.

Conflict Toolbox

Any topic can lead to controversy. Creating a culture of discourse without disrespect, managing tangents, and centering the community can support avoiding issues.

- **Discourse over disrespect and letting it sit:** Dr. Donna Oriowo teaches that disrespect gets in the way of discourse. Specifically, our emotions, especially feelings of harm and defensiveness, can impact our capacity for critical thinking. She reminds us that "feelings are not facts" and we need to take a breath to acknowledge our feelings and move towards discourse/conversation (Oriowo, 2024). She also talks about releasing urgency. If you are not in the right headspace at a particular moment, you can take some time to process before returning to the topic later
- **Tangent control:** juicy conversations can go off into a tangent. Sometimes you'll decide to follow the tangent because it's important – even if it derails your learning goals. However, if you'd like to honor the tangent without allowing it to take over, you can choose to set a transparent container of X minutes to create space for addressing whatever has entered the room and then letting it rest.
- **Calling on:** Sonya Renee Taylor talks about the use of "calling on" rather than "calling in" or "calling out." Calling out can feel like engaging in cancel culture, where a person is vilified instead of addressing harm constructively. Calling in involves emotional labor, supporting someone to understand their harmful actions or beliefs within a relationship. Calling on offers an opportunity to address problematic behavior without the emotional burden of educating the person. It fosters accountability and repair, making it valuable in learning spaces to name harm and invite the perpetrator to take responsibility and learn.

3. Centering Participant Interests, Dignity, and Needs

Interest

Understanding the interests, goals, and motivations of participants is vital for fostering buy-in and ensuring relevance to their needs. In single-session workshops, time constraints are significant, but information collection methods like polling, introductions with questions, post-it note and flipchart paper activities, or group activities can be effective. Sample questions include:

- What brings you here? or What do you hope to gain?
- What are you hoping we will cover during our time together?
- What would make you leave this space feeling fulfilled?

For multi-session spaces, ongoing check-ins and revisions are crucial. While covering essential topics, adapting activities and discussions based on participant input is key. Online or in-person discussion questions and surveys facilitate interaction and gather individual preferences and feedback throughout the experience.

Dignity and Needs

The outside world does not stop when we enter a learning space. We bring varying levels of what is happening around us, personally and globally, into the spaces we inhabit. Ignoring this reality in liberatory spaces can be damaging. Creating opportunities to process tensions, harm, exhaustion, fears, and hopes reminds everyone of their humanity.

For individual sessions, this may involve a check-in at the outset. For multi-session settings, in addition to check-ins, information gathering is supportive. In my classes, I start with a survey covering student interests, learning styles, responsibilities (work, family, other classes), and potential obstacles to attendance, including mental and physical health concerns. If a student's engagement changes, I reference this survey to craft a supportive check-in email that communicates concern to alleviate discomfort or any fears that a student may have in requesting assistance.

Recognizing student dignity, interests, and needs involves creating lessons aligned with their learning goals. I offer various entry points into the material and encourage continued exploration beyond the classroom. Homework assignments include multiple options accommodating different learning styles and energy levels, and I prioritize grace over punitive deadlines, respecting students' lives without requiring excuses. A broken heart, a long-awaited concert, and the flu are all valid life events – I do not need to know what happened to honor a request for more time.

Establishing an environment where feedback, suggestions, and criticism are welcomed without fear of retaliation is crucial in disrupting standard power dynamics. I encourage ongoing feedback and provide mid-course surveys for graded courses to demonstrate my genuine interest in student input. Their feedback is respectfully addressed if incorporation is not possible to demonstrate that their voices are valued. Lastly, it is important to acknowledge what you do not know and to demonstrate a willingness to learn new things. This fosters trust and models openness to growth.

What's Next?

The previous examples offer methods for nurturing a values-led liberatory learning space. Here I offer one of my favorite ways to structure a lesson plan, whether for a workshop or a course, to support engaging and effective learning environments that thoughtfully incorporate different learning and teaching styles.

(Simplified) Backwards Design

The following is a simplified three-step version of backwards design that I learned through Jennifer Gonzalez on Cult of Pedagogy during a pedagogy course by Dr. Catherine Sherwood-Laughlin:

1. Identify your learning goals (what your participants should know or be able to do as a result of this lesson).
2. Choose how you will effectively measure whether the learning goal was met (relevant assessment tool).
3. Select or develop lessons and activities that will support participants in kicking your assessment tool's butt (which will indicate that they have met the learning goals).

Lastly, don't forget to incorporate multiple learning styles (visual, auditory, kinesthetic, experiential, etc.) to reach your audience.

Example:

1. Learning goal: participants will be able to describe the different phases of the menstrual cycle and how those phases manifest internally and externally.
2. Assessment (1): creative individual or group project (if for a single workshop: song, presentation, or performance at the end; if part of a course, add diagram, video, comic strip, etc. options) where students fulfill the following for at least one phase:

    1. Identify hormones and their levels
    2. Describe reproductive system impact during a phase (e.g., shedding uterine lining, discharge production, egg release)
    3. Provide two examples of well-being impacts (e.g., energy levels, mood, arousal)

    Assessment (2): "Name that phase" ten-minute game-show activity matching symptoms or processes to relevant phases.

Three Lesson Plan Activity Examples

Activity 1: storytelling and mapping activity: students discuss the different symptoms they have experienced and/or observed in others around the menstrual cycle to invite lived experience into the room. Students map what they know about the cycle to a provided worksheet.

Activity 2: video presentation [transcript or an article with the same information also provided]: covers phases, hormones, reproductive system, and impact of hormonal contraception. Optional sensory activity: use water, egg whites, glue, and yogurt to familiarize students with discharge textures. Continue adding to the worksheet.

Activity 3: group discussion: students answer one another's lingering questions (students might use anatomical diagrams or plushies to facilitate explanations if available). Facilitator shares only when false information is being shared or there are unanswered questions.

Introspective Questions for Consideration

- Return to the example activities and structures offered in this chapter and consider where they intersect with the three liberatory practice prongs. It is not unusual for one activity to contribute to multiple purposes.
- As you move through the rest of the book, consider mapping what you read to how they interact with liberatory practices and your values.
- Where did excitement arise for you within this chapter? Where did resistance arise? Sit with these feelings and journal about what lessons the feelings may hold. Then, consider how you can incorporate acknowledgment of one's feelings and the stories they tell into the intra-personal liberatory learning experience.
- Reminder to return to the nurture/dismantle list at the beginning of the chapter.

Notes

1 Please note, the three levels are meant to be used in conjunction with one another. Otherwise, they run the risk of becoming performative and empty. One is not more than important than the other as they all are part of creating the present and future we seek.
2 The wisdom and influence of those named will continue to pop up throughout the chapter as we collaborated over the course of years and I learned much during that time from these individuals and groups.

References

Delgado, R. (1989). Storytelling for oppositionists and others: A plea for narrative. *Michigan Law Review, 87*(8), 2411–2441. https://doi.org/10.2307/1289308

Gonzalez, J. (2023, November 28). Backward design: The basics. *Cult of Pedagogy.* https://www.cultofpedagogy.com/backward-design-basics/

Gray, A., & Rosenstock Gonzalez, Y. R. (2023, June 3). *Mirror mirror: Using liberatory practice for resisting replication of White supremacy culture in antiracist DEI work* [Conference Workshop]. NCORE 2023, New Orleans, LA.

Hooks, B. (1994). *Teaching to transgress: Education as the practice of freedom.* Routledge.

Mariam Davis, A. (2021). Dignity is the bedrock for workplace belonging. *Stanford Social Innovation Review.* https://doi.org/10.48558/3P1Y-9H13

Oriowo, D. [@dr.donnaoriowo and @annodright]. (2024, February 20). We can choose to do better. Discourse is awesome AF but disrespect should not be encouraged and will not be tolerated. https://www.instagram.com/p/C3lnmZBM2yf/

23 From Concept to Community

Ethical Practices in Event Organization

Steph Zapata

Key Terms

- **We:** 1: collectively as organizers, 2: as a larger society, 3: Spidermen
- **Praxis:** 1: exercise or practice of an art, skill. 2: the process by which a theory, lesson, or skill is enacted, embodied, realized, applied, or put into practice.

Organizing a well-rounded, inclusive and impactful space for guest speakers is a bit like being Spiderman; "with great power comes great responsibility." To ensure inclusivity and impact, organizers entrusted with this power must carefully assess the "who, what, where, when, how, and why" not just of the event, but of the potential guest speakers.

It should come as no surprise that capitalism and racism (and all other -isms) impact the sexuality education realm. These sneaky systems negatively impact the broad field by embedding expectations of how a "professional" should look, speak, and express. Even the most well-meaning organizer may fawn to professionalism; bypassing Black, Brown, Indigenous, People of Color (BIPOC) educators, requiring speakers detach from authenticity, tokenizing marginalized educators as mere props, and centering certifications over lived experience and profound impact.

Think of your invited guests as extensions of your community and manifestations of the impact you hope to have. What stories and strategies might they offer outside of traditional academia and data? In this context, they are not just a topic presenter but the embodiment of its lived experience.

But how do we know when we perpetuate this model? How do we intentionally cross-examine our invited speaker process? This chapter serves to guide organizers through assessments, strategies, and practices in identifying, outreaching, and booking experts through a framework that centers educators, audience, and community without exploitive hierarchy.

One need only look at the Reproductive Justice timeline to understand a small portion of the sex-negative effects of white supremacy. Given these experiences, we must acknowledge that *organizers are asking educators to share personal*

DOI: 10.4324/9781032615479-28

or communal trauma to the audience's educational advantage. Most often this truth is overlooked in the name of productivity and capitalism; we dismiss it with thoughts like, "Well this is just their job." But we, dear Spidermen, are wrong – this is their history, their life.

Choose to place the most eye-opening, system-disrupting voices center stage and experience the inevitable ripple effect of changing tides. With critical intentionality, we can move towards creating a space that centers revolutionary wellness for participants *and* speakers.

You, my friend, have been bitten by the radioactive spider and now hold the power. How will you wield it and for/with whom?

In this next section we begin our analysis with ourselves because we cannot assess the multiplicity of speakers without knowing who *we* are and what we value.

Who Are We and What Are Our Values?

1. Intentional Analysis

Before approaching a speaker with an invitation, we've got to do some internal questioning because our identities and lived experiences inform how we see the world and others in it. What characteristics do we value? What forms of speech do we consider inappropriate and why?

Intentional Organizers are in awareness and acceptance of:

- Their own identities/privileges,
- Their agencies positionality/history
- And the cumulative biases between the two.

Prior to building out your event, fill in the following table:

Your identities/communities	Identities of leadership and program/planning team	Identities of the communities you/your organization serves

After you have completed this table, notice the identities not included. If you realize that marginalized communities are not equitably represented in the positions of power, organizers, or leadership, spend some time reflecting on why that is.

Through centuries of colonialism fueled by the delusion of white supremacy, non-BIPOC communities have come to believe that BIPOC communities need saving, adults have come to believe that youth need saving, and heteronormative communities have come to believe that queer communities also need saving. This exploitative framework utilizes those "in need of saving" to fulfill organization/program deliverables, while actively refusing to hire, center, and pay these communities for time and labor. We are conditioned to see *certain* communities as in need of saving but not quite capable of saving themselves, let alone others.

Next, let's look at who we deem an expert worthy of an invitation. Do you consider the following:

- What are their identities?
- What are the requirements and prerequisites of a guest speaker?
- How might their authenticity (speech, dress, presentation modality, etc.) contribute to the success of your event?

Explicitly hiring educators with myriad degrees and certifications helps to maintain systemic status quo, as you are choosing to center a singular identity: the academic, while ignoring intersectionality. Organizers must think critically about the foundational saviorism and systemic racism within academia and the non-profit industrial complex alike. When we require all speakers to be of elite higher education, rather than inviting self-made guests with relevant experience, we're limited to a very shallow pool.

Language Justice refers to the right of all to communicate in the language they are most comfortable in. Outsiders of cultural lingo may deem non-English or non-academic speech as unprofessional and an ineffective educational tool. The use of non-English, slang, and/or African American Vernacular English (AAVE) serves a connective purpose from community member to community member, while offering the opportunity for cultural outsiders to bear witness to its power. Think of how you may speak to a group of teens, versus a group of toddlers: we adjust our vocabulary accordingly to connect with our learners. Encouraging educators to speak as themselves without the performativity of academia uplifts authenticity as a valued and effective tool.

Put simply, everyone you hire should not look, speak, and present like you.

Once you have a list of educators/speakers you're interested in booking, complete the following table to help you better assess your rationale for booking or not booking a specific person:

Identity of guest speakers	How might these identities uphold traditionality/status quo?	How might these identities disrupt traditionality/status quo?

2. Offer Advocacy

While "offering" publicity/promo in exchange for labor has become common, we with "Great Power" have a responsibility to advocate for our invited guests to be financially compensated. Because you want to honor the educator's well-being, and because you see them as a whole-person – not just a temporary independent contractor, the first things to consider when drafting an offer are:

- How can I ensure this opportunity is beneficial for speakers, too? (What can I offer them?)
- How can I mitigate potential and actual harm by acting as the presenter's advocate? (What can I do/say to support/protect them?)

Monetary Compensation

Now onto the (sometimes) uncomfortable subject of monetary compensation. By now we agree that education is labor, and labor warrants recompense. We can also hold that it may not always be the case that you or your agency have unlimited funding to directly pay guest speakers. Let's compassionately explore strategies for in-kind payment vs unethical practices, with the expressed ideal goal being to financially compensate our speakers as often as we can.

Many sexuality educators are employed in underfunded agencies, barely earning a livable wage. Others pilot their sovereign entrepreneurship without the financial backing of a steady 9am–5pm paycheck or financial grants.

The principle concept of compensation is a physical (usually monetary) acknowledgement of an exchange of labor; "you have provided this service, this good, here is what I have to offer back." It is a recognition of basic human needs under inhumane capitalism.

In today's digital age, offers of "exposure" and "publicity" are dime a dozen and do next to nothing to support speaker sustainability. Answering "but why not?" is simple: speakers cannot pay bills or feed families with concepts like "exposure" or "publicity," because these are abstract and immaterial. While exposure may be a bonus, it does not consider the speaker's preparation, travel, arrangement of home/family care, supplies, or delivery time. These intangible concepts do not guarantee incoming *paid* opportunities. Therefore, such offers do not align with ethical organizing.

Part of our role as advocates is to secure funding to compensate individuals for their work. Part of our role as an advocate is to find appropriate funding to pay folks for their work, even if it feels uncomfortable to ask or if there may be anticipated pushback. This practice offers us the opportunity to affirm that our labor, our supervisor's labor, is no more worthy than that of our invited guest. Review your budget, make the request of leadership to find *something* that honors the labor of the guest. If it is **impossible** to pay your experts, consider postponing the event until you've made the impossible **possible.** With time we can earmark and reallocate funds, find new grants, and even fundraise for this specific project. Remember that not everything has to be done right now at this moment. Organizing ethically means we are detaching from urgency and instead moving with care and honor.

"What if it really *is* impossible to pay presenters *and* impossible to postpone?" In cases like this it is imperative to be transparent with your hopeful educators by clearly stating you:

- Are not able to offer financial compensation
- Recognize this lack of payment may impact them negatively or cause them to turn down your invitation
- Want to offer them something beneficial in turn and are willing to hear their thoughts/ideas

In place of dollars and exposure, additional offerings may include:

- Using existing funds to purchase a book/product of theirs
- Gifting them some of your books/products
- A public statement/press release/testimonial of their great work
- Promoting their brand through your networks for the next six months
- Travel/lodging/meal/per diem compensation
- Exchanging your client email listserv so they can grow theirs
- An invitation to attend your organization's future events for free
- Offering royalties and licensing agreements for distributed work (refer to the following section on Recorded Workshops for Distribution)

Recorded Workshops for Distribution

As you and your team discuss protocol and offers, let's consider the concept of workshop recordings. A traditional organizer model says, "Your session will be recorded." An intentional organizer model says, "Your session will be recorded *and* made available for X amount of time. It will also be shared with our full network including non-event attendees *and* it will be sold as a replay, of which you will not receive a portion of sales."

Operating through an ethical lens means that organizers do not capitalize on the labor of others without their explicit understanding and legal permission. This means recordings should be limited to event attendees, ensuring consideration of the speaker's financial interests. While you may offer a $600 honorarium and think, "now my entire network can access this training," it is essential to view this as exploitation and a form of wage theft. Offering speaker content to affiliate networks makes it unlikely that the speaker will be invited and paid by these new organizations, given they have already received the content needed.

If it is necessary to distribute recordings, organizers must practice transparency with their experts. This means we are not hiding the replay sale language in the fine print of a four-page contract, but we are literally adding bold or italics to the text, highlighting it with color so that it stands out to speakers for review. Ethical disclosure looks like:

> Thank you so much for the willingness to collab with us on this event! Our structure is one where the event is recorded, and replays are (1) available to attendees for 1 year, **and** (2) sold to the public/non-attendees.

Now, let's bring in some advocacy:

> We acknowledge that this is your intellectual property and labor, and would love to offer you 40% of sales. The replays and recordings will be accessible for 1 year, with an option for you to renew and continue sales through our platform.

Under no circumstance should you require presenters to sign a Non Disclosure Agreement specifically related to payment and overall experience with your agency. Additionally, under no circumstance should you claim intellectual property over your presenters' materials, taglines, training, or recording.

By taking this approach, you are not positioning yourself to gain at the expense of your presenter. You are not looking to exploit them; you genuinely want to support and compensate them. Acknowledging this to presenters fosters an environment conducive to community building.

3. Drafting a Speaker Invitation

Inviting a presenter to your space is not so different from inviting someone into your home; you want to give them a clear picture of the environment, your asks, and who will be there. What do speakers need to know about your event/project? The following is a place to start:

- Audience/staff demographics (ex. race, ethnicity, age), neighborhood setting (rural, suburban, city, etc.), number of attendees
- The purpose/objectives of your event and how that aligns with their work
- Requested length and content of their session
- Is this an online or in-person event? Will it be recorded, and is there a possibility to opt out of having their session recorded?
- If you are aware of or expecting any antagonists' presence (think people protesting Drag Queen Story Hour at local libraries or abortion clinics). **If so, describe in detail what you plan to do to offer safety.**
- The financial or barter compensation you *are* able to offer and the recognition that this offer may be significantly under their traditional rate.

When drafting your initial message to presenters, include as much relevant information as possible, including why you are requesting them from among all the wonderful experts in the world. This message forms the first impression the educator will have of you and your organization, so it is important to make it a positive one. To achieve this, we need to affirm and highlight a few key points.

Valuing the Speaker

Let speakers know that you value them, get specific about the things they do really well, the things you want to spotlight at your event. If you are unsure of what this presenter does well or why their voice is so important, postpone reaching out until you have done your homework.

Value Impact and Avoid Tokenization

When reaching out to educators of communities you do not belong to, what you are looking to do is name the value/impact of that difference without tokenizing them. "I'm inviting you because you are Puerto Rican and diversity matters to us" can be perceived as ingenuine and exploitive. Because we are not looking to tokenize presenters, try to expand: "I'm inviting you because you can shed light on an experience of continued colonial harm that many of us don't know happened – and is still happening today." It is incredibly powerful to transparently name your lack of belonging to a community while simultaneously advocating for your audience to see themselves reflected in your event speakers.

Intentional and Proactive Speaker Disclosure

We know that most disclosure of sexuality and sexual experiences comes with the possibility of activation, triggering/re-traumatization for speakers. Therefore, it is an organizers responsibility to clearly state that such disclosures are neither a necessity nor a request. Offer in your initial approach that, while there will likely be discussions on some heavy things, there is no expectation or ask that educators disclose their personal experiences of trauma or answer any questions from the audience that compromise their well-being. They are the experts of their experience, with full agency to say "no, I won't answer that," "I don't want to go there," or to set boundaries on their shares.

I'll say this one piece and nothing more on the topic. "You, dear Organizer, **get** to be the one to let them know that it is okay to draw boundaries for their self-preservation. In fact, you can let them know that it's more than okay . . . that you **want** them to say no and will assure your advocacy if pushback arises. Not because they need saving, but because they are an invited guest in your home.

Avoid requiring presenters to submit material for review and approval. Because you have vetted this person, read up on their work, their values and methodology *prior to* inviting them, you trust them to do their job without policing. In circumstances where this practice cannot be avoided, provide rationale and make space for the presenter's response, 'I acknowledge that this request can sometimes feel icky, as though we don't trust you or are putting you under review, and while I can't presently change the organization's procedure, I'm genuinely happy to hold space for feedback.'

Be as clear on what can and cannot offer. Inform presenters of your speakers budget, and if applicable, name that you recognize it may be less than their usual rate. As an organizer you have to do the internal work to be ready to accept rejection or a counter offer. This does not mean you have done something wrong, but that the educator is fully in their autonomy. You are affirming the agency of the guest presenter by proclaiming, 'I know you deserve to be paid, and paid well for this work. Here is what I have to offer, and I welcome your rejection/counter.'

Share the structure and availability of any wellness spaces or services you plan to head. Quiet rooms, affinity spaces, massage/body work, and access to mental health coaches are wonderful investments in the overall wellbeing of attendees, staff, and speakers.

Be proactive by asking educators of any accommodations they may need and inform them of the accessibility accommodations (or lack thereof) at your event. After the event, reach out to your presenters and ask if they would like to offer you feedback. If you are not able to hold space for educators to tell you the things that **did not go well**, do not make the offer; instead have someone else do so.

Depending on your event, you may or may not be ready or prepared to offer 'safe adaptability' and authenticity to your presenters. Safe adaptability refers to the acknowledgement that presenters' content may shift, and that they may change content to better align with their individual praxis without your approval. Why? Because we trust speaker approaches and ability to adjust their sails to the changing winds of new contexts and circumstances that may arise. Similarly safe authenticity is an invitation to show up, dress, express, speak, present in the ways that feel best and most accessible to the expert."

Through this Great Power and Responsibility we come to recognize biases and privileges that influence speaker selection and compensation determination. *This* way, *our* way of organizing is not **yet** the industry standard or "norm," because it intentionally disrupts the system and status quo. It encourages us to view speakers as community extensions, valuing their lived experiences and contributions beyond traditional academia or data. This is the way forward, through tradition, towards liberation.

Educators and organizers of color are welcome to join (for free) BIPOC S.P.A.C.E. sexperts in building community and sharing resources. If interested email StephanieSpeaksHere@gmail.com.

24 Maximizing Sexual Health Education for Youth

Sam Carwyn

Key Terms

- **Youth:** those between the ages of 11 and 18.
- **Askable Adult:** an adult who is approachable, easy for youth to talk to about anything, independently accessible to youth, and centers the youth when sharing information and answers.
- **Bodily Autonomy:** the ability to choose what happens to your body without others' influence or control that conflicts with your choices.
- **Developmental Age:** the age at which youth functions on a social, physical, intellectual, cultural, and emotional level and can process content.

Comprehensive sexuality education is a phrase used by most sex educators and often within reproductive justice work. The goal is to ensure individuals have the knowledge and skills to engage in safe, healthy behaviors and develop equitable relationships, which is aligned with Sexuality Information and Education Council of the United States sexuality education goals (National Guidelines Taskforce, 2004). Comprehensive sex education (CSE) normalizes development, is science-based, and utilizes evidence-based methods. When developing my community-based sex education programming, I used the acronym BASICS. The acronym breaks down into body knowledge, age-appropriate safety consciousness, intersectional, conversations, and self-determination.

Prevention initiatives take into account various factors. Prevention researchers and health experts utilize a socio-ecological model to address what is occurring at different levels. The model has levels that outline healthy traits, concrete prevention strategies, and the multiple factors that might affect youth's health. I developed a socio-ecological model focused on sexual health and preventing sexual harm. To zone in on the characteristics of individuals, I have included the 40 developmental assets outlined by the Research Institute. The developmental assets needed include both external and internal characteristics. You will get an overview and critique of five curriculums that focus on CSE by educating adults.

DOI: 10.4324/9781032615479-29

Also, an examination of how the curriculum fosters healthy development and prevents sexual harm.

BASICS

Body Knowledge: when one comprehensively understands bodies, one can develop an appreciation for all bodies. In CSE, there is a focus on medically accurate information, physical development, and bodily autonomy. Youth are informed about how different bodies function based on sex, when they are going through puberty, and for reproduction. The goal is to normalize various changes and support youth in learning to care for their bodies.

Age-appropriate: this information takes into account both chronological and developmental age. It focuses on vocabulary, what is happening in their current developmental stage, and information critical to the next stage. Youth are learning more about gender, peer pressure, sexual orientation, and how to evaluate different outcomes. Youth are also provided with an opportunity to think through appropriate ways to express their emotions, birth control options, and goals.

Safety Conscious: being safety conscious is about what impacts one's over-all safety. CSE has a focus on healthy relationships, consent, and sexually transmitted infections or diseases. Youth are informed about signs of abuse, barriers to utilize during various sex acts, and testing for sexually transmitted diseases and infections. They are learning to address power dynamics, non-consensual interactions, and what safety will entail for them.

Intersectional: sex education must be intersectional to be comprehensive. CSE provides an opportunity to learn how the combination of one's identities impacts how one thinks about and engages in relationships. The focus is on how geographic region impacts access to information, essential services, and culturally responsive care. With more understanding, youth recognize how to show respect for different faith traditions, levels of ability and not engage in biased behaviors.

Conversations: this mode of education is the most effective way to support youth. There is a focus on being real, communication styles, effective communication, and nonverbal communication. Educators are providing an opportunity to work through discretion, relationships online, their habits, and the impact of differing platforms utilized. Ultimately, youth learn what is appropriate communication based on the relationship, in particular settings, group dynamics, and desired degree of privacy.

Self-determination: this is a critical component of sexual health development. It empowers youth to examine their preferences, know their values, and rec-ognize the impact of societal pressure. By naming the people and factors that help them discern what they want to do, youth can make informed decisions about limits, boundaries, and relationship dynamics that can provide them pleasure while respecting partners.

All six skills are a goal for youth, yet some adults have never obtained them. I have worked my entire career in the nonprofit sector focused on youth, families, reproductive justice, and supporting survivors of violence. I have been inside and alongside systems designed to prevent or address harm. However, providers often needed to gain knowledge regarding current experiences, be made aware of how to provide culturally competent support, or did not believe in the agency of those they are providing services to. A CSE curriculum rooted in the community, alongside and outside of systems, will create the greatest degree of change. Ultimately, my professional experiences helped me to understand that prevention work and harm reduction require education beyond the participant in front of you.

The adults in a community can create a broad impact across generations. Adults can positively impact the youth they engage with professionally and personally. Thus, more youth have the opportunity to get crucial information, especially as sex education is being removed from schools and districts across the country. Adults have more cultural knowledge and experiences within faith traditions that can ensure that more thorough information is provided. Adults may have more experience in problem-solving and awareness of the city in which they live, which allows them to lay out feasible options for youth. Partnering with adults who have already built rapport with young people will enhance the quality of support.

Centering youth begins with acknowledging that your desire to be a supportive adult must include a willingness to converse with youth instead of direct them. Adult educators will likely reduce parent apprehension if they have also developed a relationship with this adult in the youth's life. Educators provide youth with complete information and want them to create their own path. Adult educators honor youth's generational experiences and can support youth beyond a class or a curriculum implementation period. Centering youth requires recognizing that their knowledge and insight have value and they deserve autonomy.

Socio-ecological models outline the interrelated factors that lead to negative or positive outcomes. An individual's access to comprehensive sexual health information may be targeted, supported, or protected. Utilizing a prevention mindset, I designed this socio-ecological model focused on sexual health based on my professional experience and utilizing aspects of four others models. My model includes aspects of the University of Minnesota's Mental Health and Well-being Socio-Ecological Model, US Public Health Service's Health Belief Model as noted in IN-clued program summary, and Johns Hopkins University's Socio-Ecological Model of Communication and Behavior Change (University of Minnesota, 2020; Shore, 2021; Kincaid et al., 2007). This new socio-ecological model outlines distinct influences on risk-taking behavior throughout different contexts, including personal characteristics, compound factors, health views, and specific skills that result in individuals applying their knowledge to obtain healthy sexual development outcomes.

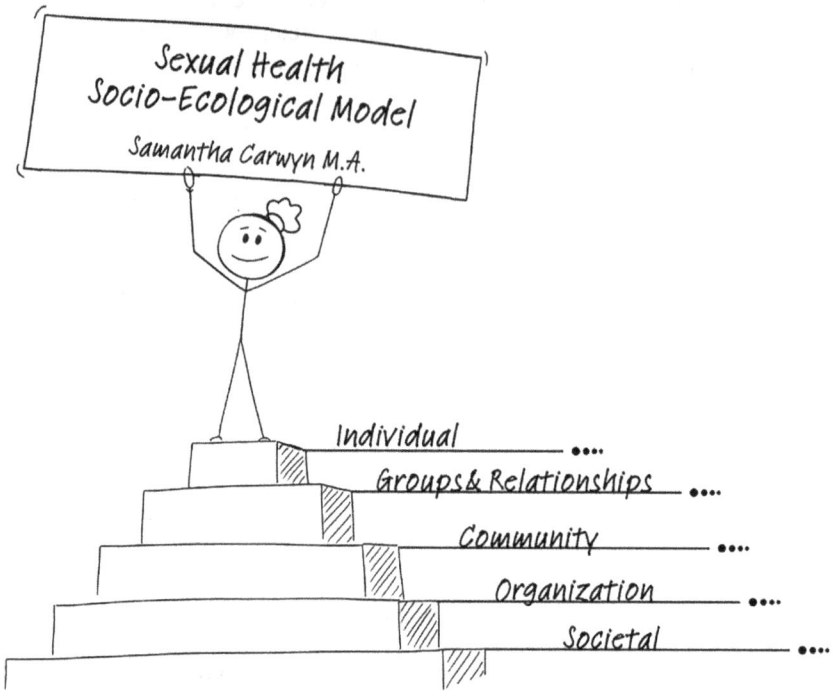

Figure 24.1 Sexual Health Socio-Ecological Model

Individual: the biological and personal history factors that increase the likelihood of risk-taking behaviors. Prevention focuses on attitudes, beliefs, and behavior choices at this level. Dialogue is utilized to build trust. The specifics that are impacting individuals are identity, personal characteristics, religion, emotions, health history, culture, shared heritage, beliefs, values, history of abuse, sibling interactions, attitudes regarding sex, increasing knowledge, technology in the household, impulsive behaviors, youth's perceived susceptibility, and risk, parent-child communication, parental guidance, passing on traditions, self-image, family dynamics (supportive, patriarchal, emotional stability, violence, routines)

Groups and Relationships: the social relationships that increase the likelihood of risk-taking behaviors. Can prevent harm by promoting positive peer norms, improving problem-solving ability, and strengthening relationship skills. Communication is socially influenced to support greater participation and personal development. Individuals are impacted by self-perception, a sense of purpose, power, emotional support, social well-being, leadership skills, emotional intelligence, bias, isolation and cohesion, bounded normative influences, others' tolerance of inappropriate behaviors, social networks, social identity, self-sufficiency, teamwork abilities, desire to fit in or stand out, time limitations, understanding of safe dating, support systems, youth's perceived benefits of behavior, sexually aggressive peers, social connections, opportunities for social interaction, healthy relationship skills, and conflict resolution proficiency.

Community: the physical settings in which people have social relationships, i.e., school, workplace, and neighborhood. Prevent harm by coordinating all community members to improve the physical environment, community resources, and social environment. Communication is direct and persuasive, providing education. Community includes accessibility, norms, stereotypes, social policies, gender equity, access to information, community centers, local events, youth's level of engagement with their surroundings, transportation, institutions, partnerships, neighborhood relationships, the availability of resources, services, and care.

Organization: a social environment that meets an individual's needs or wants. Prevention promotes staff behavior change, addresses discrimination, and analyzes policies and practices to advance equity. Communication is instructive, practiced, and reinforced. The focal points for an organization are staff's experiences of inequities based on their identity, a youth's perception of barriers within the organization, attitudes displayed, discrimination, expectations enforced, marginalization, formal and informal guidelines, cultural competence, cross-sectional understanding, resource allocation, health campaigns within the organization, accessibility including the building, materials, communication etc.

Societal: the broad community, political environment, and government in which an individual lives. Must develop and enforce laws that increase beneficial health behaviors, provide choices, and improve individual freedoms for prevention to be achieved. Communication is directive using advocacy and regulations to get compliance. The emphasis is on geographic barriers, economic programs, mass media, systemic inequities, protected classes, legal incongruence, rules, rights, and responsibilities individuals have, laws alignment with current behaviors and technology, uncertain or biased enforcement of the distribution of state-wide resources, obstruction to services due to age, immigration status, or criminal history.

The five youth empowering programs below represent distinct areas within the model.

Families Talking Together is an intervention program designed specifically for African-American and Latino caregivers of 10- to 14-year-olds. It is delivered in two parts: one meeting with the caregiver(s) and a follow-up meeting or call. During the first portion, the educator discusses the program, common caregiver barriers, current statistics, most effective communication strategies, crucial monitoring habits, and ways to approach sexual health with their youth. Then, after the caregiver talks to their youth, they will reconnect with the educator for specific support via a follow-up call. Alternatively, an educator could deliver all general information to a small group, meet one-on-one with caregivers to identify youth-specific plans, and then have one-on-one calls for additional guidance. The curriculum's primary focus is promoting direct, honest communication and appropriate monitoring habits to delay when youth begin engaging in sexual activity. This curriculum aligns with the individual level of the model as a parent will gain the skills to discuss in detail their youth's behaviors, beliefs, and intentions while being mindful of their youth's personal history. Parents can break down perceived risks and support the ongoing development of the youth in their care.

This program builds support, guides boundaries, and has parents name their expectations. As a result, youth will have greater family support and more positive family communication. This curriculum builds internal assets of integrity, restraint, planning, and personal power. The information parents receive explains strategies to help youth reject peer pressure and promote self-determination. It builds on families' core beliefs, has youth talk through how they'll address sexual interactions, recognize what's within their control, and why it's important for them not to be sexually active and act with conviction.

Caregivers and youth are provided with CSE materials. The parent workbook covers nine topics, and parents are given two books for their youth. It is almost entirely about conversations for self-determination. Though the program was designed for African-American and Latino families, the majority applies to caregivers as a whole. The broad framing makes the program applicable to families from various religious backgrounds, with differing educational levels, and regardless of the sexual orientation of the caregiver or youth.

Athletes As Leaders and Coaching Boys Into Men was designed to be implemented to a team by coaches. Athletes As Leaders can be implemented with any player on a girls' team. Coaching Boys Into Men does not distinctly identify that it can be implemented with transgender athletes. Though two distinct curricula, they have comparable frameworks and components. These curricula have coaches attend a four-hour training session with a sex educator, whom they refer to as a community advocate. The curriculum is entirely conversation-based, with coaches going through discussion points with their secondary athletes in ten or twelve sessions. Students learn to be positive peer role models, especially regarding rumors, consent, bias, and healthy relationship behaviors. Students deepen their relationships with teammates, peers, and coaches. Thus, the model-level relationships and groups are the most relevant. The curriculum enhances natural support systems and quality relationships while reducing isolation. Coaches share their experiences, which show understanding and help youth problem-solve while promoting trust.

This curriculum builds authentic, encouraging relationships that impact entire school communities with external assets of support, empowerment, and positive influences. Youth can get support from and converse with a role model in a non-parenting role. Youth are recognized as positive influences for peers, constructively using their time and valued by adults. This curriculum builds the internal assets of caring for others, equality, self-esteem, responsibility, and interpersonal competence. Youth are allowed to identify how they want to show up and actions to develop pride in the school community they are creating. The lesson topics examine and enforce typical gender roles, e.g., beauty standards in Athletes As Leaders, as well as anger and aggression in Coaching Boys Into Men. However, the curriculum's goal is positive peer interaction within and across genders. Regarding CSE components, the lessons align with the real experiences of secondary students and approach safety head-on. Students explore personal responsibility, unhealthy relationship characteristics, the role of bystanders, and marginalized identities.

Elevatus was designed for individuals with intellectual disabilities from high school through adulthood. The adults taught are professional service providers, special education teachers, and employment support staff. This curriculum is intended to be taught over several weeks and consists of 22 lessons. The adults educated in this curriculum align with the community level of the model as prevention strategies are implemented in schools, work settings, and neighborhoods. Elevatus provides a few assets for youth and addresses several components of CSE. This curriculum builds a sense of safety in the home, school, and neighborhood. When teachers are trained, they can hold appropriate high expectations, and all those in the program develop supportive relationships with youth. Youth can gain personal power, greater self-esteem, resistance wordage, and clarity of their plans. CSE components include online safety, healthy relationships, sexually transmitted infections, and diseases. It provides thorough information about bodies, conversation skills, and self-determination for their relationships.

IN-clued program educates healthcare providers to care for 14–19-year-old LGBTQ youth more effectively. The full curriculum has a workshop delivered to youth by a sexuality educator and then a three-hour workshop for healthcare providers, which a sexuality educator leads with a youth trained in peer education. This curriculum aligns with the organizational level as it is implemented within the health care setting. For consistency and effective implementation, youth educators should be part of a program or have dedicated support from an adult mentor. Organizations can build partnerships, allocate resources, address system inequities, and align their policy with best practices. Although this program is most beneficial to adult healthcare providers, there are particular strengths that youth can gain.

The youth who co-teach during the workshop and youth patients benefit differently from this curriculum. Specifically, the youth who co-teach are provided an opportunity to be a resource while serving others. This curriculum creates a safer community for youth by confronting heteronormative expectations, bias, and misinformation. On a more personal level, providers can assist youth patients in developing honesty, restraint, self-esteem, and a positive outlook by implementing the recommendations given during the workshop. Even though this curriculum focuses on a particular subset of professionals, all adults can learn skills to be better listeners. Utilizing the program's six recommendations will ensure more direct conversations and open disclosure, providing safety for youth. The In-clued workshop creates an opportunity to honor the full range of bodies, increase communication skills, and promote self-determination. The curriculum is built with multiple identities in mind and provides specific implicit bias lessons and activities.

Askable Adults Matter is a training for those supporting youth 11–19. It is most relevant for after-school program staff, educators, mentors, and foster parents. It is generally delivered over four hours, with the time being broken into discussing one's perception, current data (preferably local), and a specific framework for answering different types of questions. When provided regularly throughout a city, this training can ground advocacy work, promote science-based regulations, create greater access across districts, and advance policies impacting the sexual health of youth. This affects not only the society in which youth live but also individual youth.

This training strengthens youth relationships and provides components of comprehensive sexual health information. Youth are encouraged to speak with parents and have encouraging conversations with peers. Based on the target training population, youth will likely gain caring adults who role model responsible behaviors and are part of a youth program. Youth can better understand integrity, honesty, equality, and interpersonal skills. Since a key component is promoting inclusive access to services and providers, it supports intersectional identities and self-determination. In addition, utilizing the data shown during the training and resources provided to attendees, they can implement core CSE areas, including knowledge about the body, safety, resources for sexual health needs, conversation skills, and boundaries in age-appropriate ways, thus increasing self-determination.

Things to Consider About Yourself as an Educator

- What has your personal experience been with askable adults as a youth?
- Do you want to support adults and youth in their skills to communicate their expectations?
- What genuine relationships and partnerships have you or your organization cultivated?
- Where could you provide adult-focused sex education that benefits a new group of people?

Things to Consider About Your Community

- Is your community focused on prevention efforts or being reactionary?
- Does your community educate adults to provide a greater depth of support for youth?
- Has your community collaborated across organizations to reach shared goals?
- How does educating adults address the restrictions being placed on schools and districts?

Things to Consider When Implementing

We can measure the impact beyond the number of people directly participating, so start small. These programs should be offered as an opt-out rather than opt-in to ensure greater engagement. Specific communities could benefit from implementing sex education in this way. Allow the process of learning alongside each other.

Always focus on comprehensive education, thus not sacrificing crucial information for an adult's comfort. Unfortunately, we have been conditioned to think of talking about sex, our bodies, and so much of this as taboo. Not everyone will be enthusiastic, and only some adults will be able to honor the youth's needs first. However, every adult should have the opportunity to learn how to become an approachable and knowledgeable role model.

References

Kincaid, D. L., Figueroa, M. E., Storey, D., & Underwood, C. (2007). *A social ecology model of communication, behavior change, and behavior maintesssnance* [working paper]. Johns Hopkins Center for Communication Programs, Johns Hopkins University.

National Guidelines Taskforce. (2004). Guidelines for comprehensive sexuality education. In siecus.org. *Sexuality information and education council of the United States* (p. 19). https://siecus.org/resource/the-guidelines/

Shore, A. (2021). IN•clued program summary. In etr.org. *Planned parenthood of the Great Northwest and Hawaiian Islands*. https://www.etr.org/ebi/assets/File/INclued-Program-Summary.pdf

University of Minnesota. (2020, July 14). *Mental health and well-being ecological model | Leadership education in maternal & child public health*. Mch.umn.edu. https://mch.umn.edu/resources/mhecomodel/

25 Faith, Fear, and Freedom

Redefining Sexuality in Religious Spaces

Kara Haug

Key Terms

- **Purity Culture:** a period of time between the late 1980s and early 2000s when churches directly responded to the AIDS crisis by creating a culture based on being "pure," defined as not having sex until marriage. One of the most popular books written in the spirit of this time period was *I Kissed Dating Goodbye* by Joshua Harris. Purity rings and balls and virginity contracts and pledges were commonplace in church communities, most often made between daughters and their fathers.
- **Deconstruction:** the process of revisiting the beliefs one has been taught to assess them and redetermine what still feels true in the present.
- **Religious Trauma:** experiences of abuse and/or mental anguish leveled at individuals who do not live up to standards of purity and/or respectability established by religious institutions. In most cases, these authoritarian narratives disproportionately devalue women and queer people.
- **Saint Augustine of Hippo:** a philosopher and theologian from the 4th century whose theology greatly influenced the Catholic church.

If you're ever attended a dinner party among friends or relatives, you may have heard the little phrase, "Don't discuss sex, religion, and politics" rattle around in your brain (Steinfeld, 2020). The particular topics have been known to cause any emotionally sound person to overreact and lose their cool. In recent years, however, people have been challenging this notion and are finding ways to broach these contentious topics. These topics are important and can quickly make us wonder and question our worth the most deeply. When they are heavily debated, it can make us feel that our personhood is being questioned and that our worth is being compromised. With religion and sex there seems to be a lot of rights (with even more wrongs), which can be challenging when it comes to our sense of eternity, because we fear what may happen if we are wrong. This makes talking about it tricky. Though it is tricky, that doesn't mean we should shy away, as that may cause more harm than good.

DOI: 10.4324/9781032615479-30

As a white cisgender woman who grew up in the Evangelical Lutheran Church of America, I grew up being impacted by purity culture; I have attended seminary and am married to a pastor. The communities I have spoken with are in a place of curiosity: wanting to understand youth culture, willing to engage in conversation, and recognize the effect that religion and sex are having on our politics and, therefore, the wellness of their community. In the ten years I have been teaching about sex, I have learned that talking about it within a faith community is an artform, in which you need to be willing to change course at any moment. For our society to move to a place of wellness we need to be able to talk about these two things together with compassion and not hostility.[1]

How Church Has Harmed

Currently in America there is an abundance of people who are leaving church ("In U.S., Decline of Christianity Continues at Rapid Pace," 2019). Seminaries are closing their doors or are needing to merge with other institutions just to stay afloat, and religious trauma centers are opening nationwide, with an estimated one in five Americans reporting having had that experience (Slade et al., 2023). Many people are turning to social media to follow hashtags like #deconstruction, #purityculture, and #religioustrauma. All of this is indicative of how many messages we have received growing up about sexuality within the religious context that doesn't add up to our lived experiences. People have become confused, disheartened, hurt, and are grieving.

So why is talking about sex important in faith communities if, at the rate we are currently moving, churches may soon be obsolete? The reality is that many of these puritanical views inform the development of this country, shaping our views on sex, gender, identity, and more. As a result, we are continually impacted by these narratives. In a lot of ways, we continue to experience religion as the guidepost, using it to justify taking away human rights for many people – in ways that don't, however, speak to the larger foundations of Christianity (Abdulla, 2018). Like it is with many other religions, there is a deity of authority in whom we worship and look to resemble; however, in the pursuit of power humans have mistaken this authority for an excuse to create strict rules, strip dignity away from others, and create a hierarchy of people based on gender, race, behavior, class, and sexuality.

Beyond this point, there are also still a number of people who are very active in church and operate with the tenets of their faith as their guide or are helping to reform the institution. There are others who have left yet still love God passionately. About 5.3 million LGBT individuals in America in particular identify as religious, including many who experience other marginalizations and find comfort in their faith for withstanding those oppressions (Conron et al., 2020). In order for us as a society to come to a place of sex positivity for all people, we need to foster nurturing environments where we can have conversations about sex that recognize and speak to all those of faith.

Understanding Those Who Are Faithful

I have learned that one of the first ways to lose people in faith spaces is to indicate, whether through tone of voice, direct indication, or presentation style, that they are out of touch with the current culture or are doing it "wrong." This is a demographic that has been trying to "be good" for most of their life; it carries a lot of weight for them to follow the rules they have been given. If I say things related to gender identity, orientation, or non-monogamy that lie outside of the script they have been given or indicate that their way of doing things is "old fashioned and out of touch," I will make no impact on their learning.

As an educator I work to honor a person's faith, because much of it is built from a personal relationship they have established from their own experiences in which they find comfort. When I go into these spaces, my goal is never to change what a person believes but rather to provide more information, theological ponderings, a chance to talk about sex, and – more importantly – a place to feel cared for in the process. Here are five suggested strategies that I believe support me in achieving this aim:

1. Start Small

One of my favorite phrases for sex education is, "Start small, build from there." This is the way I approach so many of my classes as it helps me stay in a space where I can welcome all levels of knowledge. I have found through my teaching that most people, even if they may know quite a bit in one area of sexuality, still need a level of simplicity to hold space for the areas that were overlooked or silenced. Starting small is a place of great care and intention, particularly in church spaces where messages are starkly binary yet conceptually fuzzy.

2. Setting the Space

Whenever I teach I always ask for food to be present and for the room to be comfortable. Food can be comforting, as it can get people into their bodies to talk about a topic that often wasn't discussed, or that even made many of us dislike our bodies and/or detach from them. When I provide food, I find it helps take some of the edge off. At the beginning of a lesson I will also calmly introduce myself, and share the story of why I got into sex education. I set up guidelines for how we will operate in the collective space together, naming things like:

- "We all come here with different knowledge and understanding and this is okay. We will have open hearts and minds and will learn from one another."
- "This is a place where we learn together and when we learn we make mistakes. Mistakes will happen today, this is also okay. We welcome our chance to grow from them."

- "We all come from different families, cultures, upbringings, and religious understandings that affect our views of sexuality. We will approach this time together with curiosity."
- "When sex is discussed we can have sensations that may arise in our bodies. This may feel too much for you. If you need to take a break or leave, that is okay."

A lesson that a former professor of mine taught me that I also have used and feel is extremely valuable as an educator is asking the question: "what do you hope to get from our time together today?" If it is a small group I ask everyone to respond; if it is a large group I'll ask four people who are willing to share. I may also ask if they have anything more to add before proceeding. Once I have their consent, we dive in.

3. Naming the Hard

I make a point to name the challenging aspects of how religious folk have learned about sex within the first few slides of my presentation. We talk about the messages we have received, the lack of education, the guilt and shame each of us carry, the secrets we may keep, and the harm we might have experienced. I also talk about how we have been taught to treat sex and spirituality as separate entities, when in reality the two are intimately woven together. As an educator who invites participants to think about what sex positivity means to them within my presentation, I also find it very important to acknowledge the pain that sex has caused in many lives, and the fact that many of us have experienced trauma. Naming this experience lets those in attendance feel validated, and it also lets them know that I am also not out of touch with reality. This validation allows them to open, to hear that even though this is a reality for some, it doesn't need to be the whole story.

4. Holding Space for Grief

There have been times when as a presenter I thought I was failing immensely. These were the times when the room was eerily quiet and there was little engagement. I felt discouraged but kept on going with the presentation. When I was finished and felt pretty lousy about myself, my mood changed when a line started to form to talk to me. What I thought was me failing from the silence that filled the room was actually a room filled with people processing and remembering, as many of them do not hear on a day to day basis what I present about sexuality and how it pertains to them spiritually.

Though we move away from grief it doesn't mean that grief is gone. Grief tends to linger in a room like smoke from a candle. You can see this in hesitant body language, long pauses of silence, and/or disengaging eye movements. In some cases, grief can render us silent. It demands our attention when it steps into the room. I have grown accustomed to letting the silence not be an awkward experience, but that of a sacred meeting between self and a new beginning:

> There's nothing like grief to goad you into meeting a raw, true, and honest you. As you work through your grief, be prepared to engage in the process of revealing the Self to the Self.
>
> (Nathan, 2018, p. 132)

I now can see the moment it happens for people, this sense of awakening in their lives. When I see it, I pause. I let the moment linger. I then ask if there are any questions, or if people need a moment. Sometimes people take that invitation, either by taking a respite to stretch or take a bathroom break. Allowing that time for stillness, when needed or requested, is important.

5. Offer Permission to Wonder . . . and Doubt

I do believe the greatest gift we can offer people in faith based settings is the permission to wonder and doubt. Too often in religious settings we are told what to believe and how to live, with little freedom to question. From my understanding, some of the greatest theologians and religious thought leaders spent their time wondering and doubting. Creating a space where learners can openly discuss and question freely can feel novel and exciting. This can be done by providing lots of group activities involving movement vs. only listening. I think of the quote by Albert Einstein that says, "I never teach my pupils. I only attempt to provide the conditions in which they can learn." This means there are a lot of open ended questions, activities that can go many different ways based on who is in the room, and providing multiple viewpoints throughout a presentation.

Let's Talk About It

Getting people to talk about sex is my main objective when I teach. This holds great value in church spaces, since many have been instructed not to talk about it. One of my favorite activities to do in Christian spaces in particular to get them talking is this: I put up two large sheets of flip chart paper, and then write at the top of one the phrase, "God Is." I then ask them to write down any adjective they can think of about God on a sticky note, and then put all those sticky notes on the sheet. On the other flip chart sheet I write, "Sex Is," then have them do the same activity. Participants usually find that God and Sex share more adjectives than not; some adjectives that have been shared over time include "loving," "passionate," "powerful," "scary," "mighty," "all-consuming," "confusing," "intense," "big," "comforting," etc. When we read these together, mental light bulbs begin to go off. I usually then say,

The Church talks about sex in four ways: Who are you having sex with? How are you having sex? When are you having sex? What and who are you thinking about? Instead, the church could be having the conversation about how closely related our relationship to God is as our relationship is to sex.

This activity strikes a chord with many and allows us to start pondering together. This activity also illustrates the complexity and layers that both sex and God hold. People clearly see the layers and not the binary way that sex had previously been introduced to them.

Special Consideration #1–Conflict

As you can imagine when discussing sex and faith, conflict can and does arise. I will say I haven't had as much conflict as I thought I would entering into this field; however, when it has come up, I've come to understand it better, in that it usually arises when someone has been triggered in some way. It is very clear that they have been triggered, because they blurt something out and become red in the face when they are talking and/or get angry. Depending on the specific issue that arises I have done different things. In the beginning when I see the dynamics of the room change, I stop everything that we are doing. In some circumstances I address what's happening with the whole group present by naming the feelings that I believe are present in the space. I check in to make sure I am accurate, and invite learners to correct me if I am not. We then talk about the situation that produced their feelings; if I believe it will add to the educational process then we talk about it as a group. If not, I will call for a break and consult with the offended person(s) individually, with their consent. Often we come to a place of understanding, and I try to follow up on that person's needs to the best of my ability in that space. If the conflict has been successfully addressed, I will then go back and address the larger group. I normalize that conflict happens, and then get an overall consensus of the climate of the room before asking if we are okay to proceed. If we are, then we do; if not, I take a bit more time and provide them with exercises that they can reflect on in their own time to recover. I have never had to stop a workshop or lesson in its entirety from conflict; however, checking in and acknowledging it with care is very important.

Special Consideration #2–Finding Pleasure

God is not just the God of authority but of love and intimacy; this is a key point I raise in faith settings to help participants see the pleasure that can be experienced from sexuality and authentic living. As humans, we are wired for connection, including intimacy; when we form connections in our lives with ourselves and with those around us, we change. I believe we also tend to live more in the present. Creating moments in workshops where participants can experience intentional conversation, being present, and remembering times of joy takes them to places of abundance rather than scarcity. And as I have utilized creation stories before to represent expansiveness I have also used them to talk about intention. If you consider when an artist creates: it's an act of intention, a process filled with emotion and wonder, moments of reflection, and then delight. God created with intention, then looked at us and said, It was very good (The Holy Bible, NRSV, Genesis 1:31). As Kelly Brown Douglas elaborates:

> [Creation] is a glimpse of God's perfect passion for life. Human passion is God's passion bursting forth from the human being as an insatiable desire to foster life in all aspects of one's living. Such an understanding and appreciation for human passion as a glimpse of God's own passion demands an embrace of human sexuality.
>
> (Douglas, 1999, p. 120)

No matter the religion, building activities around pleasure and joy helps participants recall how passion is a form of eroticism, as Audre Lorde teaches us in her writings (Lorde, 1978). To know ourselves and our community is truly erotic and pleasurable. Pleasure doesn't have to be sexual; it can be anything that feels good to us in whatever form that is. It is okay to explore what that means for us. Reframing eroticism from only being associated with objectification, lust, and – at times – scandal, is key in faith communities.

When it comes to sexuality, faith communities struggle most with the need to "be good." This is where a lot of shame lies, yet we work to debunk it with biology and science. It is also important, however, to point out the social aspects of sexuality – including those that can be found in religious texts. I do not think it is necessary to have a theology degree to teach sex in faith settings but simply to have a chance to talk about sex, be reflective, and make mistakes that allow learners to feel nourished and be brave.

In my work I've also learned that it is important to interrogate the ways that sexuality not only affects our faith but other intersections in our lives, such as race, politics, class, gender, etc. Because sex has been taught with such scarcity it is so important to emphasize this. By fostering open conversations about sexuality and spirituality, we can begin to heal the wounds inflicted by purity culture and religious trauma, moving towards a more inclusive and compassionate faith overall.

Introspective Questions for Consideration

- Take a moment to do the God is: and Sex is: exercise. What did you notice about yourself and your own adjectives?
- What are some of the myths in your own origin story that have affected you?
- What has been important for you in your own upbringing around religion that has been positive in building relationships?

- What parts of this chapter stood out to you as helpful? What parts upset you and you thought were off base? What would you change as an educator?
- What kind of exercise would you create to get people talking from various religious backgrounds?

Note

1 Though in this chapter I am speaking through a Christian lens, I invite those of similarly challenged faith traditions to consider how my thoughts can be transferable when speaking to other religions or audiences, since in many spaces the topic of sex is still one of silence.

References

Abdulla, M. R. (2018). Culture, religion, and freedom of religion or belief. *The Review of Faith & International Affairs, 16*(4), 102–115. https://doi.org/10.1080/15570274.2018.1535033

Conron, K. J., Goldberg, S. K., & O'Neill, K. (2020). *Religiosity among LGBT adults in the U.S.* The Williams Institute.

Douglas, K. B. (1999). *Sexuality and the Black Church: A womanist perspective.* Orbis Books.

The Holy Bible. (1989). *New revised standard version.* Oxford University Press.

Lorde, A. (1978). *Uses of the erotic: The erotic as power.* N.p.: Out & Out Books.

Nathan, E. (2018). *It's grief: The dance of self-discovery through trauma and loss.* As I Am Press.

Pew Research Center. (2019). *In U.S., decline of Christianity continues at rapid pace.* Retrieved October 17, 2019, from https://www.pewresearch.org/religion/2019/10/17/in-u-s-decline-of-christianity-continues-at-rapid-pace/

Slade, D., Smell, A., Wilson, E., & Drumsta, R. (2023). Percentage of U.S. adults suffering from religious trauma: A sociological study. *Socio-Historical Examination of Religion and Ministry, 5*(1), 1–28. https://doi.org/10.33929/sherm.2023.vol5.no1.01

Steinfeld, J. (2020). How to ruin a good dinner party: We're told not to discuss sex, politics, and religion at the dinner table, but what happens to our free speech when we give in to that rule? *Index on Censorship, 49*(1), 22–23. https://doi.org/10.1177/0306422020917602

Part V

Navigating the Business and Limitations of Sex Education

26 Be Sexcessful! Navigating Sex Education Entrepreneurship

Marla Renee Stewart

Be Good or Be Good At It.

– Goody Howard (2017), Sex Educator

When we start our journeys as sex educators, we often try to find the perfect fit and what feels good to us. Some of us start off working with youth, as college health educators, and with adults selling sex toys as avenues of exploring what sex and sexuality has to offer to society and ourselves. We strive to learn about safer sex, healthy relationships, communication, and how to enhance our sexual experiences to help others who struggle with various sexuality issues. However, a lot of us enter this industry without the business acumen needed to start and maintain our business.

There are many pros and cons to deciding if entrepreneurship is for you. There are advantages to being employed in various settings: corporate, school, or an organization, and there are advantages to entrepreneurship. To help you decide which avenue might be the right for you, make a list of pros and cons of being an entrepreneur and being in the other worlds and weigh them depending on what is most important to you. Things to consider when doing your list:

1. Scheduling
2. Time Off/Vacation
3. Finances
4. Healthcare
5. Clients
6. Social Media
7. Marketing
8. Team
9. Education/Leadership Development
   . . .and most importantly
10. Your Intersecting Identities.

DOI: 10.4324/9781032615479-32

Considering these will help you to determine what's best for you. Remember, it's never too late to become an entrepreneur and it is common to work another job while you're trying to get established. Try not to get sucked into the chatter to quit your full-time paid gig so you can concentrate on your own work. If you need something more reliable, know that you will have to work additional hours on your business, which may be more physically and emotionally demanding. This is an important consideration when taking on multiple jobs. The fact is entrepreneurship takes commitment, effort, and passion. Balance and harmony are the things needed to help you to become successful. This chapter invites you to note what will help you to become successful in your sex ed business, as well as thoughtful considerations to help your business thrive.

Defining Your Sex Education Business

Identifying Audience and Passion

There are many ways of being an educator and ultimately, it is about who you want to serve. This will help you establish what kind of educator you want to be and who you want to educate. As my interests in sexuality grew, so did the type of education that I wanted to pursue. Consider these questions if you're struggling to find your niche:

• Who do I want to serve? What are three identities and/or characteristics they hold?
• What goals do they have?
• What do they care about?
• What subjects/topics excite me? (Hint: name all the things that interest you and then narrow it down to top three)

My responses led me to focus on seduction and confidence (not pick-up artist skills), effective communication (for seduction), and enhancing sex skills. Unfortunately, I had a hard time figuring out my audience, and sometimes, I still do, and for the most part, my audience tends to be queer or queer-adjacent (socially, politically, and/or sexually) and ready to enhance their confidence and sex skills. This is where I shine because I found what makes me unique from any other educator.

Your Uniqueness

As an entrepreneur in the South, abstinence-only education was rampant. To talk about seduction, kink, and the importance of pleasure in relationships was very nuanced and I was able to capitalize on the university circuit as I became highly sought after. I found paid workshops each year at universities before I started to get recommended at universities beyond the South.

I was interested in the way people learned new information. I began reading Robert Greene's *Art of Seduction* (2001) and realized that people are seduced when their learning style is utilized. I branded this the Seduction Learning Styles© and it became the foundation of my work. I believe connecting with people begins with seduction and when we learn how to do it our life becomes easier to navigate when effectively communicating. When you try to find your niche, it's imperative that you know what makes you special and different from any other educator. Knowing this builds confidence in your practice, as it provides value to the people you teach, inherently helping you to market yourself by word-of-mouth.

Here are some questions to ask yourself:

- What makes you different from other sex educators?
- What theories or models inspire you? How can you put your unique spin on them? (Hint: nothing is entirely new, but how you look at it may be)
- What do people love about you?
- Why would someone want to work with you? (Hint: your mission and vision matter)
- What makes you an expert?

As you answer these questions, you'll realize you may have a specialty. This specialty is going to be the foundation of your business. This aspect should not be lost, as it helps you weed out an audience that isn't a good fit.

Your Business Model and Delivery

A key piece of conducting your business is figuring out how you want to deliver the education you teach. There are several ways to effectively deliver your message such as: teaching in-person or online in a/synchronous ways and writing. Consider your skillset and your personality type. For charismatic and/or extroverted people, teaching in-person and online synchronously will be a great fit because it allows you to connect in real-time and find energy from others. If you are an introvert, designing self-paced courses may be a great choice because you too can do it at your own pace, alone, and you do not have to deal with other peoples' energy unless it's in an email format. I highly recommend writing in addition to any other mediums that you execute. The emotional labor is going to be low and less taxing on you, as opposed to you doing this in person.

Education and coaching go hand-in-hand; you may want to do 1-on-1 coaching, group coaching, retreats, small or large themed events, parties, create and/or sell toys, training, podcasts, video, or workshops and classes. Depending on your business model, you are going to need to decide if scaling up is also in your future. Consider putting together a business plan, in case you want to have someone invest in your business and make it a scalable business model that could earn considerable profits. Whatever you decide, the most important thing is that you have one excellent offer and push that in every way you can.

Building a Strong Brand

Your Values, Your Vision, Your Mission

Defining your personal and business values will help you understand yourself and who you serve. Search for a list of values, you may get overwhelmed as there are many. Start to think deeply about them and you'll realize some stand out more than others. Narrow those values down and choose the top ten that you want your business to uphold.

Next, write your mission statement with these values reflected. Keep your values centered as they will help you as you take on more clients who may challenge you and your values. These will be opportunities to uphold your values and offer referrals.

Your Vision Statement needs to be macro in nature. This is what you understand as the big picture of how your business is creating change for your target audience. Ask yourself these questions when crafting your vision statement:

1. What do you envision for your business?
2. What is the greater public good that you are doing?
3. How are you making the world a better place?

Answering these questions and putting them in a simple statement will allow your potential clients to understand how they fit into your practice. Clients also get an idea of your intentions and your belief systems. If you enjoy vision boards, these could be a visual representation for your goals and beliefs.

Your Mission Statement must reflect your values in a micro nature way catering to how you and your business will help and support the change the individual seeks. This could include your methodology, impact, and you help solve their challenges. Questions to form your mission statement include:

1. What are you doing with your clients?
2. How does the work you do impact them?
3. What are some of the results your (potential) clients (will) have had?

This statement is probably the most important because your clients want to know how you will be able to impact them. They want to feel confident that you have the tools to solve their problems and help them achieve their goals.

Your Company Name and Logo

If you're an individual and you don't plan to expand your business, your name or a pseudonym is a good company name. Think about what inspires you. When you name your company after your inspiration, it's a constant reminder of your values. Because we are in sex education, it's best to have a business name that stays under the radar of filters which will target your work due to sexual content. You want to be able to bypass the AI that scans and filters your content. Think about marketing. If your name is not marketing friendly, you will miss out on business opportunities. For instance, Tia and I came up with the Sex Down South Conference and tried to register that as a business. The government was quick to inform us with a response of "no" to our business name and we renamed our business officially to SDS Conferences LLC, and most people know us as Sex Down South. One of the best ways to figure out if your name will be accepted is to do a Gmail filter test. Place the name you are considering in the subject line and in the content of the email and send it to another email address and you'll notice if it passes through the filters into your inbox. Our sexdownsouth.com domain is often flagged for spam. We combat this by instructing people to save us as a safe sender. Learn from our mistakes and find a name that is suitable for other peoples' work environments.

Your logo needs to reflect your brand, and it's best to keep it simple. Imagine your logo as an app favicon. Although you can design a logo yourself, I recommend finding a graphic designer. Working with a designer allows you to modify the design, ensure that you can use it in the way you like, and that your color palette is what you desire and works for years to come. Record everything for your brand kit (logo variations, font text, and color scheme) and make sure that you can have access to it whenever you need. Fall in love with your logo.

Craft Your Brand Messaging

Your brand voice is going to help you convey your message to potential clients. One of the best ways to understand your brand voice is through your writing. Helping the client in real time picture and understand you compels them to come and stay. Your brand must be authentic; you need to show your personality. Remember if you are bored with your writing, your audience is going to be also. Seek feedback on our writing and notice if your brand voice is accurate to how you are in real life (IRL). Ultimately, it is a system to understand other peoples' perspectives on their view of your work.

Create Your Website

A Facebook page or LinkTree is fine for marketing yourself, yet it will only get your business so far. You don't own those sites and if either one goes down, your links go down too. It's imperative you have a website; it doesn't matter if it's bare bones or pleasantly robust, a website is a must. Luckily, you don't need much on your website to get clients. If you have been struggling with your website, the necessary pages would be the following:

- About you, mission, vision, and values
- Your Services/Products

- Your Contact Information
- Your Company Policies

With these basic pages and a place where you can collect email addresses for your listserv, you are set to keep cultivating your audience for your services/products. You won't have to hire a graphic designer for this project; simply use a template from your website provider and drag-and-drop items as needed. If you don't have the time and you can afford to hire someone, make sure that you have full access to the backend of your website, even if you don't know how to manage it.

Attracting Clients

Establishing Yourself in the industry

Establishing yourself in the industry requires deep thought. Find the educators that are teaching similar subjects to you. These folks are your "competitors" in a sense, but not how competition is traditionally understood. There's room for everyone and it's more important for you to view them as collaborators. Understanding what they are doing to establish themselves is going to help you find what works. Experimentation and finding tactics that work for you is imperative.

As an educator I encourage you to:

1. Write: blog, guest posts on other blogs, seek out print media like magazines or organizational newsletters.
2. Teach: guest lecture at organizations/sex shops/corporations, offer your own workshops and classes, reach out to universities, or apply to different conferences that are in alignment with your work.
3. Create content for social media. If you are great with social media and know how to gain followers, those followers may become clients.
4. Offer advice: through traditional media via journalists, pitching stories and content that you want to reach the general public. It's best to pitch to journalists.

Content Market Strategy

It's best to be up-to-date on the various sexuality celebrations and un/official holidays. Create a content calendar, find the holidays that are relevant to your work, cross reference holidays explicitly for sexuality educators (Dr. Jill Sexologist, 2019) and others for the general public (411 Holidays, 2012). Mark these as ways to connect with your audience which will give you "forever content" that can resonate with your audience throughout the year. Utilize strategies such as collaborations, giveaways, and quizzes to boost your presence. Your posts may be educational, fun, inspirational, promotional, interactive, or holiday themed. If you decide on a social media system, which is software that schedules your posts, most systems offer templates. Create a template that can be used year after year and that you can add to the queue (evergreen content) and essentially not have to worry about content until there is something that is relevant at the current moment. This will make your job easier and you will be able to navigate your time more wisely.

Networking

Networking is an incredible way to establish yourself and scout potential collaborators. There are many ways to network:

- Join groups focusing on sexuality or affinity groups (Women of Color Sexual Health Network, Sex Educators of TikTok, SPACE, etc.)
- Attend conferences (Sex Down South Conference, North Carolina Sexual Health Conference, SLAM, etc.)
- Identify events for your industry (Exxxotica Expo, etc.)
- Do non-sexuality education things
- Attend local business networking events once a quarter
- Ask for a warm introduction
- Collaborate

Achieving Success

Self-Care/Love and Managing Burnout

As an entrepreneur, you work hard and that means you must take care of yourself. Prevent burnout every way you can. Doing what helps you to feel good in your body and mind is key to keeping balance. It's important to invest in yourself and in where you spend your time. If you're in front of a computer all day, invest in some blue blocker glasses, a great computer, an elite webcam, and a chair or desk for support. Enforce your boundaries and let people know when you're taking a break and/or if you're going to be slow to respond.

Managing burnout is valuable. More important is to do the things that fuel you with love and happiness. Celebrate your wins by treating yourself. Form good morning habits and a daily sleep routine to ensure you are cultivating the habits that bring you comfort. Reflecting on how you're managing your time is an indicator to how balanced you are with your body and mind. Consider a bucket list of things that you want to do bring you joy.

Setting Goals

Do some quarterly and yearly planning with the projects that fuel your business. Set goals and think about how to achieve them. Break the goals down, give them due dates, and mark them on your calendar. Every six months, re-evaluate your goals and projects, and re-shape them to move forward. It's helpful to map your daily and weekly goals to ensure they are accomplished. Add an accountability partner to ensure you get the work done and that you have some support to help you reformulate, if necessary.

Measuring Your Success

Keeping track of your reach and numbers offer a realistic picture of your business. Reflecting on your time helps you understand if your business is sustainable and where to concentrate on in the future. If you notice what is making you the most or least money, you can focus on those things. Once you reach those goals, identify new opportunities and move towards those goals. Participation in groups offers opportunities for new announcements and new pitches to companies, organizations, non-profits, sex shops, and more. Remember to celebrate each success that you accomplish.

Things to Consider

Always consider how you are negotiating your prices with individuals and organizations. Many people will try to convince you that "exposure" is enough for you to work. This is subjective. As full- and part-time sex educators, we must tell people exposure does not pay our bills. In the beginning of your career, exposure may be useful when it comes to marketing, and you must understand that exposure arrives in many different ways: teaching for nonprofits, serving on organizational boards, being a guest on podcasts, and being featured at community events. Assess if an event is worth your time or going to help you to get more clients.

As you get farther in your journey of entrepreneurship, it's helpful to understand your pricing of your labor. It's helpful if you have certain parameters that need to be carried out such as slides, handouts, worksheets, and more. You can negotiate things such as flight arrangements, childcare stipend/travel, housing accommodations, and/or meal stipends. If you bring value to the community, communities will want you to be present and will make sure that they can get you there.

Consider finding a mentor. All too often we don't seek mentors who are doing similar work and this leads to isolation. A mentor can teach you how to be successful. If they are doing what you want to do, this is an opportunity to learn from them and maximize their expertise.

Certifications are contentious when it comes to this industry. Depending on your audience, certifications may grant you access to people who value them. Many people in our industry are successful without certifications. Depending on the certification a sex educator holds, it might expand their ability to do the work they want to do. It's important to gauge if a certification you are considering is reflective of your business and the teaching modalities. Are certifications necessary? No. Are they helpful? Yes. Can you be successful without them? Absolutely. It might take time to build rapport and your reputation so people know you have knowledge, training, and that you are capable of helping them.

Introspective Questions for Consideration

- Why are you considering becoming an entrepreneur?
- What do you like about being in sex-positive communities?
- What is your capacity to work for yourself?
- What are your support systems that will allow you to flourish?
- How would a certification help you?
- How dedicated are you to continuous learning and improvement?
- Who holds you accountable and will hold space for hard conversations?

References

411 Holidays. (2012, December 12). Human sexuality holidays and observances. *Holidays and Observances*. Retrieved July 23, 2024, from https://www.holidays-and-observances.com/

Dr. Jill Sexologist. (2019, April 19). *Human sexuality holidays and observances.* Retrieved July 23, 2024, from https://www.thesexologist.org/library-content/human-sexuality-holidays-and-observances

Howard, G. (2017). *Be good or be good at it* [Audio podcast]. In *A good 15 with Goody Howard*. Apple Podcasts. Retrieved from https://podcasts.apple.com/us/podcast/a-good-15-with-goody-howard

27 Sex Ed and Social Media

Mariah Caudillo

Welcome to the world of sex education in the digital age! The power of social media platforms are at our fingertips and can revolutionize the way we teach and learn about sexuality. This chapter uncovers shortcomings of traditional sex education methods and examines how social media offers a unique opportunity to bridge those gaps, providing a more inclusive, accessible, and engaging platform for learning. Whether you're just starting as a sex educator or looking to become a "sexedfluencer," this chapter is a guide to navigating the ever-evolving landscape of social media in the world of sex education.

Traditional sex education methods are still a valuable starting point in providing foundational knowledge and skills related to sexual health. However, we must recognize the limitations of traditional sex education and the evolving needs of learners in today's digital age.

Social media can complement traditional methods by offering additional routes for learning, engagement, and support. Through social media, sex educators can enhance the reach and impact of their efforts, address diverse learner needs and provide real-time support in response to emerging issues and trends.

Gaps in Traditional Sex Ed

Unlike traditional sex education, social media allows learners to find valuable resources anytime, anywhere, with only an internet connection. Social media creates safe spaces where individuals can learn about taboo topics in an anonymous, non-judgmental environment, and find representation and resources that resonate with their identities.

Rather than relying on one-way communication through lectures and presentations, social media helps facilitate interactive and engaging communication through features like comments, likes, shares, direct messaging, polls, and live streams.

Social Media Landscape

The social media landscape is ever-changing, but platforms like TikTok, Instagram, and YouTube have emerged as some of the more powerful tools for

DOI: 10.4324/9781032615479-33

shaping conversation around sexuality and relationships. While our discussion centers on these platforms, the principles and strategies discussed are applicable to any platform.

TikTok is a popular platform where users create and share short videos to engage with an audience. According to Welch (2023)

> Researchers found that 42% of social media users agree that TikTok is the most accessible way to obtain more sexual health information. The rise in interest about sexual health online is undoubtedly related to the lack of proper knowledge being taught in schools today.

It is characterized by its algorithm-driven content discovery, trending challenges, and creative editing tools. Sex educators can use TikTok to create engaging and informative videos on sexual health topics, leveraging trends, challenges, FAQ sessions, and storytelling techniques to capture a diverse audience of all ages.

The TikTok hashtag #sexualhealth has over 2 billion views from videos created by thousands of users (Welch, 2023). In Nguyen and Carvalho's article *Sex Education in Social Media*, they highlight that

> some obstetrics and gynecology doctors use TikTok to engage youth with medically accurate sexual health information. This platform allows users the space to create content that is inclusive and accessible to marginalized populations, like LGBTQ+ youth, who traditionally have trouble finding community and support in the classroom.
>
> (Nguyen & Carvalho, 2023)

Instagram is a visually driven platform where users share photos, videos, and stories. Sex educators can create visually appealing content with infographics, images, and short videos regarding sexual health. Engage users through hashtags and by hosting Q&A sessions and live streams that facilitate real-time interaction and discussion.

YouTube is known for its extensive library of educational content, tutorials, and vlogs. Sex educators can create long form, in-depth videos on sexual health topics. YouTube's search feature and recommendation algorithms make it easier for users to find educational content tailored to their needs.

The Pew Research Center asked US teens if they use ten specific online platforms: YouTube, TikTok, Instagram, Snapchat, Facebook, Twitter, Twitch, WhatsApp, Reddit, and Tumblr. YouTube was most common, and many also said they used TikTok, Instagram, and Snapchat. When it comes to frequency, teens use YouTube and TikTok most. The survey results confirm that video content is highly desired and sought out by teens.

If you are ready to embrace the world of social media to provide sex education you will need to know the following: (1) content creation considerations, (2) principles of effective sex education content on social media, and (3) helpful tools and tips.

1. Content Creation Considerations

- Do I truly want to make sex education content on social media? Do I feel equipped to handle the responsibilities and challenges it brings?
- Am I comfortable putting my face on the internet for potentially millions of people to see?
- What are my boundaries/limitations?
- What is the purpose of my content?
- Who is my target audience?
- Am I prepared to engage with my audience?
- Is my information accurate and evidence-based?
- Do I want to present information objectively as in a professional setting, or should it reflect my personal opinions?
- Am I fostering a shame-free environment?
- How will I address sensitive topics or trigger warnings?
- What are the potential risks or consequences?
- How will I handle feedback and criticism?

2. Principles of Effective Sex Education Content on Social Media

I. Understand the Algorithm

Social media algorithms are highly complex rules and calculations that determine which content appears in users' feeds or search results. Every social media platform has a unique algorithm for content display, and by knowing what the algorithm favors, you can tailor your content to maximize visibility and impact.

Social media algorithms tend to prioritize digestible content that generates high levels of engagement. The more engagement, the higher the chance of "going viral." One complication is that the algorithm decides if your content is useful and it is not uncommon for sexual health content creators to struggle with algorithm restrictions no matter how "educational" their content is. Regardless, high-quality, engaging content that sparks conversation and encourages participation is more likely shown to a wider audience.

Additionally, timing plays a crucial role in algorithm optimization. Sex educators can experiment with posting at key times when their audience is most active, and schedule content accordingly. Leveraging features (i.e., hashtags, trends, and collaborations) can also help increase content reach.

II. Create Accessible Content

- Use clear and inclusive language, and respect diverse identities and experiences. Avoid jargon, slang, or offensive terms that may be exclusionary or alienating.
- Offer content in multiple formats to accommodate different learning styles, including captions or transcripts for videos, alt text for images, and audio descriptions for visually impaired users.
- Feature high-contrast colors and clear and readable fonts.
- Caption your videos for deaf and hard of hearing viewers. Synchronize captions with the audio.
- For images or graphics, provide detailed text descriptions or alternative text (alt text) that conveys the same information for the visually impaired.
- Encourage feedback from your audience and address it.

III. Avoid Sharing Misinformation

Social media is flooded with misinformation. Sex educators can work around this by thoroughly researching topics before discussing them and rely on reputable sources such as peer-reviewed journals, academic publications, and credible health organizations like the CDC and WHO. Citations can be included in captions or text overlays.

IV. Be Adaptable

Adjust and iterate content, strategies, and messaging to meet evolving needs based on audience feedback. On social media, it's possible to embrace change while staying true to oneself, which leads to the key principle of effective sex education content on social media: authenticity.

V. Authenticity

People who are authentic are often more relatable and trustworthy and prompt more engagement by viewers. Use your tone of voice and facial expressions to create unique content. For some, that will mean reflecting on your values, beliefs, and personal experiences.

3. Helpful Tools and Tips

Planning: successful content creators plan ahead, generating ideas, scripting, calendaring and ensuring a diverse range of topics and formats. Here are ideas for generating content:

- Organize a space to write down your content ideas
- Conduct audience research to understand the interests, needs and preferences of the target audience, then ask for audience feedback and ideas through polls, surveys, and Q&A sessions

- Use social media analytics to identify content topics that resonate with your audience
- For video content like TikTok videos or Instagram Reels, write a script to maintain structure and flow when recording. Outline key points, messages, and takeaways. Incorporate storytelling techniques and practice delivering scripted content
- Stay informed about current sexual health trends
- Brainstorm ideas collaboratively with fellow creators

Content calendars (ex. Buffer, Google Sheets, Hootsuite, Later, Notion, Sprinklr, and Sprout Social) help you to . . .

- Organize your ideas, themes, and topics
- Schedule posts in advance
- Incorporate content based on holidays, awareness months, or relevant events
- Maintain a balance of themes and formats
- Regularly review content performance

Topics and Formats:

- Rotate among educational, informative, entertaining, and interactive content
- Explore different formats such as videos, infographics, blog posts, podcasts, live streams, and interactive quizzes to appeal to diverse learning styles
- Incorporate intersectional perspectives to ensure inclusivity and representation
- Regularly review and adjust content strategy to identify gaps or areas for improvement

Example topics that can be transformed into content for social media include relationships, LGBTQ+ experiences, reproductive health, birth control, and sexual wellness. To tailor topics like these to specific social media platforms, content creators should use the approach best suited to their style, personality, audience, and goals.

- Instagram: create infographics and reels, share personal stories in video or text format. Host live Q&A sessions or collaborate with other educators for joint posts
- TikTok: produce short educational videos using popular trends and sounds, create a series addressing common misconceptions or FAQs in a fun and engaging manner
- YouTube: develop comprehensive tutorials or educational series on specific topics; conduct interviews with experts or individuals sharing their experiences

Technical aspects

Lighting, camera setup, sound quality, and editing are important, but you can also create simple yet incredible social media content from your smartphone.

Lighting

If natural lighting is not possible in your recording space, there are affordable solutions such as ring lights or softbox lights that enhance visibility, reduce shadows, and make your videos and images look professional.

Camera

Familiarize yourself with your personal camera equipment. Understand how to adjust settings such as exposure, focus, and white balance. Experiment with different camera angles. Perhaps invest in a simple background.

Horizontal videos are more suitable for desktop and tablet devices (ideal for YouTube). Vertical videos are popular on mobile-centric platforms such as Instagram, Snapchat, and TikTok. I recommend purchasing a small tripod to keep your camera steady. In addition, you may want to get a camera shutter remote control with Bluetooth wireless technology. It eliminates the risk of moving the camera when you trigger the shutter.

Sound

Quality microphones capture clear audio and minimize background noise, and lapel microphones record dialogue or voiceovers. Most smartphones produce great sound quality.

Editing

Add music, text and image overlays, special effects, filters, and captions, to refine content flow:

1. Create images and graphics with Canva, PicMonkey, and Adobe Creative Cloud Express
2. Create videos with Capcut, Splice, InShot, Promo, and KineMaster

Delivery style

Deliver content in a clear and approachable manner:

- Enunciate words and speak at a moderate pace
- Use plain language to make it feel they are learning from a friend
- Avoid looking down or away from the camera for extended periods
- Convey enthusiasm, sincerity, or empathy, as appropriate
- Ask questions and prompt discussions
- Use storytelling techniques, anecdotes, or real-life examples
- Utilize props (i.e., uterus model)

- Respond to audience comments in real time
- Practice multiple times to refine your pace

As content creators master effective delivery styles in discussing sexual health, it's equally important to ensure the learning environment is safe, inclusive, and affirming for all. This can be accomplished by using inclusive language and prioritizing representation to include people of all genders and sexual orientations (i.e., using "they" pronouns.)

Here are several other steps to cultivate a safe, inclusive environment:

- Identify potentially sensitive topics, such as discussions about sexual, gender, and racial violence and trauma
- Prepare your audience through topic and volume warnings. Topic warnings clearly indicate at the beginning of the content or certain sections if sensitive topics will be discussed
- Offer support resources that are relevant and accessible to individuals from diverse backgrounds, including in multiple languages and formats

Nurturing a Supportive Online Community

As we have established, what sets social media apart from traditional school-based sex ed is the community people can discover, specifically LGBTQ+ folks of color. Social media platforms provide a level of anonymity that may not be available in school-based sex education settings. Individuals can engage with content in the privacy of their own space and participate in discussions without fear of judgment, stigma, or disclosure of personal information.

Here are strategies for building a supportive community:

- Respond to audience engagement
- Offer resources, links, or referrals to additional information or support services
- Ask follow-up questions, encourage others to share their perspectives, and acknowledge contributions made by community members
- Establish clear guidelines for respectful and inclusive communication and encourage participants to engage in constructive dialogue and avoid personal attacks or derogatory language
- Block or report people who cross those boundaries

Strategies for managing inappropriate behavior:

- Monitor discussions and interactions within the community
- Intervene promptly to address conflicts, inappropriate comments, or violations of community guidelines
- Remove offending content or issue warnings
- If needed, limit comments or adjust settings to flag inappropriate comments or words so they are not posted

Social Media Limitations

Sex educators work hard to create safe digital spaces where individuals can find support without fear of judgment, but despite our best efforts, we often find ourselves navigating a minefield of confusing community guidelines and unfair restrictions. Access to sexual health information is a human right, and it can be frustrating when basic information everyone should know is censored or deemed "inappropriate" by these platforms.

How to navigate these limitations:

- **Age-restrict content:** mark content as age-restricted or limit access to mature audiences only.
- **Implement censoring techniques:** to avoid triggering content filters or restrictions, consider censoring words or phrases related to sex. This can include using asterisks, abbreviations, emojis, euphemisms to convey the message. Emojis can sometimes be a playful and effective way to communicate words and concepts related to sex. You can spell words differently in captions and graphics to "bypass this censorship" on social media. Spell words like "seggs" or "secks," "le$bean," "masterbacon," "SA" (pronounced "ess-ay" is used in sexual assault awareness content), "ab0rti0n," or "b00b." We should not have to censor the word sex, but on social media it is becoming increasingly impossible and more likely than not, your content will be flagged if you do so (Cowsert, 2024).
- **Add background music to video content**: background music enhances engagement and can mask sexual content so that algorithms will not pick up on the creator talking about sex. Always use royalty-free music and adjust the volume so your speaking voice is the focal point.
- **Provide content introductions:** provide context or disclaimers to clarify the educational intent and distinguish it from explicit or adult material. Some sex educators begin their content with: "my name is ___ and I'm a certified sex educator, reminder that this is educational content."
- **Create a backup account:** in case your primary account is suspended, have a backup account to ensure that you can continue sharing content with your audience.
- **Apply for verification:** apply for verification on social media platforms to lend credibility and authenticity to your account. Verified accounts also receive additional benefits (i.e., increased visibility and protection against impersonation).
- **Block trolls and haters:** people may target sex education content with negative comments, harassment, or mass reporting. Utilize platform features to block or mute them.
- **Engage with support teams and make appeals:** if you encounter content moderation issues, engage with platform moderators to seek clarification or resolution. Advocate for fair treatment and consideration of educational intent.

Social Media Boundaries

Establishing boundaries around the time and cost associated with content creation, engagement with followers, and decisions about brand partnerships helps prevent burnout and maintain a healthy balance between your online presence and personal life. Effective time management includes setting dedicated time slots for content creation and engagement, and being selective about brand partnerships and opportunities, collaborating only with those that align with your values. Embrace your social media boundaries and prioritize your mental and emotional well-being.

Looking Forward to the Future

This chapter has revealed the ways social media is shaking up sex education and how to make the most of it as a content creator. Traditional school-based methods have limitations including lack of inclusivity, one-way communication that does not engage learners and curricula that may not cover taboo or sensitive topics comprehensively. Social media platforms are bridging those gaps, extending the reach of traditional sex education programs by making resources available to individuals who may not have access to formal classroom settings and supporting lifelong learning beyond the classroom. While social media faces its own limitations and challenges, there's no denying it is a powerful tool for creating accessible and relatable sexual health education. Whether creating videos, infographics, or hosting livestreams, sharing expertise and passion online contributes to a world where everyone has access to life-saving sex education.

Introspective Questions for Consideration

- How do I perceive the role of social media in addressing the gaps and challenges I've encountered in traditional sex education settings?
- What specific steps can I take to integrate social media into my sex education programs, curriculum, workshops, or outreach efforts?
- What steps can I take to ensure that my social media content is trauma-informed, considering the diverse backgrounds and experiences of my audience?
- How do I navigate the evolving algorithms and policies of social media platforms to maximize the reach and impact of my sex education content while remaining ethical and responsible?

References

Cowsert, M. (2024, March 22). Navigating sexual and reproductive health censorship on social media. *Healthy Teen Network.* https://www.healthyteennetwork.org/news/sexual-and-reproductive-health-censorship-social-media/

Nguyen, K., & Carvalho, P. (2023, July 13). Sex education and social media – public health post. *Public Health Post*. https://www.publichealthpost.org/viewpoints/sex-education-and-social-media/

Welch, A. (2023, November 1). Social media picks up the slack when it comes to sexual education. *The Voyager*. https://uwfvoyager.com/3927/uncategorized/social-media-picks-up-the-slack-when-it-comes-to-sexual-education/

28 Sex Ed and Working with the Media

Dirty Lola

Key Terms

- **Personal Brand:** your personal brand is a culmination of the experiences, skills, and values that differentiate you.
- **Media:** newspapers, magazines, radio, and television
- **Media Boundaries:** your media boundaries are the limits you set around what you share with the media, where you share it, and whether it aligns with your ethics. These boundaries help maintain professional integrity.

Media is being utilized more than ever to educate people, creating an ideal platform for sexuality professionals to contribute their expertise. However, it is also being used for fearmongering and to spread misinformation, signaling a call to action for sex educators to engage with the media. This is a new and challenging area for many, and sex educators need to understand the role of media in sex education and learn how to work with various forms of media effectively.

Your teaching experience may have encompassed various settings, such as in-person and online workshops, classrooms, or one-on-one consultations. These experiences have undoubtedly sharpened your public speaking skills. However, the use of media to disseminate sex education information presents a distinct set of challenges that you may not have encountered before. Understanding these challenges makes you feel more prepared and aware of your approach.

In classroom and workshop settings, you have more control over what you share, how it is received, and who you share it with. You can also handle any questions or misunderstandings the moment they arise. When you work with the media, much of that control is reduced. You no longer have a say in how what you are sharing is consumed or who it is consumed by, and what you share could be restructured to fit the narrative of the form of media you are working with. You also lose the direct link to your audience, leading to unanswered questions and misunderstandings taking on a life of their own.

DOI: 10.4324/9781032615479-34

Other Pros and Cons

Pros:

- You get to share your message with a broader audience
- You get to tap into demographics you hadn't considered before
- A new audience will discover your brand and previous work
- Your voice will become synonymous with the topics you speak on regularly

Cons:

- You will expose your work, brand, and appearance to public scrutiny and criticism
- The work you contribute to the media can and will be disassembled and discussed without allowing you to comment
- You may be harassed by those who do not agree with or understand your work
- Once something you have shared is out in the media, you cannot take it back

Traditional media refers to forms of mass communication, including newspapers, magazines, television, radio, and podcasts. It is defined as static, one-way communication to a broad audience.

Though social media is often used similarly to traditional media, it does not fall under the traditional media umbrella because it offers a more personalized and interactive experience that caters to a specific group of people based on the target audience of its internet or app creator.

Traditional media still has a demographic focus but tends to be broader. For instance, traditional media may focus on working moms in general, while social media may refine that focus to working BIPOC moms living in the suburbs.

There are three factors to consider when collaborating with any media:

1. Determine if their audience is local, national, or international.
2. Decide whether their audience aligns with your brand's target demographic.
3. Will working with a specific form of media expose you to a new demographic you have wanted to tap into?

Here Are Some Additional Factors to Take Into Account for Each Type of Media

Understanding the various options available when working with traditional media can significantly assist you in making informed choices about which formats are best suited for your brand and career path. If you are aiming to gain visibility and credibility within the media industry, there are several options that you should consider.

Newspapers and Magazines

These include both print and digital formats. Print and digital versions often overlap in information, but some brands only run certain content on their digital sites.

- Writing articles, opinion pieces, or reviews for digital and print publications on specialized topics
- You can be featured as a quoted expert in an interview or article
- You can be the subject of an interview

Contact a writer if you are interested in being quoted as an expert or featured in an article or interview.

- Cultivate relationships with writers who write on topics that align with your interests and branding
- Respond to prompts on sites like Connectively. Respond to writers' calls for quotes and interviews on social media
- Working with a PR firm can be a good option if you want to be considered for interviews or as a featured expert. While you could write and release a statement about your project, a PR firm has the necessary contacts and resources to get your project in front of the right audience

Contact an editor if you want to write articles, opinion pieces, or reviews for a publication.

- Editors are not as easily accessible as writers, but many publications provide information on how to submit your work on their websites or social media
- Smaller independent publications sometimes use social media to call for article submissions

Television

This form of media covers various categories, such as reality shows, news shows, talk shows, docuseries, and documentaries.

- You can be an expert guest on a morning or evening news program
- You can also appear as a guest on a talk show
- Another option is to appear as an expert on a docuseries or documentary as a host or talking head. The host is a featured player prominently featured throughout the show and may ask questions and lead discussions. A talking head is shown only from the shoulders and speaks on a specific topic. While they may be seen throughout a show, a talking head is not its focus

- Additionally, you can work as a content consultant. Sometimes, productions look for content consultants to advise on projects on specific topics. This role can be more challenging to source if you do not have connections with producers

Due to the nature of the industry, television is much more challenging to break into. Producers of TV media content are looking for talent. Even when looking for experts, they seek entertaining and informative individuals.

- Casting call sites like BackStage allow you to sort listings, sign up for email notifications, and look for city-specific opportunities
- Production companies sometimes announce projects they are working on on social media. Occasionally, they will hold open calls for experts or talking heads
- Talent Scouts work with various production companies. They will post open calls on social media or sites like BackStage
- This is another instance where working with a PR firm can be beneficial. They have access to contacts and job openings that are not publicly advertised

Radio

Radio shows are similar to podcasts, except they are live, and some encourage live on-air audience involvement. While radio shows are less prevalent than they were in the past, they still exist and are great for connecting to wider local audiences.

- You can be an expert speaking on a specific topic
- You can be a guest speaking on a topic specific to your brand or personal lived experience

Podcasts

There are a massive number of podcasts, and many of them cover sexuality and sexual wellness topics.

Most radio shows and podcasts are easily accessible since they constantly seek guests. Getting on popular and celebrity-hosted shows and podcasts may be more challenging, but it is still possible.

- Many radio shows and podcasts offer guest submission forms or provide instructions in their websites' FAQ section on applying to be guests on their shows
- Keep an eye on their social media accounts for any calls for guests
- Working with a PR firm can increase your chances of appearing on popular shows or shows hosted by celebrities.

Be Aware and Beware

Gaining entry into specific forms of media can be challenging at times because they are not designed to facilitate the entry of individuals who are not part of them. Unless you have connections to production companies or know where to look for casting calls, you must depend on word of mouth and your public presence. On the more accessible side of things, you have podcasts. While it can be helpful to have a PR person to connect you with podcast producers and hosts (especially for popular podcasts), many podcasts have public-facing contact information and often respond to messages on social media, making it very easy to reach out on your own.

When you contribute to media such as TV, newspapers, and magazines, you will not have a say in editing. However, most podcasts offer the option to remove parts of the conversation after the fact if you no longer feel comfortable with what you shared being part of the final episode.

Avoid Being Misquoted

To avoid being misquoted in print media, you can always ask to see the piece before it goes to print, though this option is rarely offered for TV and other visual media. If the writer can't provide this opportunity, consider it when deciding whether to contribute. Another effective strategy is to provide your answers in writing or voice notes, allowing you to retain an original copy of your quotes for reference.

When working with traditional media, it is crucial to respond quickly to opportunities. Having a digital folder containing all the necessary items helps you stay ready. This way, you can be prepared whenever opportunities arise. The required items include your bio(s), professional title, Chyron, social media handles, and contact information can be placed on one document to make it easy to copy and paste items as needed.

Professional Title

Your professional title is the name of your job role or your membership in a professional organization. When quoted in articles or any other platform, it identifies your expertise in a specific area. Your professional title serves as a shorthand for the readers to understand your professional background and knowledge in the field quickly. If you have multiple professional titles, choose the one that best suits the platform and content you are being quoted for.

Examples of professional titles: Sex Educator, Sex Therapist, Shop Owner, Dating Coach

Bio

Have a few versions of your bio because they will be used differently.

- A lengthy introduction bio: this version gives the full story of your career
- This short–medium-length bio: this version can be used on social media, as a writer's bio, or when a shorter bio is requested. It should include your title, a bit of your career story, what you're known for, and your current work
- A two- to three-line bio: this version is a short blurb that will be used to quickly tell an audience who you are during radio, podcast, and TV appearances. It should include your title and the work you do.

Chyron

A chyron is a text-based graphic usually located on the lower third of a screen. It is commonly used on news shows, sporting events, and interviews to communicate information pertinent to the background event and to introduce the person on camera. As an expert, our Chyron should include your name, your professional title, and what you're speaking about.

Social Media Handles

Share only the accounts/platforms you use for your sex ed business.

Contact Information

This includes website(s), email(s), and your business phone number.

When creating your emails and domain names, keep in mind that these things will be shared professionally at some point, so it's better to opt for straightforward emails over cute or overly creative emails. It's also important to note that domains and emails with the word "sex" in them will get caught up in porn filters or be sent to spam folders.

Elevator Pitch

An elevator pitch is a brief and persuasive speech that communicates your identity, your offerings, and the benefits they can provide to your audience. It should be 1–2 minutes at maximum. Elevator pitches are used in networking to quickly and memorably introduce yourself to others.

Rate Sheet

A rate sheet is a single-page document that lists all your offerings and what you charge for them. Offerings include consulting, workshops, reviews, social media posting, products, and speaking fees. You should consider having different rates for local and long-distance gigs. You should revisit your rates after milestone moments such as receiving a new certification, degree, or award, publishing a book, or being featured in a media project such as a TEDTalk or streaming service show.

Visual Media

Images and video for your website, social media, and media kit.
- Headshots: have a few different headshots that can work for various needs and are up to date
- Event photos/action shots and candids
- Video from your show or event

Media Kit/Press Kit

Media or press kits are promotional materials to promote you, your brand, event, or product. They are multiple pages and can be formatted as a presentation deck. What to include in a

Media Kit:

- Long-form bio
- Headshot
- Contact information
- Introduction to your brand, business, or project
- Your mission
- Demographics and who you serve
- Testimonials (if applicable)
- Frequently asked questions
- A summary of your packages and rates

One-Sheet

A one-sheet is a page used to promote a particular product, service, or event. Its primary purpose is to provide a snapshot of a specific aspect of your business. It is important to note that a one-sheet is designed to summarize only some of your services. What to include in a

One-Sheet:

- Headline of . . .
- Headshot or event image
- Short bio

- Short project intro
- Social and website links
- Contact information
- Rates

If you are planning to pursue working in audio and visual media, such as television and podcasts, there are other things you'll need to consider, such as your attire, public speaking skills, body language, and setting up your space for remote interviews.

Setting Your Boundaries When Considering Projects

Before working in any part of media, you must create media boundaries that help you decide which projects align with your personal brand and if you want to dedicate your valuable time to working on them. Here are a few questions that will help you craft your media boundaries:

- Are there individuals/groups with whom you prefer not to work? There are various reasons why you may choose not to collaborate with someone: you may disagree with their ethics or politics, they may have caused harm to you or your community, or you may simply find them insufferable. Whatever your reasons, it's important to be firm in your decision and be able to justify it
- Do you have criteria by which you judge projects you are considering?
- What topics are you drawn to, and which do you want to avoid?
- What are your compensation needs?
- How much time are you willing to dedicate to a project?

Navigating and Negotiating Compensation

The misconception is that working with the media automatically means you will be paid well. That is patently false. Here is a snapshot of what compensation looks like across the various forms of media:

Newspapers and Magazines

Writers are either paid a salary, by the hour, or by the word. Some publications pay guest and independent writers a flat fee. Writers cannot pay for their sources, so you will not be compensated if quoted or interviewed for a publication.

Television

Unless you are a lead talent on a reality series, an actor, or an extra on a series, you will not receive payment for your work on the TV side of the media. Most talk shows and news programs do not pay their guests, though a few may offer a small fee or honorarium. Depending on their budget, documentaries and docuseries may pay a small fee to their experts and participants, but this is not always the case. Occasionally, you may have the opportunity to consult on a project you are involved in or offer a service outside of the role you are taking on. In those cases, you should negotiate fees for those services.

Radio Shows

Radio shows do not pay their guests.

Podcasts

Most podcasts do not pay their guests, but a handful pay a small honorarium. Ask for audio/video assets, collaboration posts, and other ways to use their platform to showcase yours.

Navigating the Media With Marginalized Identities

The lack of representation of diverse racial and ethnic groups, disabilities, sexual and gender identities, and body types in media makes it harder for individuals with one or more of these identities to be considered for roles and other opportunities. One must also be aware of whether their inclusion is a step towards actual inclusivity or to perpetuate certain stereotypes. To navigate these problems in the industry and ensure the project you are choosing to work on aligns with your personal brand, it is important to ask questions when considering a project such as:

• Why were you chosen to be a part of the project?
• What is the final vision of the project? Often, you will find you are only given information on the project pertaining to your part. Ask about the whole story and how your part will be utilized.
• Who is working on the project? Who are the director, producer, and fellow performers, and are they people you are okay working with?

Advocate for those not in the room. This is not a question, but it is important to note who is being left out. Speaking up about who needs to be represented, especially early in production, could change how things are constructed.

Navigating Bad Press

The pitfalls of working in the media while teaching and talking about sex for a living are the backlash and bad press that can arise if a project you are working on becomes popular or goes viral for the wrong reason. How do you navigate negative pieces written about you that are not great? Here are a few Dos and Don'ts:

Do...

- Have a plan: dealing with negative comments and an influx of private messages can take an emotional toll on anyone. Knowing what steps you'll take before facing an onslaught of negativity will help you navigate future turmoil
- Designate a trusted person to catalog and keep track of articles written about you that you want to keep
- Remove personal contact information from social media platforms, such as your email, phone number, and location
- Limit comments on your posts or make your social media accounts private altogether
- Block trolling accounts, and be sure to save screenshots of the harassment
- Save any harassing emails you receive and block the sender. You can block people from sending you emails through Gmail, Outlook, Proton, Yahoo, and Apple Mail
- Use keyword filters to filter out trolls and folks harassing you from their social media accounts
- Prepare a statement to address the backlash in your own words if necessary
- Take some time away from social media
- Take a break from your public-facing work or any projects that must be promoted via social media channels
- Utilize your press connections (if you trust them) to push your prepared statement

Don't...

- Panic
- Give the attack pieces clicks or views by opening or resharing them. If you must read it, download the PDF so you don't reopen them
- Try to respond to all of the negative comments or private messages
- Try to clear your name using the press unless you trust the writer and the news outlet to allow you to tell your story without spinning it in a worse/more negative direction

Working with the media can be challenging, but it can also be gratifying. In a world where misinformation spreads rapidly, it's not just crucial; it's our responsibility to have people equipped with accurate information on the frontlines, especially about sex. Traditional media is a powerful tool when used correctly. It can amplify your messages and advance your career but also have negative consequences. Being cautious and mindful of the potential drawbacks of a public persona is essential. With this knowledge, you can establish a productive and valuable relationship with the media.

Index

Note: Numbers in *italic* indicate a figure and numbers in **bold** indicate a table on the given page number.

and 64–65; thinking critically about structures and styles 125, 127–131; unhealthy 31, 225; youth 91, 226; *see also* monogamy; polyamory; sexual relationships; throuples

religion 29, 31, 41, 72, 112, 122, 147, 222, 228–229, 234, 235n1; *see also* religious beliefs

religious beliefs 4, 45, 171

reporting requirements 33–34; mandatory reporting 33

reproductive event 80–81

reproductive health 11, 13, 193, 252

reproductive intelligence 80, 82; *see also* Black Girl Reproductive Intelligence

reproductive justice (RJ) 6–7, 11–13, 16, 191, 193, 195, 219, 221; movement 13, 193; timeline 13, 211

reproductive politics 79, 82

reproductive rights 6, 17n1, 151

reproductive technology 76, 79, 108

reputation management 96

resilience 28–36, 94–95, 98; -informed approach 36; *see also* resilient zone

resilient zone 28, 30–36

resistance 4–5, 89, 210, 225

Rich, Adrienne 127

risk(s): of abuse 143; BDSM 179–180; depression 137; dignity of 134, 138, 140, 149, 154; health 87; hookup 96; mitigation 135; online 95, 100, 163; pregnancy 87, 131; re-traumatization 32, 69; sexual 1, 21, **23**; sexual assault 138; STI 87, 89; and youth 222, 224

Roe v. Wade 13, 77

role models 50, 224–227

romantic orientation 115

safer sex **23**, 69, 87, 239

safety 14, 17, 28–36, 69, 90–91, 99, 103, 108, 131, 135, 157, 165, *173*, 185, 200, 216, 225–226; body 160; consciousness 219–220; digital 96; emotional 32, 90; internet 144, 163, 165; language of 33; mental 90; online 161–163, 165, 225; personal 150; physical 32, 90; psychosocial 199; resources 226

Sanger, Margaret 193

scare tactics 22

Second World War 78

security 95; in- 93

seduction 240–241

Seduction Learning Styles© 241

self-acceptance 95

self-advocacy 5, 150

self-care 29, 57, 203, 245

self-determination 78, 134, 194, 219–220, 224–226

self-discipline 21

self-esteem 62, 65, 95–97, 179, 225–226

settler colonialism 7, 118, 122–123, 191

sex (biological): assigned at birth 22, 118, 120, 122, 136–137; "biological" 22; binary 103; vs gender 104–105; heteronormative, cisnormative ideals and representations of 21; as a spectrum 103–104; *see also* endosex; gender; intersex; transgender

sex (sexual activity) 21–22, **23**, 48, 81, 87–88, 91, 130, 132, 143, 228, 233; anal 22, **23**; "intercourse" 22, 85–87, 92; interracial 178; risky 99; "safe" **23**, 88, 107; "safer" **23**, 69, 87, 239; societal attitudes towards 4; unprotected 94; unsafe 100; vaginal **23**; *see also* sexual behavior

sex avoidance 85, 89

sex-avoidant society 85–92

sex characteristics: primary 102; secondary 93, 102, 104–105

sex ed *see* sex education

"sexedfluencer" 248

sex education: abstinence-based (ABSE) 21; accessible 2–3; addressing stigma within 131–132; contemporary sex ed values in United States 21–25; critical 2–3; curriculums 2; emotional literacy in 48–54; gaps in 2–3; gaps in traditional 248; implementing CNM expansive activities and conversations within 129–133; importance of critical pedagogy in 3–4; inclusive 2–3, 5, 135, 140, 143–144, 196; beyond intercourse 86–87; intersectional and trauma-informed approaches to 1–8; liberatory 6; for neurodivergent learners 142–148; for people with IDD 149–155; for people with physical disability 134–140; porn literacy and 157–165; school-based 20; sexual racism in 63–64; and social media 248–256; trauma-informed 2–3;

30; intergenerational 30; intersex medical 106; multigenerational 30; personal 211; physical 106; religious 228–229, 234; responses 28–29, 31–33, 35; re-traumatization 32–35; sexual 57, 106; survivors of 30–31, 35; symptoms of 28; toxic/chronic stress 30; *see also* trauma-informed; traumatic invalidation
trauma-informed: applications 1, 3; approaches 1, 28–36, 40, 136, 196, 199; care 35; comprehensive sex education 194; consent education 69–71; education 68, 70, 72; framework 69; lens 70, 137; manner 181; professionals 165; seven steps 32–34; sex education 2–3, 196, 199; sex educator 136; sexuality education 29; strategy 172
traumatic invalidation 68, 70, 73
Trevor Project 119
tribalism 30
Trump, Donald 79
Tumblr 249
Turtle Island 122
Tuskegee Syphilis Study 60
Twitch 249
Twitter 249
Two-Spirit 123–124
Two-Spirit, lesbian, gay, bisexual, transgender, queer/questioning, intersex, and/or asexual (2SLGBTQIA+) 135, **139**

United Kingdom (UK) 167
United States 28, 76, 79, 119, 123, 193–194, 219; contemporary sex ed values in 21–25; Criminal Justice System 69; current education in 68–69; law 121; sex education in 6, 21; slavery in 57; Supreme Court 13, 77, 79, 193; weaponization of values in 20
universal "truths" 19
unlearning/un(learning) 5, 25, 125, 143, 200

values 3–4, 17, 19–26, **23**, *24*, 39–42, 46, 71, 99, 125, 129, 161, 164, 171, 193, 202–203, 206, 208, 210, 212, 218, 220, 222, 242–243, 251, 256,

258; abolitionist 204; identifying and neutralizing 21–25; personal 26, 99, 131, 199; philosophical 131; professional 26; religious 22; social 125; societal 93, 135; transformative justice 204; weaponization of 20; white supremacist 204–205
victim-blaming 33–34
violence 167–175; colonial 6; dating 34, 150; gendered 6; physical 30, 35, *169*; racial 11, 254; in sex education 171; against sex workers 169–170, *169*, 174; survivors of 221; *see also* sexual violence
virginity 22, **23**, 81, 228
"voluntary motherhood" 78

Western imperialism 118, 121
WhatsApp 249
whiteness 60–61; valorization of 60
white people 7, 11, 14, 191
White Racial Folklore Theory 58; and sexual racism 60–61
white supremacy (WS) 7, 11, 13–14, 20, 25, 61, 69, 71, 118, 191, 193–194, 197–198, 204, 211–212; history of 58–60
WHO 251
whorearchy 169–170, *170*, 172–174
whorephobia 167, 169–174; and colonialism 174; definition 167, 169; internalized 169
Williams, Serena 60
Williams Institutes 119
woman of color 77, 195
Women's Liberation Movement 78
workshops 100, 164, 206–207, 233, 240–241, 244, 256, 258, 263; online 258; recorded 215–216

youth: culture 229; definition 219; digital awareness among 162–164; disabled 136, 143; educators 90, 92, 225; LGBTQ/LGBTQAI+/LGBTQAI2S+ 95, 119, 195, 225, 249; maximizing sexual health education for 219–227; with physical disability 136; queer 95, 181; relationships 91, 226; and risk 222, 224; sexuality **23**
YouTube 12, **139**, 185, 248–249, 252–253

For Product Safety Concerns and Information please contact our EU
representative GPSR@taylorandfrancis.com
Taylor & Francis Verlag GmbH, Kaufingerstraße 24, 80331 München, Germany